CentOS 7 Server Deployment Cookbook

Deploy and manage today's essential services on an enterprise-class, open operating system

Timothy Boronczyk

BIRMINGHAM - MUMBAI

CentOS 7 Server Deployment Cookbook

Copyright © 2016 Packt Publishing

First published: September 2016

Production reference: 1270916

Published by Packt Publishing Ltd.
Livery Place
35 Livery Street
Birmingham
B3 2PB, UK.
ISBN 978-1-78328-888-5

www.packtpub.com www.packtpub.com

Credits

Author

Timothy Boronczyk

Reviewer

Mitja Resman

Commissioning Editor

Kartikey Pandey

Acquisition Editor

Rahul Nair

Content Development Editor

Mehvash Fatima

Technical Editors

Devesh Chugh

Siddhi Rane

Copy Editor

Tom Jacob

Project Coordinator

Kinjal Bari

Proofreader

Safis Editing

Indexer

Pratik Shirodkar

Graphics

Kirk D'Penha

Production Coordinator

Shantanu N. Zagade

About the Author

Timothy Boronczyk is a native of Syracuse, New York, where he works as a lead developer at Optanix, Inc. (formerly ShoreGroup, Inc.). He's been involved with web technologies since 1998, has a degree in Software Application Programming, and is a Zend Certified Engineer. In what little spare time he has left, Timothy enjoys hanging out with friends, studying Esperanto, and sleeping with his feet off the end of the bed. He's easily distracted by shiny objects.

About the Reviewer

Mitja Resman comes from a small, beautiful country called Slovenia, located in southern Central Europe. Mitja is a fan of Linux and is an open source enthusiast. Mitja is a Red Hat Certified Engineer and Linux Professional Institute professional. Working as a system administrator, Mitja got years of professional experience with open source software and Linux system administration on local and international projects worldwide. The swiss army knife syndrome makes Mitja an expert in the field of VMware virtualization, Microsoft system administration, and lately, also Android system administration.

Mitja has a strong desire to learn, develop, and share knowledge with others. This is the reason he started a blog called GeekPeek.Net (https://geekpeek.net/). GeekPeek.Net provides CentOS Linux guides and How to articles covering all sorts of topics appropriate for beginners and advanced users. He wrote a book, *CentOS High Availability* by Packt Publishing, covering the topic of how to install, configure, and manage clusters on CentOS Linux.

Mitja is also a devoted father and husband. His two daughters and wife are the ones who take his mind off the geek stuff and make him appreciate life, looking forward to things to come.

www.PacktPub.com

For support files and downloads related to your book, please visit www.PacktPub.com.

Did you know that Packt offers eBook versions of every book published, with PDF and ePub files available? You can upgrade to the eBook version at www.PacktPub.com and as a print book customer, you are entitled to a discount on the eBook copy. Get in touch with us at service@packtpub.com for more details.

At www.PacktPub.com, you can also read a collection of free technical articles, sign up for a range of free newsletters and receive exclusive discounts and offers on Packt books and eBooks.

https://www.packtpub.com/mapt

Get the most in-demand software skills with Mapt. Mapt gives you full access to all Packt books and video courses, as well as industry-leading tools to help you plan your personal development and advance your career.

Why subscribe?

- Fully searchable across every book published by Packt
- Copy and paste, print, and bookmark content
- On demand and accessible via a web browser

Table of Contents

Preface

For over a decade, the CentOS project has provided the community with a free, enterprise-grade operating system through the rebranding and recompilation of the Red Hat Enterprise Linux source. Since CentOS users rely almost exclusively on the community for their support needs, I was keen to write this book when Packt approached me about the project's latest release, CentOS 7. The recipes we chose cover a wide range of topics, from getting started to managing many common web services, and hopefully administrators of any skill level will find something of interest.

However, writing a book is a huge undertaking. Because of this, I want to thank the staff at Packt, my family, and my friends, for their support. The dog needs to be taken for a walk, family engagements need attending, and emergencies arise at the workplace. Without the understanding and encouragement of those around me and the editorial staff, you wouldn't be reading this book.

What this book covers

The recipes presented in this book aim to make even the most difficult configuration tasks easy by providing step-by-step instructions and discussion. Here's a quick rundown of what you can expect from each of the 12 chapters.

Chapter 1, *Getting Started with CentOS*, contains recipes for installing CentOS using graphical, text-based, and kick-start approaches. How to set up a CentOS platform for projects running Docker and on Amazon Web Services is also discussed.

Chapter 2, *Networking*, contains recipes to help you complete common networking tasks, such as how to set up a static IP address, assign multiple addresses to a single network interface, bond multiple interfaces with the same address, and configure the system's firewall using FirewallD and iptables. It also presents recipes for configuring network services such as DHCP, NFS, and Samba.

Chapter 3, *User and Permission Management*, shows you how to increase the security of your system by enforcing password restrictions, adjusting the default permissions given to newly created files and directories, and the use of sudo to avoid circulating the root password. How to work with SELinux is also discussed.

Chapter 4, *Software Installation Management,* provides recipes focused on working with software repositories and installing software. You'll learn how to register the EPEL and Remi repositories, prioritize the repositories packages are installed from, and update your software automatically. You'll also learn how to compile and install software from source code.

Chapter 5, *Managing Filesystems and Storage,* presents recipes that show you how to set up and work with RAID and with LVM. These services leverage your system's storage to maintain availability, increase reliability, and to keep your data safe against inevitable disk failures.

Chapter 6, *Allowing Remote Access,* aims to help you provide remote access to your CentOS system in a secure manner. Its recipes cover using SSH, configuring a chroot jail, and tunneling VNC connections through an encrypted SSH tunnel.

Chapter 7, *Working with Databases,* collects recipes that provide you with the necessary steps to get started with various database services such as MySQL, MongoDB, and OpenLDAP. You'll also learn how to provide backup and redundancy for these services.

Chapter 8, *Managing Domains and DNS,* takes us into the world of DNS. The recipes show you how to set up a resolving DNS server to decrease latency caused by domain lookups and how to manage your own domain with an authoritative DNS server.

Chapter 9, *Managing E-mails,* will help you set up your own mail server. The recipes discuss configuring Postfix to provide SMTP services, configuring Dovecot to provide IMAP and POP3 services, and securing these services with TLS. You'll also find instructions on how to set up SpamAssassin to help reduce unsolicited bulk e-mails.

Chapter 10, *Managing Web Servers,* contains recipes about configuring Apache to server web content. You'll learn how to set up name-based virtual hosting, server pages over HTTPS, and perform URL rewriting. How to set up NGINX as a load balancer is also discussed.

Chapter 11, *Safeguarding Against Threats,* contains recipes to help protect the investment you've made in your CentOS server. They cover logging, threat monitoring, virus and rootkits, and network backups.

Chapter 12, *Virtualization,* shows you how CentOS can function as a host operating system to one or more virtualized guests. This allows you to take better advantage of your hardware resources by running multiple operating systems on the same physical system.

What you need for this book

To follow the recipes in this book, first and foremost you'll need a system capable of running CentOS 7. The minimum requirements (and maximum capabilities) are documented in the Red Hat Enterprise Linux knowledge base available online at `https://access.redhat.com/articles/rhel-limits`. In brief, you'll need a system that has the following:

- x86_64 processor (RHEL/CentOS 7 does not support x86)
- 1 GB RAM
- 8 GB Disk capacity

Apart from a system to install CentOS on, you'll also need a copy of the CentOS installation media and a working network connection. You can download a copy directly from `https://www.centos.org/download/` or using BitTorrent.

Who this book is for

This book is for Linux professionals with basic Unix/Linux functionality experience, perhaps even having set up a server before, who want to advance their knowledge in administering various services.

Sections

In this book, you will find several headings that appear frequently (*Getting ready, How to do it..., How it works..., There's more...,* and *See also*).

To give clear instructions on how to complete a recipe, we use these sections as follows.

Getting ready

This section tells you what to expect in the recipe, and describes how to set up any software or any preliminary settings required for the recipe.

How to do it...

This section contains the steps required to follow the recipe.

How it works…

This section usually consists of a detailed explanation of what happened in the previous section.

There's more…

This section consists of additional information about the recipe in order to make the reader more knowledgeable about the recipe.

See also

This section provides helpful links to other useful information for the recipe.

Conventions

In this book, you will find a number of text styles that distinguish between different kinds of information. Here are some examples of these styles and an explanation of their meaning.

Code words in text, database table names, folder names, filenames, file extensions, pathnames, dummy URLs, user input, and Twitter handles are shown as follows: "The repositories' configuration files are found in the `/etc/yum.repos.d` directory."

A block of code is set as follows:

```
[sshd]
enabled=true
bantime=86400
maxretry=5
```

Any command-line input or output is written as follows:

```
firewall-cmd --zone=public --permanent --add-service=dns
```

New terms and **important words** are shown in bold. Words that you see on the screen, for example, in menus or dialog boxes, appear in the text like this: "Select your desired language and click on **Continue**."

Warnings or important notes appear in a box like this.

 Tips and tricks appear like this.

Reader feedback

Feedback from our readers is always welcome. Let us know what you think about this book-what you liked or disliked. Reader feedback is important for us as it helps us develop titles that you will really get the most out of.

To send us general feedback, simply e-mail feedback@packtpub.com, and mention the book's title in the subject of your message.

If there is a topic that you have expertise in and you are interested in either writing or contributing to a book, see our author guide at www.packtpub.com/authors.

Customer support

Now that you are the proud owner of a Packt book, we have a number of things to help you to get the most from your purchase.

Errata

Although we have taken every care to ensure the accuracy of our content, mistakes do happen. If you find a mistake in one of our books-maybe a mistake in the text or the code-we would be grateful if you could report this to us. By doing so, you can save other readers from frustration and help us improve subsequent versions of this book. If you find any errata, please report them by visiting http://www.packtpub.com/submit-errata, selecting your book, clicking on the **Errata Submission Form** link, and entering the details of your errata. Once your errata are verified, your submission will be accepted and the errata will be uploaded to our website or added to any list of existing errata under the Errata section of that title.

To view the previously submitted errata, go to `https://www.packtpub.com/books/content/support` and enter the name of the book in the search field. The required information will appear under the **Errata** section.

Piracy

Piracy of copyrighted material on the Internet is an ongoing problem across all media. At Packt, we take the protection of our copyright and licenses very seriously. If you come across any illegal copies of our works in any form on the Internet, please provide us with the location address or website name immediately so that we can pursue a remedy.

Please contact us at `copyright@packtpub.com` with a link to the suspected pirated material.

We appreciate your help in protecting our authors and our ability to bring you valuable content.

Questions

If you have a problem with any aspect of this book, you can contact us at `questions@packtpub.com`, and we will do our best to address the problem.

Getting Started with CentOS

This chapter contains the following recipes:

- Installing CentOS using Anaconda in graphics mode
- Installing CentOS using Anaconda in text mode
- Coordinating multiple installations using Kickstart
- Running a cloud image with Amazon Web Services' EC2
- Installing a container image from the Docker Registry
- Installing the GNOME desktop
- Installing the KDE Plasma desktop

Introduction

This chapter's recipes focus on getting up and running with CentOS using a variety of installation methods. You'll learn how to perform interactive graphical and text-based installations using Anaconda and perform an unattended installation using Kickstart. You'll also see how to run CentOS in the cloud with Amazon Web Services and in a Docker container image. Most of the recipes in this book take place at the command prompt, but some require a graphical desktop, so we'll finish up with a look at installing the GNOME and KDE Plasma desktops.

Installing CentOS using Anaconda in graphics mode

In this recipe, you'll learn how to install CentOS using the graphical installer Anaconda. This is the most common way that CentOS is installed, although there are other ways too (some of which are discussed in later recipes). This approach is also the easiest installation method, especially for setting up single-server deployments.

Getting ready

This recipe assumes that you have a copy of the CentOS 7 installation medium. If you don't, visit `https://www.centos.org` and download a minimal ISO image. You'll also need to make a physical disc from the image. Instructions for burning the ISO image to disc can be found at `https://www.centos.org/docs/5/html/CD_burning_howto.html`.

If your system doesn't have an optical drive and its BIOS supports booting from a USB device, you can also write the ISO image to a USB stick.

How to do it...

Follow these steps to install CentOS using the graphical installer Anaconda:

1. Insert the installation disc into your system's optical drive (or USB stick into a USB port) and reboot. The system should boot to the CentOS 7 installation menu:

The installer is launched from the installation menu

If your system doesn't boot to the installation menu then the drive may not be configured as a boot device. The exact steps to verify and adjust the configuration vary between BIOS vendors, but in general you'll press *Esc, F1, F2,* or *Delete* while the system is booting to gain access to the BIOS settings. Then you'll find the list of boot devices and change the order in which each is searched for a boot record.

2. Using the arrow keys, make sure that the **Install CentOS 7** option is highlighted and press *Enter.*

3. The **WELCOME TO CENTOS 7** screen confirms which language to use during the installation process. Select your desired language and click on **Continue**:

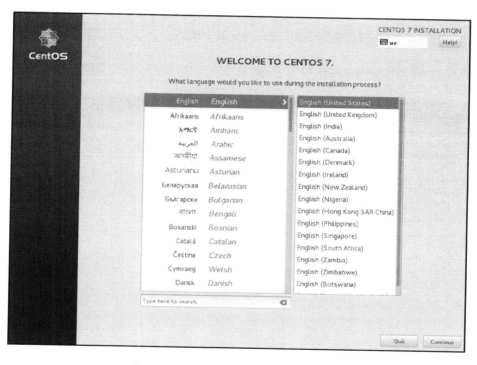

You can change the language used during the installation process

4. The next screen is a menu that organizes the installation options by category. We'll configure networking first—click on **NETWORK & HOST NAME** under the **SYSTEM** category:

If your system doesn't have a mouse, you can navigate using *Tab* to cycle through the input fields, use the arrow keys to select the entry, and press *Enter* to select or activate an input.

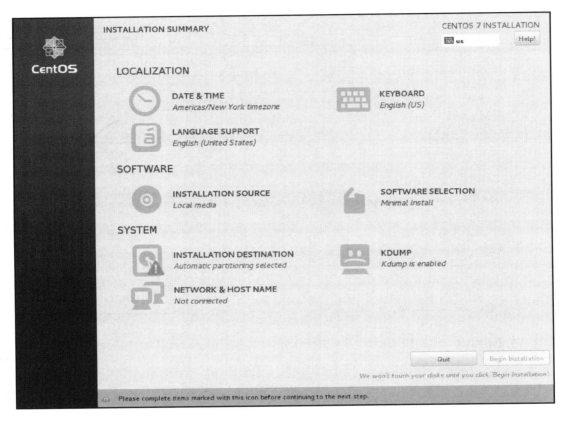

The installation summary screen organizes the installation options into categories

5. Enter the system's hostname in the **Host name** field. Then, select the system's primary network interface and toggle the switch at the right to **ON** to enable it. Click on the **Done** button when you're finished to return to the **INSTALLATION SUMMARY** menu:

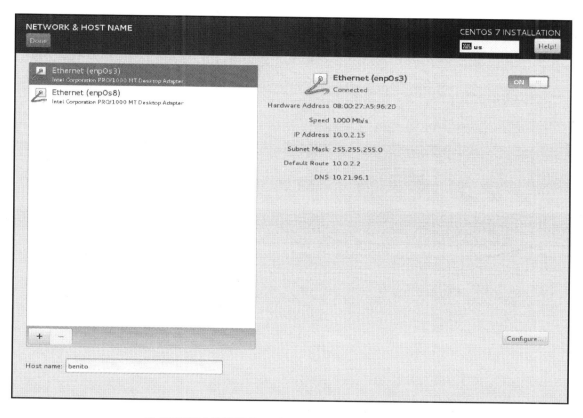

The NETWORK & HOST NAME screen lets us configure the system's network interfaces

6. Click on **DATE & TIME** under the **LOCALIZATION** category.
7. Set your time zone by either selecting your region and city or by clicking on your location on the map. Then, click on **Done** to return to the **INSTALLATION SUMMARY** menu:

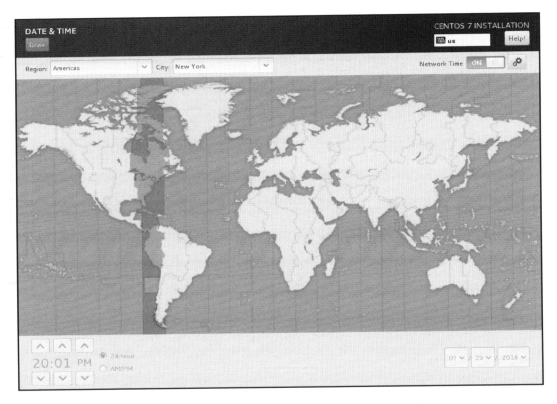

The DATE & TIME screen lets us configure the system's time zone

8. If you know what purpose the system will serve on your network and require something more than a minimal installation, click on **SOFTWARE SELECTION** under the **SOFTWARE** category. Select the environment and any additional add-ons to install the desired packages. When you're finished, click on **Done**:

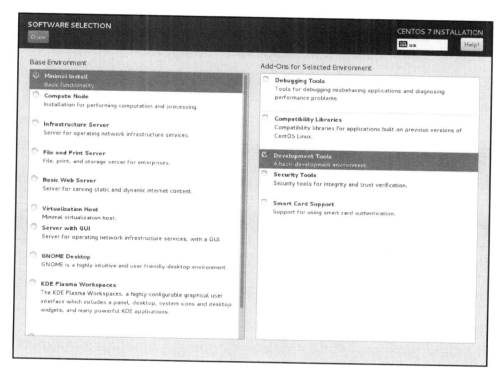

The SOFTWARE SELECTION screen lets us install purpose-based software

Software can easily be installed using yum, so don't worry if you need to install additional software after you already have CentOS up and running. The **SOFTWARE SELECTION** section is purely for convenience.

9. Click on **INSTALLATION DESTINATION** under the **SYSTEM** category.

10. Click on the appropriate drive in the **Local Standard Disks** area to set the installation target. If the drive is not bootable, or if multiple drives are selected, click on the **Full disk summary and boot loader...** link at the bottom of the screen to open the **Selected Disks** window. Then, select the drive you want to be the boot device, click on the **Set as Boot Device** button, and click on **Close**. When you're finished, click on **Done**:

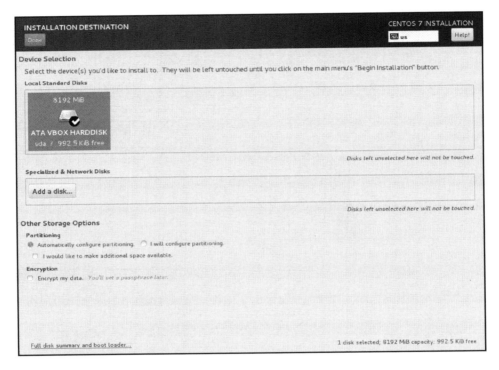

The INSTALLATION DESTINATION screen lets us set the disk where CentOS will be installed

11. Click on the **Begin Installation** button to start the installation process.

12. Click on **Root Password**. In the input fields, enter and confirm the password you want to use for the system's root account. Click on **Done** when you've finished entering these details:

You'll need to press the Done button twice to return to the configuration screen if you specify a password that's too weak. If you need help to create a strong password, visit http://www.howtogeek.com/19543/how-to-create-a-strong-password-and-remember-it/.

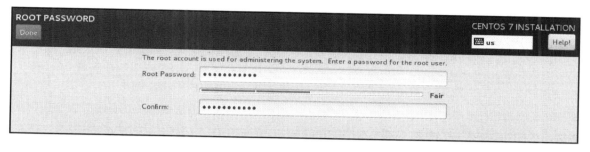

The ROOT PASSWORD screen lets us set the root account's password

13. Click on **User Creation**. In the input fields, provide your name, username, and desired password. Again, press **Done** when you've finished entering these details:

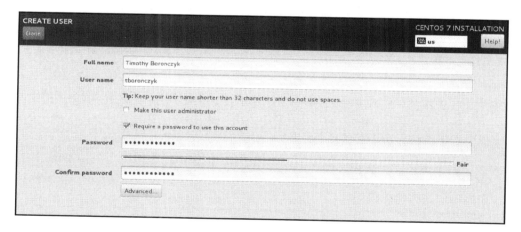

The CREATE USER screen lets us create an unprivileged user account

14. When the installation is complete, click on the **Finish Configuration** button. Anaconda will finalize the system's configuration and the button's label will change to **Reboot**.

15. Remove the CentOS installation media from the drive and reboot your system.

How it works...

After installing CentOS using Anaconda in graphical mode, you should now have a basic CentOS 7 system up and running. The process began when we booted the system from the installation disc and selected **Install CentOS 7** from the installation menu. The installer's kernel loaded into memory and Anaconda launched in graphical mode.

The **NETWORK & HOST NAME** screen shows a list of the available network interfaces and basic information about them, for instance, the card's MAC address and transfer rate. By default, the interfaces are configured to use DHCP to obtain their IP address when they are enabled. (Configuring a static IP address is discussed in a later recipe.)

The system's time zone is set on the **LOCALIZATION** screen. The date and time fields are disabled when NTP is enabled because the values will be set by the NTP service. The system clock's time can drift for many reasons, especially if the system is running on a virtual machine, so allowing NTP to manage the system's time is a good idea to ensure it stays correct. If the date and time fields aren't set by NTP, make sure the **Network Time** toggle is set **ON**. You can specify an NTP server by clicking on the button with the gears icon.

The **INSTALLATION DESTINATION** screen lets us set the installation target for CentOS and specify how the system's drives are partitioned. You can choose to configure the partitions if you have special requirements, but in this recipe I let Anaconda partition the drives automatically.

While Anaconda is busy installing CentOS and any additional software packages you may have requested, it shows us the **Configuration** screen. This screen gives us the opportunity to set a password for the system's administrative account (`root`) and create an unprivileged user account. You should only sign in with `root` when necessary; for your normal day-to-day work you should use your unprivileged account. Anaconda finalizes the installation by configuring the system's boot record and creating the user account.

After the system reboots, the Grub boot loader prompt appears and the arrow keys can be used to select a boot configuration. There's also a timer, so pressing nothing will eventually boot the system using the default configuration.

See also

For more information on installing CentOS 7, refer to the RHEL 7 Installation Guide (`https://access.redhat.com/documentation/en-US/Red_Hat_Enterprise_Linux/7/html/Installation_Guide`).

Installing CentOS using Anaconda in text mode

Next, you'll learn how to install CentOS using Anaconda in text mode. It's recommended that you install CentOS graphically because graphics mode is easier to use and offers more functionality. However, it may not be available when the system lacks sufficient resources to run the installer in graphical mode, for example, if the display adaptor's capabilities are limited or if there is reduced RAM.

Getting ready

This recipe assumes that you have a copy of the CentOS 7 installation medium. If you don't, visit https://www.centos.org to download an ISO image and then burn the image to a disc.

How to do it...

Follow these steps to perform a text-based installation of CentOS:

1. Insert the installation disc into your system's optical drive (or USB stick into a USB port) and reboot. The system should boot to the CentOS 7 installation menu.
2. Using the arrow keys, make sure the **Install CentOS 7** option is highlighted and press *Tab.* The command to boot the installer kernel appears at the bottom of the screen.
3. Add the word text to the end of the list of arguments and press *Enter.* Anaconda will launch in text mode:

```
vmzlinuz initrd=initrd.img inst.stage2=hd:LABEL=CentOS
\x207\x20x86_64 rd.live.check quiet text
```

 Anaconda will launch in text mode automatically if your system has less than 768 MB of RAM.

4. The **Installation** menu presents the installation options by category. Type **2** and press *Enter* to select **Timezone settings**:

```
Starting installer, one moment...
anaconda 19.31.123-1 for CentOS 7 started.
 * installation log files are stored in /tmp during the installation
 * shell is available on TTY2
 * when reporting a bug add logs from /tmp as separate text/plain attachments
00:57:27 Not asking for VNC because we don't have a network
================================================================================
================================================================================
Installation

 1) [x] Language settings            2) [!] Timezone settings
        (English (United States))           (Timezone is not set.)
 3) [!] Software selection           4) [!] Installation source
        (Processing...)                     (Processing...)
 5) [x] Network settings             6) [!] Install Destination
        (Not connected)                     (No disks selected)
 7) [x] Kdump                        8) [!] Create user
        (Kdump is enabled)                  (No user will be created)
 9) [!] Set root password
        (Password is not set.)
  Please make your choice from above ['q' to quit | 'b' to begin installation |
 'r' to refresh]: _

[anaconda] 1:main* 2:shell  3:log  4:storage-log  5:program-log
```

The text-based installation menu categorizes the installation options

5. The **Timezone settings** menu presents a list of regions. Enter the number for the desired value.

6. You will be given a list of available time zones in the selected region (paginate through the list by pressing *Enter* if the list is long). Enter the number for the desired time zone.

7. If you know what purpose the system will serve and require something more than a minimal installation, enter **3** to select **Software selection**. Here you can select groups of software packages for that purpose. When finished, enter *c* to continue back to the **Installation** menu.

8. Enter **5** to select **Network settings**.

9. Enter **1** to set the system's hostname. Type the desired name and press *Enter*.

10. Enter the number to configure the system's primary network interface. Then, enter **7** to mark **Connect automatically after reboot** and **8** to mark **Apply configuration in installer**. Enter *c* to go back to the **Network settings** menu and *c* again to return to the **Installation** menu:

```
=======================================================================
=======================================================================
Network settings

Wired (enp0s3) connected
 IPv4 Address: 10.0.2.15 Netmask: 255.255.255.0 Gateway: 10.0.2.2
 DNS: 192.168.1.1
Wired (enp0s8) disconnected

Host name: benito

 1)  Set host name
 2)  Configure device enp0s3
 3)  Configure device enp0s8
 Please make your choice from above ['q' to quit | 'c' to continue |
 'r' to refresh]:
[anaconda] 1:main* 2:shell  3:log  4:storage-log  5:program-log
```

The Network settings menu lets us configure the system's network interfaces

11. Enter **6** to select **Install Destination**.
12. If the desired drive is not already marked, enter the number for the drive. Then, enter *c* to continue. The **Autopartioning Options** menu is shown in the following screenshot:

```
Probing storage...
Install Destination

[x] 1) ATA VBOX HARDDISK: 8192 MiB (sda)

1 disk selected; 8192 MiB capacity; 992.5 KiB free ...

  Please make your choice from above ['q' to quit | 'c' to continue |
  'r' to refresh]: c
=======================================================================
=======================================================================
Autopartitioning Options

[ ] 1) Replace Existing Linux system(s)

[x] 2) Use All Space

[ ] 3) Use Free Space

Installation requires partitioning of your hard drive. Select what space to use
for the install target.

  Please make your choice from above ['q' to quit | 'c' to continue |
  'r' to refresh]:
[anaconda] 1:main* 2:shell  3:log  4:storage-log  5:program-log
```

The Install Destination menu let us set the installation target and the Autopartioning Options menu lets us specify how the disk will be used

13. Enter the number for the desired partitioning (**Use All Space** is the default) and then **c** to continue.

14. Select the desired partition scheme (**LVM** is the default) and then enter *c* to return to the **Installation** menu.

15. Enter **8** to select **Create user**.

16. Enter **1** to mark the **Create user** option. Provide your name and set a username for the account by entering **2** and **3** respectively. Enter **4** to mark the **Use password** option and then **5** to set your password. Then, enter *c* to return to the **Installation** menu:

You must confirm you really want to use your password if you provide a password that is too weak.

```
================================================================
================================================================
Create user

 1) [x] Create user
 2) Fullname
    Timothy Boronczyk
 3) Username
    tboronczyk
 4) [x] Use password
 5) Password
    Password set.
 6) [ ] Administrator
 7) Groups
  Please make your choice from above ['q' to quit | 'c' to continue |
  'r' to refresh]: 5
================================================================
================================================================
Password:
Password (confirm): _
[anaconda] 1:main* 2:shell  3:log  4:storage-log  5:program-log
```

The Create User menu let us create an unprivileged user account

17. Enter **9** to select **Set root password**. Enter and confirm the password you want to use for the system's root account.

18. After all of the sections that required attention have been resolved, enter *b* to begin the installation process.

19. When the installation is complete, remove the media from the drive and reboot the system.

How it works...

This recipe showed you how to install CentOS using Anaconda running in text mode. The process began when we booted the system from the installation disc, selected **Install CentOS 7** from the installation menu, and added the `text` option to the boot parameters. The installer's kernel loaded into memory and Anaconda launched in text mode.

The text-based installation is similar to installing CentOS in graphical mode, answering prompts for time zone, software, and networking information. However, Anaconda presents the prompts in a different order when running in text mode and some functionality is missing. For example, we can't perform custom disk partitioning. Nevertheless, text mode enables us to quickly install a basic CentOS system.

See also

For more information on installing CentOS 7, refer to the RHEL 7 Installation Guide (`https://access.redhat.com/documentation/en-US/Red_Hat_Enterprise_Linux/7/html/Installation_Guide`).

Coordinating multiple installations using Kickstart

If you're planning on installing CentOS on multiple servers, it's more convenient to automate as much of the process as possible. In this recipe, you'll learn how to use Anaconda's `kickstart.cfg` file to perform an unattended network-based installation.

Getting ready

This recipe requires at least two systems on your network: an existing system running an HTTP server to host the installation files and Kickstart configuration (the recipe *Installing Apache HTTP Server and PHP* in `Chapter 10`, *Managing Web Servers*, shows you how to install Apache) and the target system on which we'll install CentOS. You'll also need the installation media and administrative privileges.

How to do it...

Follow these steps to perform unattended network installations using the Kickstart method:

1. Log in to the system running the HTTP server using the root account.
2. Place the installation disc in the system's optical drive.
3. Mount the disc using the `mount` command so that its contents are accessible:

   ```
   mount /dev/cdrom /media
   ```

4. Create a new directory under Apache's web root to host the installation files:

   ```
   mkdir -p /var/www/html/centos/7/x86_64
   ```

5. Copy the contents of the installation disc to the new directory:

   ```
   cp -r /media/* /var/www/html/centos/7/x86_64
   ```

6. Copy the `kickstart.cfg` file created by Anaconda when the system was installed to Apache's web root:

   ```
   cp /root/kickstart.cfg /var/www/html/kickstart.cfg
   ```

7. Unmount and remove the installation disc:

   ```
   umount /media
   eject /dev/cdrom
   ```

8. Insert the disc into the target system's drive and reboot it. The system should boot to the CentOS 7 installation menu.
9. Highlight the **Install CentOS 7** option and press *Tab*.
10. Update the arguments used to boot the installer kernel to read as follows. Change the IP address as necessary to point to the system hosting the Kickstart file:

    ```
    vmlinuz initrd=initrd.img ks=http://192.168.56.100/kickstart.cfg
    ```

11. Press *Enter* to begin the installation process.
12. Once the installation process begins, you can eject the disc and begin the next system's installation. Repeat steps 8-11 for each additional system.

How it works...

Anaconda writes the configuration values we provide when performing a graphical or text-based installation to `kickstart.cfg`. If you plan on installing CentOS on multiple servers, it's more convenient to use the file to provide the interface's answers. The remaining installations can be performed mostly unattended and the systems' configurations will be more consistent.

This recipe showed you how to make the `kickstart.cfg` file and the CentOS installation files available to other systems over the network, and update the boot command to tell Anaconda where to look for the installation files and prompt responses. Since the software packages are retrieved from the installation server instead of the disc, you can eject the disc as soon as the installation process is underway and use it to begin the next process on your next system.

Of course, `kickstart.cfg` can be used as a starting point, and you can edit the responses using a text editor to further customize the installations. If you like, you can create multiple kickstart files in the web root, each with a different configuration. Just specify the desired file when you set the installer's boot arguments.

Although you can edit your kickstart files with a basic text editor, dedicated programs exist for editing them as well. Check out Kickstart Configurator (`http://landoflinux.com/linux_kickstart_configurato r.html`).

See also

For more information on coordinating multiple installations of CentOS 7, refer to the following resources:

- RHEL 7 Installation Guide (https://access.redhat.com/documentation/en-US/Red_Hat_Enterprise_Linux/7/html/Installation_Guide)
- Anaconda documentation (http://rhinstaller.github.io/anaconda/index.html)
- Install PXE Server on CentOS 7 (http://www.unixmen.com/install-pxe-server-centos-7)

Running a cloud image with Amazon Web Services' EC2

Amazon Web Services (AWS) is a suite of services hosted within Amazon's network infrastructure which allows companies and individuals take advantage of their computing/storage capacity and world wide data centers. Elastic Cloud Compute (EC2) is a virtualization platform that lets us set up virtual systems on demand, usually to host websites and web apps. This recipe will walk you through the process of setting up a new virtual server running CentOS on the AWS platform.

Getting ready

This recipe assumes that you have an AWS account. You can sign up for one at http://aws.amazon.com. You will need to provide a valid credit card, although you will have access to Amazon's free tier for 12 months.

How to do it...

To set up a new Amazon Machine Instance (AMI) on AWS's EC2 platform, follow these steps:

1. Log in at `https://aws.amazon.com` and go to the AWS Management console. Under the **Compute** category, click on the EC2 link to access the EC2 management page. Then, click on the **Launch Instance** button:

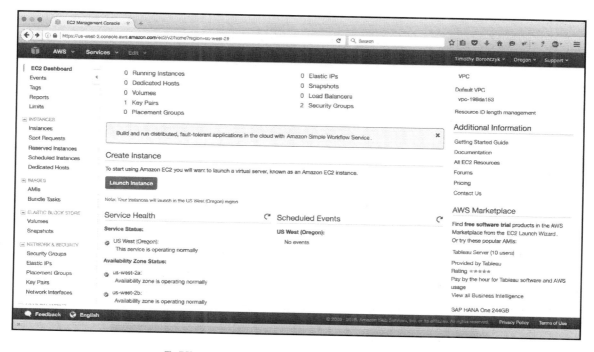

The EC2 Management Console presents an overview and quick access to resources

2. On the **Choose an Amazon Machine Image (AMI)** page, select **Community AMIs** in the side menu and then check the **CentOS** filter. A list of instances created by the community will be shown. Select the one you desire:

 Review the list of available images carefully. Many are available, created using different versions of CentOS and with various configurations.

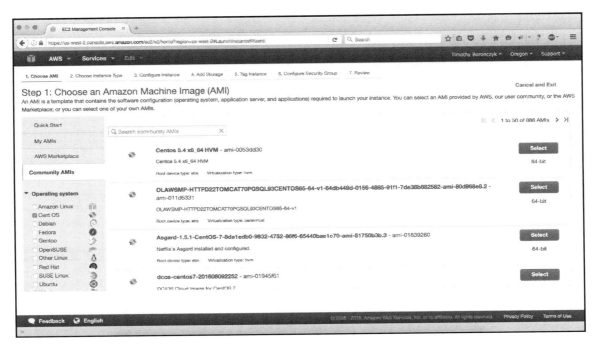

The image selection page presents a filterable list of machine images created by community users

3. On the **Review Instance Launch** page, review your instance's resources (the number of virtual CPUs, available memory, and so on) and click on the **Launch** button:

Amazon guides you through selecting an AMI and configuring it in a wizard-like fashion, listing the steps at the top of the page. The **Review** and **Launch** buttons jump directly to the last step. You can use the links at the top of the page to go back to an earlier step and adjust the instance's configuration.

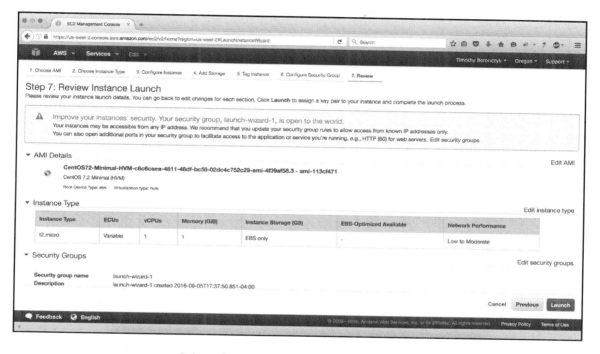

Review your instance's resources on the **Review Instance Launch** page

4. Using the drop-down list, select **Create a new key pair**, enter a suitable filename for the key, and click on the **Download Key Pair** button. After you save the downloaded private encryption key, click on the **Launch Instances** button:

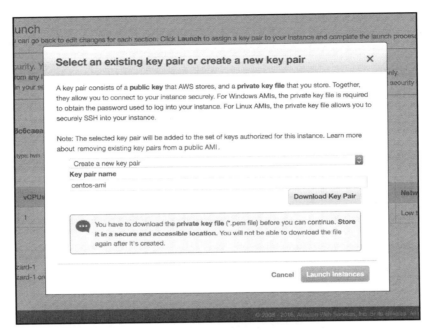

You're prompted to create a pair of encryption keys the first time you launch the image

5. On the launch status page, click on the **View Instances** button at the bottom of the page. Then, right-click on the running instance and select **Connect** from the context menu. Select the preferred connection method and follow the instructions that appear on the screen.

How it works...

This recipe walked you through the steps necessary to spin up a new CentOS AMI on AWS's EC2 platform. To log in to the system, a password or set of encryption keys is needed, and since the primary user account's password is likely to be unknown, we opted to generate a new pair of keys. The private key is downloaded and then used with your SSH client to authenticate your login.

Once you have logged in to your running system, it's worth viewing the contents of the `/etc/system-release` file to verify the running version of CentOS. Also, you should use the `passwd` command to change the root account's password if the account isn't already locked down. This is an important security precaution because you don't know who knows the default password. You'll find recipes for managing user permissions in Chapter 3, *User and Permission Management,* and recipes for managing remote access in Chapter 6, *Allowing Remote Access:*

```
● ● ●                    ⇑ tboronczyk — bash — 83×24
TB-C02P12CUG3QC:~ tboronczyk$ chmod 400 centos-ami.pem
TB-C02P12CUG3QC:~ tboronczyk$ ssh -i centos-ami.pem root@52.88.155.116
The authenticity of host '52.88.155.116 (52.88.155.116)' can't be established.
RSA key fingerprint is 9e:bf:9a:af:62:0d:14:9d:0d:a0:5a:14:80:89:18:28.
Are you sure you want to continue connecting (yes/no)? yes
Warning: Permanently added '52.88.155.116' (RSA) to the list of known hosts.
Last login: Sat Jul 30 22:37:14 from 71.176.76.158
[root@ip 172.31.31.202 ~]# passwd
Changing password for user root.
New password:
Retype password:
passwd: all authentication tokens updated successfully.
[root@ip 172.31.31.202 ~]# cat /etc/system-release
CentOS release 7.1.1503 (Core)
[root@ip 172.31.31.202 ~]#
```

After you log in, verify the system's version number and update the root password

See also

Refer to the following resources for more information on working with AMIs on Amazon's EC2 platform:

- What Is Amazon EC2? (http://docs.aws.amazon.com/AWSEC2/latest/UserGuide/concepts.html)
- Connect to Your Linux Instance (http://docs.aws.amazon.com/AWSEC2/latest/UserGuide/AccessingInstances.html)
- Remove SSH Host Key Pairs (http://docs.aws.amazon.com/AWSEC2/latest/UserGuide/building-shared-amis.html#remove-ssh-host-key-pairs)

Installing a container image from the Docker Registry

This recipe shows you how to procure a CentOS base for your development needs using Docker, a virtualization strategy based on the concept of containers. Each container wraps the target software in its own filesystem so that it can run regardless of the operating system on which it's installed. Developers like Docker especially because it helps provide consistency between development and deployment environments.

Getting ready

The recipe assumes that you have a system with Docker installed. If you don't, you can obtain the Docker installer from `http://www.docker.com`.

How to do it...

Follow these steps to install a CentOS container image from the Docker Registry:

1. Open the Docker Toolbox terminal program.
2. At the terminal's prompt, invoke the `docker pull` command to retrieve a CentOS 7 container:

```
docker pull centos:7
```

3. After the container has been downloaded, you can launch an interactive shell with `docker run`:

```
docker run -i -t centos:7 /bin/bash
```

How it works...

This recipe retrieves the official CentOS container from the Docker Registry using the `docker pull` command. By providing the version tag (`:7`), we can make sure we retrieved CentOS 7 as opposed to an earlier (or perhaps newer) version.

Alternatively, Kitematic is the graphical program which lets us search for and retrieve containers from the registry. Simply launch Kitematic and enter CentOS as the search term in the search box. Then, look for the official CentOS repository in the results list.

The default version retrieved by Kitematic is the latest. To specifically select CentOS 7 or a maintenance release, click on the entry's ellipsis button. Set the desired tag and then click on the **Create** button:

Kitematic displays the results of searching for CentOS

See also

Refer to the following resources for more information about working with Docker:

- Docker home page (http://www.docker.com)
- Understanding the Docker architecture (https://docs.docker.com/engine/understanding-docker)
- The official CentOS Docker hub (https://hub.docker.com/_/centos)

Installing the GNOME desktop

This recipe shows you how to install the GNOME desktop environment, which provides a graphical user interface (GUI) for working with your CentOS system. Usually, such environments aren't installed on server systems, but it can be convenient sometimes to have one available. For example, an administrator might feel more comfortable updating a system's configuration using graphical programs.

GNOME isn't the only GUI environment available —other popular environments include KDE, XFCE, and Fluxbox. If GNOME isn't your cup of tea, the next recipe shows you how to install KDE.

Getting ready

This recipe requires a CentOS system with a working network connection. Administrative privileges are also required by logging in with the root account.

How to do it...

Follow these steps to install the GNOME desktop environment:

1. Install the GNOME Desktop package group with yum groupinstall:

```
yum groupinstall "GNOME Desktop"
```

2. Manually start the desktop environment using `startx`:

```
startx
```

3. If more than one environment is installed, you'll need to specify the path to `gnome-session`:

```
startx /usr/bin/gnome-session
```

4. When you're done using GNOME and log out of the desktop, you'll be returned to the console.
5. To configure the system to automatically start the graphical environment when it boots, set the default start up target to `graphical.target`:

```
systemctl set-default graphical.target
```

How it works...

This recipe uses `yum` to install the GNOME desktop environment. All of the necessary components and dependencies are installed by the `GNOME Desktop` package group. Package groups saves us time and hassle because they let us install a collection of packages for a common task at the same time instead of individual packages one at a time.

```
yum groupinstall "GNOME Desktop"
```

Unlike Windows, where the graphical desktop is part of its operating system, Linux systems delegate basic graphics and input handling to a graphics server. This approach is one reason why there are several desktop environments to choose from —it abstracts many of the specifics and provides a common platform on top of which any number of environments can run, both locally and across a network. CentOS's default graphics server is X Window System.

If GNOME is the only desktop environment installed, it'll be run by default when we launch X with `startx`. However, if more than one desktop is installed, we need to tell X which one we want to run. For GNOME, we provide the path to `gnome-session`:

```
startx /usr/bin/gnome-session
```

The GNOME desktop provides a graphical interface for working with the system

The systemd service manager is responsible for starting various servers and processes when the system boots. The `systemctl` command is our interface to the service manager and can be used to set the default boot target. The default target dictates whether the system boots to a terminal or GUI-based login screen:

```
systemctl set-default graphical.target
```

When set to graphical, systemd starts X and the GNOME Display Manager when the system boots, which presents us with a graphical login to provide our account details. Once we're authenticated, the desktop session is initiated and we find ourselves at the GNOME desktop.

If you no longer want to boot to the graphical environment, you can set the default target back to multiuser and the system will boot to the terminal-based login screen again:

```
systemctl set-default multi-user.target
```

You can choose which desktop environment you want to use if more than one environment is installed by selecting it from the gear button on the login screen:

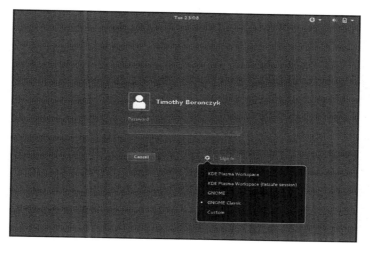

You can select your preferred desktop from the login screen

See also

The following resources will provide you with more information about installing graphical desktop environments and using the GNOME desktop:

- GNOME Library (https://help.gnome.org)
- RHEL 7 Desktop Migration and Administration Guide (https://access.redhat.com/documentation/en-US/Red_Hat_Enterprise_Linux/7/html/Desktop_Migration_and_Administration_Guide)
- *Guild to X11/Starting Sessions* (https://en.wikibooks.org/wiki/Guide_to_X11/Starting_Sessions)

- How to install desktop environments on CentOS 7 (`http://unix.stackexchange.com/questions/18153/how-to-install-desktop-environments-on-centos-7/18154#18154`)

Installing the KDE Plasma desktop

Separating the graphical interface from the operating system gives users the power to choose the graphical environment they like best. Don't worry if you're not a GNOME fan because there are still many other desktops you can explore! This recipe shows you how to install another popular desktop environment, KDE Plasma Workspaces.

Getting ready

This recipe requires a CentOS system with a working network connection. Administrative privileges are also required by logging in with the root account.

How to do it...

Follow these steps to install the KDE Plasma Workspaces desktop environment:

1. Install the KDE Plasma Workspaces package group:

   ```
   yum groupinstall "KDE Plasma Workspaces"
   ```

2. Manually start the desktop environment using startkde. When you're done using KDE and log out of the desktop, you'll be returned to the console:

   ```
   startkde
   ```

3. To configure the system to automatically start the graphical environment when it boots, use systemctl to set the default start up target to graphical.target:

   ```
   systemctl set-default graphical.target
   ```

How it works...

This recipe installs the KDE Plasma Workspaces desktop environment via Yum's package groups. All of the necessary software components and dependencies to run KDE are installed by the KDE Plasma Workspaces package group:

```
yum groupinstall "KDE Plasma Workspaces"
```

The startkde script starts the X server and launches the KDE environment together. Unlike with GNOME, we're not invoking startx directly, so we don't need to provide additional paths when more than one environment is installed:

```
startkde
```

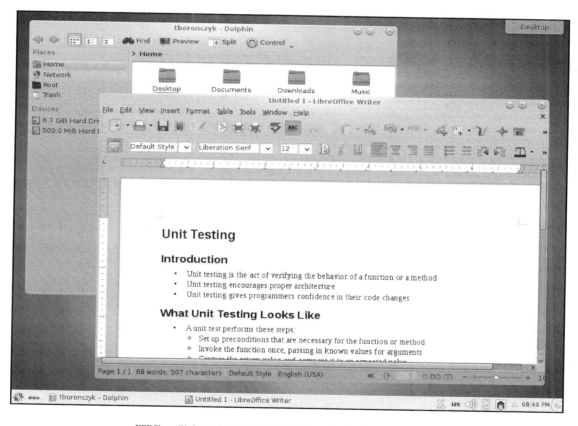

KDE Plasma Workspaces is a popular graphical desktop environment for Linux-based systems

See also

The following resources will provide you with more information about installing and using KDE Plasma Workspaces:

- How to install desktop environments on CentOS 7 (`http://unix.stackexchange.com/questions/18153/how-to-install-desktop-environments-on-centos-7/18154#18154`)
- KDE documentation (`https://docs.kde.org`)

2
Networking

This chapter contains the following recipes:

- Setting a static IP address
- Binding multiple addresses to a single Ethernet device
- Bonding two Ethernet devices
- Configuring the network firewall with FirewallD
- Configuring the network firewall using iptables
- Installing a DHCP server
- Configuring an NFS server to share a filesystem
- Configuring an NFS client to use a shared filesystem
- Serving Windows shares with Samba

Introduction

The recipes in this chapter cover various networking tasks that should prove useful to you as a CentOS administrator. You'll learn how to configure a static IP address, bind multiple addresses to a single Ethernet device, and bond two devices together. You'll also see how to configure the system's firewall using FirewallD and iptables, and how to set up a DHCP server to distribute IP addresses, which allows other computers using dynamic networking configurations to access the network. The remaining recipes will teach you how to set up centralized file storage using NFS and Samba.

Setting a static IP address

This recipe shows you how to configure a static IP address. Unless you configured a static address during installation, CentOS uses the Dynamic Host Configuration Protocol (DHCP) to obtain an IP address to communicate across the network. Using a dynamically assigned address is fine for most desktop and laptop systems, but those that host e-mail servers, file sharing and print services, and web servers should have an address that doesn't change. The static address provides a stable, known location on the network where users can access a system's services.

Getting ready

This recipe requires a CentOS system with a working network connection and administrative privileges provided by logging in with the `root` account. It assumes that your primary Ethernet device is named `enp0s3` and is currently configured with DHCP. If your device is named differently, substitute its name appropriately in the following commands.

How to do it...

Follow these steps to configure a static IP address:

1. Open the Ethernet device's configuration file, found under `/etc/sysconfig/network-scripts`,with your text editor:

   vi /etc/sysconfig/network-scripts/ifcfg-enp0s3

2. Change the value of BOOTPROTO to none:

   BOOTPROTO="none"

3. At the end of the file, add the IPADDR, NETMASK, and BROADCAST entries to set the desired IP address. Assign them values that properly reflect your network:

```
IPADDR="192.168.56.100"
NETMASK="255.255.255.0"
BROADCAST="192.168.56.255"
```

```
TYPE="Ethernet"
BOOTPROTO="static"
DEFROUTE="yes"
PEERDNS="yes"
PEERROUTES="yes"
IPV4_FAILURE_FATAL="no"
IPV6INIT="yes"
IPV6_AUTOCONF="yes"
IPV6_DEFROUTE="yes"
IPV6_PEERDNS="yes"
IPV6_PEERROUTES="yes"
IPV6_FAILURE_FATAL="no"
NAME="enp0s3"
UUID="73aa0ca8-6ba9-460e-9095-ace519395314"
DEVICE="enp0s3"
ONBOOT="yes"
IPADDR="192.168.56.100"
NETMASK=255.255.255.0"
BROADCAST="192.168.56.255"

~
~
~
--- INSERT ---
```

The interface is configured with a static IP address

4. Save your changes and close the file.
5. Open the /etc/sysconfig/network file using your editor:

```
vi /etc/sysconfig/network
```

6. Add a GATEWAY entry to identify your network's gateway:

```
GATEWAY="192.168.56.1"
```

7. Save your changes and close the file.
8. Restart the networking service for the configuration changes to take effect:

```
systemctl restart network.service
```

How it works…

In this recipe, you learned how to assign a static IP address to an Ethernet device. It assumed the name of your primary Ethernet device to be enp0s3, thus ifcfg-enp0s3 would be the name of the device's configuration file. If your device is named differently (for example, eth0, eno1677, and so on) then you need to adjust the recipe's directions accordingly.

First, we changed the value for BOOTPROTO from dhcp, the protocol used to obtain an IP address dynamically, to none since we are setting the address ourselves. Then we added the IPADDR, NETMASK, and BROADCAST entries to provide the details of the static IP address. Next, we specified the network's default gateway using GATEWAY in /etc/sysconfig/network. This allows us to route traffic beyond the local subnetwork.

After you restart the networking service, you can confirm the new address using the ip command. ip addr show will display information about the current state of your system's network devices:

```
[root@benito network-scripts]# ip addr show
1: lo: <LOOPBACK,UP,LOWER_UP> mtu 65536 qdisc noqueue state UNKNOWN
    link/loopback 00:00:00:00:00:00 brd 00:00:00:00:00:00
    inet 127.0.0.1/8 scope host lo
       valid_lft forever preferred_lft forever
    inet6 ::1/128 scope host
       valid_lft forever preferred_lft forever
2: enp0s3: <BROADCAST,MULTICAST,UP,LOWER_UP> mtu 1500 qdisc pfifo_fast state UP
qlen 1000
    link/ether 08:00:27:a5:96:2d brd ff:ff:ff:ff:ff:ff
    inet 192.168.56.100/24 brd 192.168.56.255 scope global dynamic enp0s3
       valid_lft 410sec preferred_lft 410sec
    inet6 fe80::a00:27ff:fea5:962d/64 scope link
       valid_lft forever preferred_lft forever
[root@benito network-scripts]#
```

ip addr show displays your system's networking information

See also

For more information on configuring network settings in CentOS, refer to the *Configure IP Networking* chapter in the RHEL 7 Networking Guide (https://access.redhat.com/documentation/en-US/Red_Hat_Enterprise_Linux/7/html/Networking_Guide/ch-Configure_IP_Networking.html).

Binding multiple addresses to a single Ethernet device

This recipe shows you how to bind multiple IP addresses to a single Ethernet device. The ability to assign more than one address to the same device can be useful-the most obvious benefit is that you don't need to procure multiple Ethernet cards. The cost of hardware has dropped substantially, but IT budgets still run tight. Perhaps a less obvious benefit, but one more valuable, is the greater flexibility it gives when configuring network services. Different services, such as e-mail and websites, can run on the same system but be accessed using different addresses.

Getting ready

This recipe requires a CentOS system with a working network connection. It assumes that your primary Ethernet device is enp0s3 and is configured with a static IP address. You'll also need administrative privileges provided by logging in with the root account.

How to do it...

Follow these steps to bind multiple addresses to the same Ethernet device:

1. Make a copy of the device's configuration file:

   ```
   cp /etc/sysconfig/network-scripts/ifcfg-enp0s3
   /etc/sysconfig/network-scripts/ifcfg-enp0s3:1
   ```

2. Open the new file with your text editor:

   ```
   vi /etc/sysconfig/network-scripts/ifcfg-enp0s3:1
   ```

3. Delete the UUID entry entirely. If a HWADDR entry exists, delete that also.
4. Update the NAME and DEVICE values:

   ```
   NAME="System enp0s3:1"
   DEVICE="enp0s3:1"
   ```

5. Change the value of IPADDR to the IP address you wish to use:

   ```
   IPADDR="192.168.56.101"
   ```

6. Save your changes and close the file.

7. Restart the networking service for the configuration changes to take effect:

   ```
   systemctl restart network.service
   ```

How it works...

In this recipe, you learned how to assign multiple IP addresses to the same Ethernet device. We made a copy of one of the original network configuration files, taking care to name it appropriately to create a virtual adapter, and edited its configuration details. Since the name of the first device's configuration is ifcfg-enp0s3, the new file is named ifcfg-enp0s3:1 to create the first virtual adapter associated with that device. If you want to add more adapters (assign more IP addresses), repeat the steps using incrementing numbers, for example, enp0s3:2, enp0s3:3, and so on.

In the configuration file, we removed the HWADDR and UUID entries since they are not needed for a virtual adapter. Then we updated the DEVICE and NAME entries to give the adapter its own identify, and, of course, we updated the IPADDR entry to assign its IP address:

```
[root@benito network-scripts]# ip addr show
1: lo: <LOOPBACK,UP,LOWER_UP> mtu 65536 qdisc noqueue state UNKNOWN
    link/loopback 00:00:00:00:00:00 brd 00:00:00:00:00:00
    inet 127.0.0.1/8 scope host lo
       valid_lft forever preferred_lft forever
    inet6 ::1/128 scope host
       valid_lft forever preferred_lft forever
2: enp0s3: <BROADCAST,MULTICAST,UP,LOWER_UP> mtu 1500 qdisc pfifo_fast state UP
qlen 1000
    link/ether 08:00:27:a5:96:2d brd ff:ff:ff:ff:ff:ff
    inet 192.168.56.100/24 brd 192.168.56.255 scope global enp0s3
       valid_lft forever preferred_lft forever
    inet 192.168.56.101/24 brd 192.168.56.255 scope global secondary enp0s3:1
       valid_lft forever preferred_lft forever
    inet6 fe80::a00:27ff:fea5:962d/64 scope link
       valid_lft forever preferred_lft forever
[root@benito network-scripts]#
```

Multiple IP addresses are bound to an Ethernet device via a virtual adapter

See also

Refer to the following resources for more information on binding multiple addresses to the same Ethernet device:

- Create Multiple IP Addresses to One Single Network Interface (http://www.tecm int.com/create-multiple-ip-addresses-to-one-single-network-interfac e)
- Assign Multiple IP Addresses To Single Network Interface Card On CentOS 7 (ht tp://www.unixmen.com/linux-basics-assign-multiple-ip-addresses-singl e-network-interface-card-centos-7)
- Adding Secondary IP Addresses (https://dbiers.me/adding-secondary-ip-a ddresses-centosrhel/)

Bonding two Ethernet devices

In this recipe, you'll learn how to combine multiple Ethernet devices as a single network device in a configuration known as channel bonding. Channel bonding allows us to bind multiple devices together so that they appear as a single interface to servers running on the CentOS system. Its purpose is to improve your system's overall network performance and provide redundancy if one of the network devices fails.

Getting ready

This recipe requires a CentOS system with at least two Ethernet devices. It assumes that your primary Ethernet device is enp0s3. If your device is named differently, substitute the name appropriately in the recipe's commands. You'll also need administrative privileges provided by logging in with the root account.

How to do it...

Follow these steps to bond two Ethernet devices:

1. Install the bind-utils and ethtool packages:

```
yum install bind-utils ethtool
```

2. Create a new configuration file for the bonded interface:

    ```
    vi /etc/sysconfig/network-scripts/ifcfg-bond0
    ```

3. Add the following lines to the file, substituting values for IPADDR, NETMASK, and BROADCAST that are appropriate for your network:

    ```
    BOOTPROTO="none"
    DEVICE="bond0"
    USERCTL="no"
    ONBOOT="yes"
    IPADDR="192.168.56.100"
    NETMASK="255.255.255.0"
    BROADCAST="192.168.56.255"
    ```

4. Save your changes and close the configuration file.

5. Open the configuration file of the first device you wish to bond:

    ```
    vi /etc/sysconfig/network-scripts/ifcfg-enp0s3
    ```

6. Make sure BOOTPROTO is set to none and ONBOOT is set to yes. Then remove the IPADDR, NETMASK, and BROADCAST entries if they exist.

7. Add the SLAVE and MASTER entries at the end of the file:

    ```
    SLAVE=yes
    MASTER=bond0
    ```

8. Save your changes and close the configuration file.

9. Repeat steps 5-8 for each additional device you want to bond.

10. Create the configuration file used by the kernel to control how the bonding interface should behave:

    ```
    vi /etc/modprobe.d/bonding.conf
    ```

11. Add the following lines to the file:

    ```
    alias bond0 bonding
    options bond0 mode=5 miimon=100
    ```

12. Save your changes and close the file.

13. Register the bonding module with the system's kernel:

```
modprobe bonding
```

14. Restart networking services for the changes to take effect:

```
systemctl restart network.service
```

How it works...

We began by creating a configuration file for the bonding interface at `/etc/sysconfig/network-scripts/ifcfg-bond0`. BOOTPROTO was set to none because the IP address is set statically, DEVICE gives a name to the interface, USERCTL was set to no to prohibit nonadministrative users from bringing the interface up and down, and ONBOOT was set to yes so that the interface will be automatically activated. We also gave the IP address information with IPADDR, NETMASK, and BROADCAST:

```
BOOTPROTO="none"
DEVICE="bond0"
USERCTL="no"
ONBOOT="yes"
IPADDR="192.168.56.100"
NETMASK="255.255.255.0"
BROADCAST="192.168.56.255"
```

Then we updated the configuration files for each device we want to bond. We made sure BOOTPROTO was set to none and there was no address information since the device will no longer need its own IP address. Adding the SLAVE and MASTER entries, we identified the device as being bound to the new bond0 device:

```
SLAVE=yes
MASTER=bond0
```

By performing these steps, we have created a new virtual device known as the bonding master that will use our real Ethernet devices as slaves. If one slave device fails, the other slave will still be active, providing redundancy.

Next, we created a new configuration file with our preferences for the kernel bonding module. The module is the kernel implementation of the bonding device and is responsible for coordinating the physical devices:

```
alias bond0 bonding
options bond0 miimon=100 mode=5
```

`miimon=100` specifies that MII link monitoring will occur every `100` milliseconds to verify that the physical devices are active. `mode=5` represents a basic configuration that doesn't require any specific type of network switch support. It allows outgoing traffic to be distributed according to the current load on each slave device. There are five other modes which give you plenty of options in configuring how the devices work together, although you should be aware that some modes may require specific hardware support. Refer to `http://wiki.centos.org/TipsAndTricks/BondingInterfaces` for more information.

After making changes to the device's configuration files, we registered the bonding kernel module using `modprobe`:

```
modprobe bonding
```

```
[root@benito network-scripts]# ip addr show
1: lo: <LOOPBACK,UP,LOWER_UP> mtu 65536 qdisc noqueue state UNKNOWN
    link/loopback 00:00:00:00:00:00 brd 00:00:00:00:00:00
    inet 127.0.0.1/8 scope host lo
       valid_lft forever preferred_lft forever
    inet6 ::1/128 scope host
       valid_lft forever preferred_lft forever
2: enp0s3: <BROADCAST,MULTICAST,SLAVE,UP,LOWER_UP> mtu 1500 qdisc pfifo_fast mas
ter bond0 state UP qlen 1000
    link/ether 08:00:27:a5:96:2d brd ff:ff:ff:ff:ff:ff
3: enp0s8: <BROADCAST,MULTICAST,SLAVE,UP,LOWER_UP> mtu 1500 qdisc pfifo_fast mas
ter bond0 state UP qlen 1000
    link/ether 08:00:27:38:c2:0f brd ff:ff:ff:ff:ff:ff
4: bond0: <BROADCAST,MULTICAST,MASTER,UP,LOWER_UP> mtu 1500 qdisc noqueue state
UP
    link/ether 08:00:27:a5:96:2d brd ff:ff:ff:ff:ff:ff
    inet 192.168.56.101/24 brd 192.168.56.255 scope global bond0
       valid_lft forever preferred_lft forever
    inet6 fe80::a00:27ff:fea5:962d/64 scope link
       valid_lft forever preferred_lft forever
[root@benito network-scripts]#
```

Two Ethernet devices are bound with the same IP addresses through the bonding adapter

See also

For more information on bonding Ethernet devices CentOS, refer to the *Configure Network Bonding* chapter in the RHEL 7 Networking Guide (`https://access.redhat.com/documen tation/en-US/Red_Hat_Enterprise_Linux/7/html/Networking_Guide/ch-Configure_N etwork_Bonding.html`).

Configuring the network firewall with FirewallD

Now you'll learn how to configure the networking firewall using FirewallD. Starting with CentOS 7, FirewallD replaces iptables as the default firewall configuration utility (although iptables is still used behind the scenes by FirewallD). Based on which zones and services you configure, you can increase the network security of your server by controlling what traffic is allowed or disallowed to and from the system.

Getting ready

This recipe requires a CentOS system with a working network connection. You'll also need administrative privileges provided by logging in with the `root` account.

How to do it...

This collection of commands will show you how to perform several basic configuration tasks using FirewallD's command-line client, `firewall-cmd`:

1. To identify the currently active zones and which Ethernet devices are assigned to them, use the `--get-active-zones` flag:

   ```
   firewall-cmd --get-active-zones
   ```

2. To temporarily change which zone a device is assigned to, use the `--zone` argument to specify the target zone and `--change-interface` to specify the Ethernet device:

   ```
   firewall-cmd --zone=public --change-interface=enp0s3
   ```

3. To permanently assign a device to a zone, add a ZONE entry to the device's configuration file. This change will not take effect until the service has been restarted:

   ```
   vi /etc/sysconfig/network-scripts/ifcfg-enp0s3
   ZONE="public"
   ```

4. To identify the current configuration for a zone, use the `--zone` argument to specify the target zone and include `--list-all`:

```
firewall-cmd --zone=public --list-all
```

5. To allow traffic through the firewall, use the `--add-service` or `--add-port` arguments:

> Traffic for common services and protocols such as HTTP and SMTP can be allowed by name. The following adds the `http` service which opens port `80` (the port used by Apache and other HTTP servers):

```
firewall-cmd --zone=public --permanent --add-service=http
```

> Traffic can always be allowed directly given the port and network protocol. The following opens port 8080 to TCP traffic, another port commonly used to serve web content:

```
firewall-cmd --zone=public --permanent --add-port=8080/tcp
```

6. To disallow traffic that is currently allowed through the firewall, use the `--remove-service` or `--remove-port` arguments:

```
firewall-cmd --zone=public --permanent --remove-service=http
firewall-cmd --zone=public --permanent --remove- port=8080/tcp
```

7. To reload the firewall after making a change, use `--reload` :

```
firewall-cmd --reload
```

How it works...

The default installation of FirewallD makes several preconfigured zones available, for example, `public`, `dmz`, `work`, `home`, and `trusted`. Different interfaces can be assigned to different zones and have different rules applied. To see all of the available zones and their configuration, we can invoke `firewall-cmd` with the `--list-all-zones` flag:

```
firewall-cmd --list-all-zones
```

Most updates made to the firewall rules will take effect immediately but are temporary. We saw this earlier when we had to update the device's configuration file and restart the service to make a zone change permanent. This lets us experiment with different settings before finalizing the configuration. When configuring services and ports, the `--permanent` flag is used to make the changes permanent. If you don't provide the flag, the changes will take effect immediately but will only be temporary (not persist across a system reboot or restart of the firewall service):

```
firewall-cmd --zone=public --permanent --remove-service=http
```

Named services are preconfigured port settings that are common to a specific network service and are available for our convenience. For example, SSH traffic commonly consists of TCP packets destined for port 22, so the `ssh` service reflects this. In the examples, we used the `http` service, which configured port 80, the standard port used to serve web pages. While assigning the port directly has the same effect, services provide convenient, human-readable names and should be used when possible. To get a list of all available services, use `--get-services`:

```
firewall-cmd --get-services
```

```
[root@benito ~]# firewall-cmd --get-active-zone
public
  interfaces: enp0s3
[root@benito ~]# firewall-cmd --get-services
RH-Satellite-6 amanda-client bacula bacula-client dhcp dhcpv6 dhcpv6-client dns
ftp high-availability http https imaps ipp ipp-client ipsec kerberos kpasswd lda
p ldaps libvirt libvirt-tls mdns mountd ms-wbt mysql nfs ntp openvpn pmcd pmprox
y pmwebapi pmwebapis pop3s postgresql proxy-dhcp radius rpc-bind samba samba-cli
ent smtp ssh telnet tftp tftp-client transmission-client vnc-server wbem-https
[root@benito ~]# firewall-cmd --zone=public --permanent --add-service=http
success
[root@benito ~]# firewall-cmd --reload
success
[root@benito ~]# firewall-cmd --zone=public --list-all
public (default, active)
  interfaces: enp0s3
  sources:
  services: dhcpv6-client http ssh
  ports:
  masquerade: no
  forward-ports:
  icmp-blocks:
  rich rules:

[root@benito ~]#
```

firewall-cmd is a command-line client for configuring firewall rules

Named services are defined as XML files under `/usr/lib/firewalld/services`. If you want to allow access for some traffic but a service isn't defined, and you would prefer to perform the configuration using a service instead of the port and protocol for the sake of readability, you can create a new service file in this directory. Copy an existing file as your starting point and modify it to suit your needs.

See also

For more information on working with FirewallD, refer to the following resources:

- RHEL 7 Migration Planning Guide: Security and Access Control (`https://acces s.redhat.com/documentation/en-US/Red_Hat_Enterprise_%2Linux/7/html/M igration_Planning_Guide/sect-Red_Hat_Enterprise_%2Linux-Migration_Pl anning_Guide-Security_and_Access_%2Control.html`)
- FirewallD (`http://fedoraproject.org/wiki/FirewallD`)
- How To Set Up a Firewall Using FirewallD on CentOS 7 (`https://www.digitalo cean.com/community/tutorials/how-to-set-up-a-firewall-using-firewall d-on-centos-7`)

Configuring the network firewall using iptables

In this recipe, you'll learn how to replace FirewallD with the iptables service and perform basic firewall configurations. iptables was the default method for managing the firewall's settings in CentOS prior to version 7. Some administrators might prefer iptables because it's within their comfort level or maybe they have several older servers running in the data center and they want to maintain similarity as much as possible.

Getting ready

This recipe requires a CentOS system with a working network connection. You'll also need administrative privileges provided by logging in with the `root` account.

How to do it...

The following steps will allow you to replace FirewallD with the iptables service:

1. Stop the FirewallD service and disable it:

```
systemctl stop firewalld
systemctl mask firewalld
```

2. Install the `iptables-services` package which contains the service:

```
yum install iptables-services
```

3. Start the service and register it so that it will start automatically when the system is booted:

```
systemctl start iptables
systemctl enable iptables
```

The following collection of commands will show you how to perform several basic configuration tasks using `iptables`:

- Use the `-L` flag to print the current configuration. Add the `--line-numbers` flag to display each rule's ID number alongside it:

```
iptables -L --line-numbers
```

- Use the following command to allow TCP traffic on port 80 from the `enp0s3` interface through the firewall:

```
iptables -A INPUT -i enp0s3 --dport 80 -p tcp -j ACCEPT
```

- To remove the rule that allows TCP traffic on port 80, execute `iptables -L --line-numbers` to find the rule's ID and then use the following (replace ## with the rule's ID):

```
iptables -D INPUT ##
```

- Reload iptables after making configuration changes for them to be in effect:

```
systemctl restart iptables
```

How it works...

To replace FirewallD with the iptables service to manage the network firewall, we first stopped and disabled the FirewallD service; we don't want multiple firewall daemons running since it would lead to conflicts. FirewallD uses iptables behind the scenes so iptables is already installed, but the iptables service isn't. So, next we installed the `iptables-services` package:

```
yum install iptables-services
```

We then saw how to perform basic configurations to allow and disallow traffic. For example, the recipe presented the command to add a rule that allows TCP traffic through port 80:

```
iptables -A INPUT -i enp0s3 --dport 80 -p tcp -j ACCEPT
```

The `-A` argument indicates that we wish to add a firewall rule and is followed by the rule type. Possible values are `INPUT`, `OUTPUT`, and `FORWARD`, which apply to incoming traffic, outgoing traffic, and traffic that is routed, respectively (if the system is configured as a router, for example). Since `INPUT` is specified, our rule applies to incoming traffic on port 80.

The `-i` argument specifies the network interface that is monitored by the rule. In this case, the rule applies to `enp0s3`. Then, `--dport` specifies the traffic's destination port, in this case port 80, and `-p` specifies the transport protocol, for example, either TCP or UDP.

The `-j` argument is the target action for **jump to**. With iptables, rules are strung together to make chains of filtering logic. Imagine iptables checking traffic against each rule we've specified; if the first rule doesn't match, it goes on to check the next rule, and the next, until a match is found. When the matching rule is found, iptables stops checking and *jumps* to the desired state. Possible states are `ACCEPT` to accept the traffic, `REJECT` to actively deny the connection, and `DROP` to silently ignore it.

We also saw how to display the rules that are currently defined using the −L flag and that using −−line-numbers will display an identifier alongside each rule:

```
iptables -L --line-numbers
```

```
[root@benito ~]# iptables -L --line-numbers
Chain INPUT (policy ACCEPT)
num  target     prot opt source               destination
1    ACCEPT     all  --  anywhere             anywhere             state RELATED
,ESTABLISHED
2    ACCEPT     icmp --  anywhere             anywhere
3    ACCEPT     all  --  anywhere             anywhere
4    ACCEPT     tcp  --  anywhere             anywhere             state NEW tcp
dpt:ssh
5    REJECT     all  --  anywhere             anywhere             reject-with i
cmp-host-prohibited
6    ACCEPT     tcp  --  anywhere             anywhere             tcp dpt:http
7    ACCEPT     tcp  --  anywhere             anywhere             tcp dpt:smtp
8    ACCEPT     tcp  --  anywhere             anywhere             tcp dpt:imaps
9    ACCEPT     tcp  --  anywhere             anywhere             tcp dpt:pop3s
10   ACCEPT     tcp  --  anywhere             anywhere             tcp dpt:https
11   ACCEPT     tcp  --  anywhere             anywhere             tcp dpt:mysql

Chain FORWARD (policy ACCEPT)
num  target     prot opt source               destination
1    REJECT     all  --  anywhere             anywhere             reject-with i
cmp-host-prohibited

Chain OUTPUT (policy ACCEPT)
num  target     prot opt source               destination
[root@benito ~]#
```

iptables accepts or denies traffic based on the configured rules

Knowing a rule's identifier is convenient if we want to delete it. By providing −D, the rule type (INPUT, OUTPUT, or FORWARD), and the ID, we can succinctly remove a rule from the chain:

```
iptables -D INPUT 6
```

Alternatively, you can respecify the entire rule while substituting −A with −D to delete it:

```
iptables -D INPUT -i enp0s3 --dport 80 -p tcp -j ACCEPT
```

See also

Refer to the following resources for more information on working with iptables:

- How to Migrate from FirewallD to iptables on CentOS 7 (https://www.digitalocean.com/community/tutorials/how-to-migrate-from-firewalld-to-iptables-on-centos-7)

- How to List and Delete iptables Firewall Rules (`https://www.digitalocean.com/community/tutorials/how-to-list-and-delete-iptables-firewall-rules`)
- 25 Most Frequently Used Linux iptables Rules (`http://www.thegeekstuff.com/211/6/iptables-rules-examples`)
- Drop versus reject (`http://www.chiark.greenend.org.uk/~peterb/network/drop-vs-reject`)

Installing a DHCP server

This recipe will show you how to set up your own DHCP server on CentOS. DHCP is used to assign IP addresses and other network configuration details on demand to a client. While a system configured with a static IP address will already know all the necessary networking details, a system configured to use DHCP broadcasts a request on the network and waits to receive a response from the DHCP server.

Getting ready

This recipe requires a CentOS system with a working network connection. You'll also need administrative privileges provided by logging in with the `root` account.

 Only one DHCP server should be running on the network to prevent clients from receiving conflicting responses that can result in network instability. Many routers already have a DHCP service running on them, so check for this on your own network before proceeding.

How to do it...

Follow these steps to set up a DHCP server:

1. Install the `dhcp` package:

    ```
    yum install dhcp
    ```

2. Copy the example configuration file provided by the package to serve as the starting point of your server's configuration:

    ```
    cp /usr/share/doc/dhcp-4.2.5/dhcpd.conf.example
    /etc/dhcp/dhcpd.conf
    ```

3. Open the configuration file using your text editor:

```
vi /etc/dhcp/dhcpd.conf
```

4. Modify the configuration with values that make sense for your environment. In particular, you'll want to address the following options: domain-name and domain-name-servers, subnet, the dynamic-bootp range, broadcast-address, and routers. Here is an example configuration for a network of two subnets:

```
# option definitions common to all supported networks
option domain-name localdomain;
option domain-name-servers ns1.localdomain;
default-lease-time 600;
max-lease-time 7200;
# This DHCP server is the official DHCP server for the
# local network
authoritative;
# No service will be given on this subnet, but declaring
# it helps the server to understand the network topology.
subnet 192.168.56.0 netmask 255.255.255.0 {
}
# This is a basic subnet declaration
subnet 192.168.56.0 netmask 255.255.255.128 {
  range 192.168.56.110 192.168.56.120;
  option domain-name-servers ns1.localdomain;
  option domain-name "localdomain";
  option routers 192.168.56.1;
  option broadcast-address 192.168.56.127;
}
# This is the second subnet
subnet 192.168.56.128 netmask 255.255.255.128 {
  range 192.168.56.200 192.168.56.210;
  option domain-name-servers ns2.sub.localdomain;
  option domain-name "sub.localdomain";
  option routers 192.168.56.129;
  option broadcast-address 192.168.56.255;
}
```

5. Save your changes and close the file.
6. Start the dhcp service and enable it to start at system boot:

```
systemctl start dhcpd
systemctl enable dhcpd
```

7. Open ports 67 and 68 in the system's firewall to allow traffic:

```
firewall-cmd --zone=public --permanent --add-service=dhcp
firewall-cmd --reload
```

How it works...

A system configured to use DHCP will broadcast a request and wait to receive a response from the DHCP server. The server's response lets the client know which IP address, netmask, gateway information, and so on to use on the network. DHCP-provisioned addresses are usually leased, which means that after a set amount of time they expire and the client needs to send another request. The DHCP server, in addition to handing out connection details, must keep track of the addresses that have already been leased so that a client doesn't receive an address that's already in use by another system.

We began by installing the dhcpd package, which contains the server and example configuration files. Copying the example configuration to use as a starting point for our own saves us from having to draft the entire configuration from scratch:

```
cp /usr/share/doc/dhcp-4.2.5/dhcpd.conf.example  /etc/dhcp/dhcpd.conf
```

In the configuration file, there are several places where you need to provide values that make sense for your network. The minimal configuration file provided as an illustration in the recipe reflects a network divided into two subnets. The first subnet is 192.168.56.0/25 and the second is 192.168.56.128/25. Each subnet has its own declaration.

Examining the first subnet declaration, the subnet's ID is 192.168.56.0 with a netmask of 255.255.255.128. The range option will restrict the DHCP server in assigning IP addresses in the range of 192.168.56.110 to 120 (the other addresses are still valid and are available for static assignment). Subsequent option entries provide the subnet's broadcast-address and gateway, and override the domain name and nameservers defined globally:

```
# This is a basic subnet declaration
subnet 192.168.56.0 netmask 255.255.255.128 {
  range 192.168.56.110 192.168.56.120;
  option domain-name-servers ns1.localdomain;
  option domain-name "localdomain";
  option routers 192.168.56.1;
  option broadcast-address 192.168.56.127;
}
```

Configuring a DHCP server properly requires an understanding of computer networking. It is a complex topic and, as such, we can't discuss every option in detail. I advise you to read the manual page for `dhcpd.conf` for extra guidance. The page can be accessed using the `man` command:

```
man 5 dhcpd.conf
```

```
dhcpd.conf(5)                    File Formats Manual                    dhcpd.conf(5)

NAME
       dhcpd.conf - dhcpd configuration file

DESCRIPTION
       The  dhcpd.conf  file contains configuration information for dhcpd, the
       Internet Systems Consortium DHCP Server.

       The dhcpd.conf file is a free-form ASCII text file.  It  is  parsed  by
       the  recursive-descent  parser  built into dhcpd.  The file may contain
       extra tabs and newlines for formatting purposes.  Keywords in the  file
       are  case-insensitive.  Comments may be placed anywhere within the file
       (except within quotes).  Comments begin with the # character and end at
       the end of the line.

       The file essentially consists of a list of statements.  Statements fall
       into two broad categories - parameters and declarations.

       Parameter statements either say how to do something (e.g., how  long  a
       lease  to  offer),  whether to do something (e.g., should dhcpd provide
       addresses to unknown clients), or what parameters  to  provide  to  the
       client (e.g., use gateway 220.177.244.7).

       Declarations  are  used  to  describe  the  topology of the network, to
Manual page dhcpd.conf(5) line 1 (press h for help or q to quit)
```

The configuration file for dhcpd is documented in a manual page

Once the DHCP server was configured and running, we then needed to poke a hole in the firewall to allow requests and responses to flow freely. DHCP requests occur using UDP and ports 57 and 58 (you can allow them using the service defined for FirewallD):

```
firewall-cmd --zone=public --permanent --add-service=dhcp
firewall-cmd --reload
```

See also

For more information on setting up a DHCP server, refer to the following resources:

- The `dhcpd.conf` manual page (`man 5 dhcpd.conf`)
- RHEL 7 Networking Guide: DHCP Servers (`https://access.redhat.com/docum entation/en-US/Red_Hat_Enterprise_Linux/7/html/Networking_Guide/ch-D HCP_Servers.html`)

- Quick Start: Setup CentOS 7 as a DHCP Server
  (`www.yoyoclouds.com/2015/01/quick-start-setup-centos-7-as-dhcp.html`)
- Subnet Calculator (`www.subnet-calculator.com`)

Configuring an NFS server to share a filesystem

Network File System (NFS) is a protocol for a distributed filesystem. That is, we can store files to a directory on a remote server and clients can mount the share. The remote directory will appear to the client as if it were local, although all data saved to it resides on the server. This recipe shows you how to configure NFS on a server and expose the storage as a network share. (The next recipe will show you how to configure NFS on a client.)

Getting ready

This recipe requires a CentOS system with a working network connection. You'll also need administrative privileges provided by logging in with the `root` account.

How to do it...

Follow these steps to set up an NFS server:

1. Install the `nfs-utils` and `libnfsidmap` packages:

   ```
   yum install nfs-utils libnfsidmap
   ```

2. Create a globally accessible directory which will serve as the root of the file share:

   ```
   mkdir -m 777 /var/nfsshare
   ```

3. Open `/etc/exports` and add the following entry to mark the directory for export by NFS. When done, save and close the file:

   ```
   /var/nfsshare 192.168.56.0/24(rw,sync,root_squash)
   ```

   The `exports` file is very picky. Make sure there's no space between the network and the parenthesized options as well as no spaces around the commas that separate the options.

4. Start the necessary services and register them so that they will start when the server boots:

```
systemctl start rpcbind nfs-server
systemctl enable rpcbind nfs-server
```

5. Open ports 111, 2048, and 2049 in the firewall to allow traffic through:

```
firewall-cmd --permanent --zone public --add-service rpc-bind
firewall-cmd --permanent --zone public --add-service mountd
firewall-cmd --permanent --zone public --add-service nfs
firewall-cmd --reload
```

How it works...

In this recipe, you learned how to set up a shared network directory using NFS. After installing the appropriate packages, we created the shared directory, registered it to be exported, and started the necessary system services.

/etc/exports is the configuration file that manages which filesystems are exported and how. We added an entry that identified the directory we want to export, followed by which clients they are exported to and the options that govern how the export will be treated:

```
/var/nfsshare 192.168.56.0/24(rw,sync,root_squash)
```

In the example, we make the share available to 192.168.56.0/24, in other words, any host on the network. Alternatively, you can share the directory a single host or a range of hosts. An entry that shares the directory with a specific host looks like the following:

```
/var/nfsshare 192.168.56.101(rw,sync,root_squash)
```

The rw++ option allows both read and write access to the share. sync flushes any changes to a file immediately to disk. While writing to disk might make access to the file slower at times, the delay won't be noticeable unless your system is under high load, and it would seem like a fair trade-off for the safety that immediate flushes provide in the event of a crash.

NFS will effectively squash the root user's ownership when root_squash is provided by changing the owner to nfsnobody. This is a security measure that mitigates the risk of a root user on the client system attempting to write a file to the share with root ownership (otherwise a malicious user could store a file and mark it executable where it might be run with root privileges). If you want to squash the ownership of all files to nfsnobdy, you can use the all_squash option.

NFS relies on a few other services, which is why we also enabled rpcbind and opened firewall ports for rpcbind and mountd. NFS works on top of the Remote Procedure Call (RPC) protocol, and rcpind is responsible for mapping the RPC-based services to their ports. An incoming connection from a client first hits the rpcbind service, providing an RPC identifier. Rpcbind resolves the identifier to a particular service (NFS in this case) and redirects the client to the appropriate port. There, mountd handles the request to determine whether the requested share is exported and whether the client is allowed to access it.

See also

Refer to the following resources for more information about configuring an NFS server:

- The Network Filesystem (http://www.tldp.org/LDP/nag/node14.html)
- RHEL 7 Storage Administration Guide: NFS Server Configuration (https://access.redhat.com/documentation/en-US/Red_Hat_Enterprise_Linux/7/html/Storage_Administration_Guide/nfs-serverconfig.html)
- How to setup NFS Server on CentOS 7 (http://www.itzgeek.com/how-tos/linux/centos-how-tos/how-to-setup-nfs-server-on-centos-7-rhel-7-fedora-22.html)

Configuring an NFS client to use a shared filesystem

This recipe continues where the previous recipe left off, showing you how to configure NFS on a client system.

Getting ready

This recipe requires a CentOS system with a working network connection. It assumes that an NFS server has been configured as explained in the previous recipe. You'll also need administrative privileges provided by logging in with the root account.

How to do it...

Follow these steps to configure an NFS client:

1. Install the `nfs-utils` and `libnfsidmap` packages:

   ```
   yum install nfs-utils libnfsidmap
   ```

2. Create the directory which will serve as the mount point for the remote filesystem:

   ```
   mkdir /mnt/nfs
   ```

3. Start the `rpcbind` service and register it so that it will start when the server boots:

   ```
   systemctl start rpcbind
   systemctl enable rpcbind
   ```

4. Mount the NFS share to the mount point:

   ```
   mount -t nfs 192.168.56.100:/var/nfsshare /mnt/nfs
   ```

How it works...

Like the server side, the client side of NFS relies on RPC. So, we started and enabled the rpcbind service. The `mount` command is then used to mount the remote share:

```
mount -t nfs 192.168.56.100:/var/nfsshare /mnt/nfs
```

The `-t` argument indicates the share's filesystem type, which, of course is, `nfs`. The location of the remote share is also provided, the IP address of the server and the directory of the shared data separated by a colon. Finally, the mount target is given.

To manually unmount the share, the `umount` command is used with the mount point:

```
umount /mnt/nfs
```

We can also configure the system to mount the NFS share automatically at boot time. Open `/etc/fstab` using your editor and add the following line:

```
192.168.0.100:/var/nfsshare /mnt/nfs/var/nfsshare nfs defaults 0 0
```

The share will be automatically mounted when the system boots. Since `mount` can look up information in `/etc/fstab`, the invocation to mount the share manually becomes much simpler once it's registered in this manner. You can now mount the share manually by providing just the `mount`:

```
mount /mnt/nfs
```

See also

Refer to the following resources for more information about configuring an NFS client:

- The `mount` manual page (`man 8 mount`)
- Setting up an NFS Client (`http://www.tldp.org/HOWTO/NFS-HOWTO/client.htm l`)
- RHEL 7 Storage Administration Guide: NFS Client Configuration (`https://acce ss.redhat.com/documentation/en-US/Red_Hat_Enterprise_Linux/7/html/St orage_Administration_Guide/nfs-clientconfig.html`)
- How to setup NFS Server on CentOS 7 (`http://www.itzgeek.com/how-tos/lin ux/centos-how-tos/how-to-setup-nfs-server-on-centos-7-rhel-7-fedora- 22.html`)

Serving Windows shares with Samba

In this recipe, you will learn how to serve a Windows share from a CentOS system using Samba. Like NFS, a Windows share is a directory on a remote server that a client may access to store files. Samba is a server that understands the SMB protocol used by Windows so that it can export directories that a Windows client can mount.

Getting ready

This recipe requires a CentOS system with a working network connection. You'll also need administrative privileges provided by logging in with the `root` account.

The name of your Windows workgroup is needed to configure Samba properly. Before you begin, on your Windows system in your network, run `net config workstation` and record the `Workstation domain` value:

```
Command Prompt                                              —    □    ×

Microsoft Windows [Version 10.0.10586]
(c) 2015 Microsoft Corporation. All rights reserved.

C:\Users\Timothy>net config workstation
Computer name                           \\SPECTRUM
Full Computer name                      Spectrum
User name                               Timothy

Workstation active on
        NetBT_Tcpip_{A3AADBFB-8EA3-4A29-9DDB-486C77C71A45} (005056C00001)
        NetBT_Tcpip_{B99928ED-5BB3-428F-A3C7-0904B23A5EC1} (78E3B5C32991)

Software version                        Windows 10 Home

Workstation domain                      WORKGROUP
Logon domain                            Spectrum

COM Open Timeout (sec)                  0
COM Send Count (byte)                   16
COM Send Timeout (msec)                 250
The command completed successfully.


C:\Users\Timothy>
```

net config workstation displays information about the Windows system's workgroup and domain

How to do it...

Follow these steps to set up Samba to share directories with Windows systems:

1. Install the `samba` package:

   `yum install samba`

2. Create a dedicated group for Samba users:

   `groupadd smbgroup`

3. Create the directory which will serve as the root of the file share. Set its group ownership to the new Samba users group:

```
mkdir -m 770 /var/sambashare
chgrp smbgroup /var/sambashare
```

4. Open Samba's configuration file using your text editor:

```
vi /etc/samba/smb.conf
```

5. Update the workgroup parameter in the [global] section to match the Windows workgroup name. Feel free to review the other parameters in the configuration file as each is clearly documented with helpful comments:

```
Workgroup = WORKGROUP
```

6. At the end of the configuration file, add the following content:

```
[share]
path = /var/sambashare
guest ok = no
valid users = @smbgroup
writable = yes
create mask = 0755
```

7. Save your changes and close the file.
8. Start the necessary services and register them so that they will start when the server boots:

```
systemctl start smb nmb
systemctl enable smb nmb
```

9. Open ports 137–139 and 445 to allow the network traffic:

```
firewall-cmd --permanent --zone public --add-service samba
firewall-cmd --reload
```

10. For each user who will connect to the share, assign them to the users group and register the password they will use:

```
usermod -a -G smbgroup tboronczyk
smbpasswd -a tboronczyk
```

How it works...

In this recipe, you learned how to install and configure Samba to share a directory which a Windows client can access.

We started by doing a bit of research using the `net config` command to discover the Windows workgroup that our client belongs to. This is important because two systems on the same network but identifying themselves as part of different workgroups will not be able to communicate with one another. In the example, the workgroup's name was simply WORKGROUP.

Next, we installed the `samba` package and created a special group named `smbgroup`. We'll configure Samba so that any user account on the CentOS system will be able to access the share as long as it's assigned to the `smbgroup` group. Then we created the directory we would be sharing and set its group ownership to the new group.

We then edited Samba's configuration file, specifying the name of the Windows workgroup we looked up earlier for the `workgroup` value, and added a section to define the new share. We restricted the share so that only authenticated users belonging to `smbgroup` can access it by setting `guest ok` to `no` and `valid users` to `@smbgroup`. The `writable` entry allows users to create and update files on the share (otherwise the files would be read-only), and the `create mask` entry was used to specify the default file permissions that new files will be assigned in the Linux filesystem. The name `share` within brackets not only starts that configuration section but also serves as the name the share will be exported as (that is, `\\192.168.56.100\share`). You can export multiple shares as long as each name is distinct.

For each user account that will be used to connect to the share, we made sure it belonged to the `smbgroup` and used the `smbpasswd` command to specify a password the account would use to authenticate its SMB sessions. This password is maintained separately from the system's credentials and is valid only for authenticating to Samba, so a password different from the account's login password should be chosen.

Managing Samba users is done using `smbpasswd`. The `-a` flag adds an entry in Samba's account database, and we can delete a user from the database using the `-x` flag:

```
smbpasswd -x tboronczyk
```

On the Windows system, you can use the `net use` command to map the remote share to a drive letter. Once it's mapped, the drive appears in the list of available drives:

```
net use Z: \\192.168.56.100\share /USER:tboronczyk
```

Alternatively, you can map the drive through the Windows GUI, navigating through `Computer` | `Map network drive` | `Map network drive` in File Explorer while the **This PC** bookmark is selected:

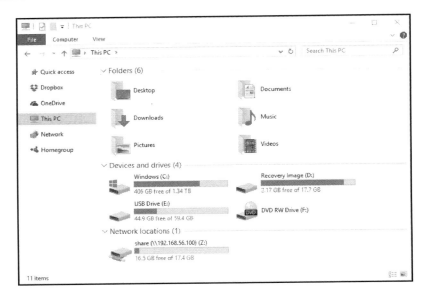

The Samba share is available as a network mapped drive

See also

For more information on working with Samba, refer to the following resources:

- The `smb.conf` manual page (`man 5 smb.conf`)
- Using Samba on CentOS With Windows 7/8 (`https://rcollier.me/213/7/3/using-samba-on-centos-with-windows-78/`)
- Install And Configure Samba Server In CentOS 7 (`http://www.unixmen.com/install-configure-samba-server-centos-7`)

3

User and Permission Management

This chapter contains the following recipes:

- Escalating privileges with sudo
- Enforcing password restrictions
- Setting default permissions for new files and directories
- Running binaries as a different user
- Working with SELinux for greater security

Introduction

Each of the recipes in this chapter pertain to users and permissions. You'll learn how to let users temporarily escalate their privileges without requiring the root password and how to enforce complexity requirements for users. You'll also learn how to specify what access permissions are given to new files and directories by default and how the traditional Unix permission system can allow a program to run under a different security context than that of the user who launched it. Finally, we'll look at SELinux, a secondary permission system that hardens the security of your CentOS server.

Escalating privileges with sudo

The `root` account is Linux's **god account**, and it has the ability to perform pretty much any activity on the system. For security reasons, you should use an unprivileged user account for your day-to-day activities and use `root` only when it's necessary for administration tasks. It's also important to keep the root's password secret; the more people who know its password, the harder it is to keep it secret. A quote by Benjamin Franklin comes to mind: *Three can keep a secret if two of them are dead.*

If more than one administrator has been tasked with managing a system, keeping `root` secure can be difficult. `sudo` solves this problem by giving users a way to execute commands with the privileges of another user (most commonly `root`). Each of the administrator accounts can be configured using one of the methods presented in this recipe to escalate their privileges temporarily with `sudo`, and root's password can remain secret.

Getting ready

This recipe requires a CentOS system and administrative access provided by logging in with the `root` account. You'll also need one or two unprivileged user accounts to configure (refer to the `useradd` man page `man 8 useradd` for information on creating user accounts).

How to do it...

One way to allow an unprivileged account the use of `sudo` is to assign it a membership in the `wheel` group. This is done with the following steps:

1. Use `usermod` to add the user account to `wheel`:

   ```
   usermod -a -G wheel tboronczyk
   ```

2. Verify the update using the `groups` command. `wheel` should list one of the groups which the account is a member of:

   ```
   groups tboronczyk
   ```

Another way to grant access to `sudo` is by configuring the sudoers policy which identifies which accounts can use `sudo` and in what manner. You can easily add an account to the policy with the following steps:

1. Create a new file in the `/etc/sudoers.d` directory named after the user account:

   touch /etc/sudoers.d/tboronczyk

2. Open the file and add the following directive. When finished, save your update and close the file:

   tboronczyk ALL = ALL

How it works...

For a user to use the `sudo` command they must be somehow listed in the sudoers policy. This is checked by `sudo` to verify whether the account is authorized to perform the attempted action. This recipe presented two ways of accomplishing this: by assigning the user account to the `wheel` group (which is already registered in the policy) or by adding the account directly to the policy.

In the first approach, the `usermod` command assigns the user membership in `wheel`. The `-G` option specifies the name of the group and `-a` instructs `usermod` to add the user to that group. It's important that you provide `-a` since without it the list of assigned groups is overwritten with only what is given with `-G` (that is, the account would belong only to `wheel`).

   usermod -a -G wheel tboronczyk

The second approach registers the account with the sudoers policy by creating a file for the user under `/etc/sudoers.d`. We alternatively could have added the user's information to the `/etc/sudoers` configuration file, but the policy already includes any files found in the `sudoers.d` directory as part of its configuration. Creating a file for each user in the directory will be more manageable given a large number of users when it is time to revoke access.

Both approaches allow a user the use of `sudo` to execute commands they wouldn't ordinarily have sufficient rights to. For example:

   sudo umount /media

The first time a user invokes `sudo`, a message is displayed that reminds them to be responsible with their new-found power. The user must provide their password to verify their identity; the verification is cached for five minutes from the last invocation as an extra bit of protection against malicious users who might walk up to a terminal that was carelessly left logged in.

```
[tboronczyk@benito ~]$ sudo umount /media

We trust you have received the usual lecture from the local System
Administrator. It usually boils down to these three things:

    #1) Respect the privacy of others.
    #2) Think before you type.
    #3) With great power comes great responsibility.

[sudo] password for tboronczyk:
```

sudo reminds the user that with great power comes great responsibly

The sudoers policy is flexible enough to allow a user account to execute certain commands instead of giving carte blanche access. Recall the configuration directive for our unprivileged user account:

```
tboronczyk ALL = ALL
```

The username is specified followed by assigning the `ALL` alias to `ALL`. As you might determine by looking at this, `ALL` is the predefined alias that represents all commands. We can redefine the alias for the given user as a list of allowed commands:

```
tboronczyk ALL = /bin/mount /bin/umount
```

Now the account can invoke any command it normally has access to, but only the `mount` and `umount` commands with elevated privileges (assuming the account isn't a member of `wheel`).

Are you tired of typing `sudo` before your commonly-used administrative commands? You can create aliases for a smoother command line experience. Suppose your unprivileged account is allowed to use the `mount` and `umount` commands with `sudo`. Adding the following lines to your `~/.bashrc` file will let you invoke them commands without explicitly typing `sudo`:

```
alias mount sudo /bin/mount
alias umount sudo /bin/umount
```

Multiple directives in the policy can apply to an account in which case they are applied additively, first to last. To see this in action, suppose an account already has full `sudo` usage by assignment in the `wheel` group. By default, the user needs to provide their password to execute a command. We can relax this requirement and allow the user to use `ls` to display the contents of restricted directories without a password:

```
tboronczyk ALL = NOPASSWD: /bin/ls
```

The `wheel` group's policy is applied first, establishing the default behavior. Then our new directive uses the `NOPASSWD` tag to grant the user unauthenticated access to the `ls` command. The user will still need to provide their password for commands such as `mount` and `passwd` but won't need to provide it to list restricted directories.

See also

Refer to the following resources for more information on working with `sudo` to temporarily elevate an account's privileges:

- The `sudo` man page (`man 8 sudo`)
- The `sudoers` man page (`man 5 sudoers`)
- Code Snipcademy: Using `sudo` and `su` and their differences (`https://code.snipcademy.com/tutorials/linux-command-line/permissions/sudo`)

Enforcing password restrictions

A weak password can be one of the weakest security points of any system. Simple passwords are susceptible to brute-force attacks and long-lived passwords, if they are compromised, provide a wide window of opportunity for malicious activity. Because of this, it's important to ensure that your users choose sufficiently complex passwords and change them regularly. This recipe shows you how to strengthen your system's security by enforcing various restrictions on users' passwords. You'll learn how to specify the minimum complexity requirements for a password, how long before a password must be changed, and how to lock down an account after a number of failed login attempts.

Getting ready

This recipe requires a CentOS system and administrative access, either provided by logging in with the `root` account or by using `sudo`.

How to do it...

Follow these steps to enforce password restrictions that will increase the security of your CentOS system:

1. The parameters governing password aging are found in `/etc/login.defs`; open the file using your text editor of choice:

   `vi /etc/login.defs`

2. Locate the password aging controls section and update the value of `PASS_MAX_DAYS`, `PASS_MIN_DAYS`, `PASS_MIN_LEN`, and `PASS_WARN_AGE`:

   `PASS_MAX_DAYS   90`
   `PASS_MIN_DAYS   0`
   `PASS_MIN_LEN    8`
   `PASS_WARN_AGE   15`

3. Save your changes and close the file.

4. The values specified in `login.defs` will be applied to new accounts when they are created. Existing users must have their password parameters set separately using the `chage` command:

   `chage --maxdays 90 --mindays 0 --warndays 15 tboronczyk`

5. The parameters governing the acceptable complexity for passwords are found in `/etc/security/pwquality.conf`; open the file for editing:

   `vi /etc/security/pwquality.conf`

6. Uncomment the `minlen` value to specify the desired minimum password complexity plus 1. For example, an eight-character password consisting of all lowercase characters would require a `minlen` of 9:

   `minlen = 9`

7. You may uncomment other values and set them as well if you like. Each value is preceded by a brief descriptive comment of what it does. To require a minimum number of characters to be from a certain class (uppercase, lowercase, digits, and other/special), specify the value as a negative number. For example, if passwords require at least one numeric digit and one uppercase character then both `dcredit` and `ucredit` would be set to -1:

```
[tboronczyk@benito ~]$ cat /etc/security/pwquality.conf
# Configuration for systemwide password quality limits
# Defaults:
#
# Number of characters in the new password that must not be present in the
# old password.
# difok = 5
#
# Minimum acceptable size for the new password (plus one if
# credits are not disabled which is the default). (See pam_cracklib manual.)
# Cannot be set to lower value than 6.
minlen = 9

# The maximum credit for having digits in the new password. If less than 0
# it is the minimum number of digits in the new password.
dcredit = 1

# The maximum credit for having uppercase characters in the new password.
# If less than 0 it is the minimum number of uppercase characters in the new
# password.
ucredit = 1

# The maximum credit for having lowercase characters in the new password.
# If less than 0 it is the minimum number of lowercase characters in the new
# password.
# lcredit = 1
#
# The maximum credit for having other characters in the new password.
# If less than 0 it is the minimum number of other characters in the new
# password.
# ocredit = 1
#
# The minimum number of required classes of characters for the new
# password (digits, uppercase, lowercase, others).
# minclass = 0
#
# The maximum number of allowed consecutive same characters in the new password.
# The check is disabled if the value is 0.
# maxrepeat = 0
#
# The maximum number of allowed consecutive characters of the same class in the
# new password.
# The check is disabled if the value is 0.
# maxclassrepeat = 0
#
# Whether to check for the words from the passwd entry GECOS string of the user.
# The check is enabled if the value is not 0.
# gecoscheck = 0
#
# Path to the cracklib dictionaries. Default is to use the cracklib default.
# dictpath =
```

Options for configuring your system's password complexity requirements are found in pwquality.conf

8. Save your changes and close the file.

9. Next we'll update PAM's `password-auth` and `system-auth` module configurations to lock out an account after a number of unsuccessful login-attempts. Open the file `/etc/pam.d/password-auth`:

```
vi /etc/pam.d/password-auth
```

10. Update the group of `auth` lines at the beginning of the file to read as follows. The second and fourth lines have been added and include `pam_faillock` to the authentication stack:

```
auth     required      pam_env.so
auth     required      pam_faillock.so preauth silent audit  deny=3
unlock_time=600
auth     sufficient    pam_unix.so nullok try_first_pass
auth     [default=die] pam_faillock.so authfail audit deny=3
unlock_time=600
auth     requisite     pam_succeed_if.so uid >= 1000  quiet_success
auth     required      pam_deny.so
```

11. Update the group of `account` lines to read as follows. The second line has been added to include `pam_faillock` to the account stack:

```
account  required   pam_unix.so
account  required   pam_faillock.so
account  sufficient pam_localuser.com
account  sufficient pam_succeed_if.so uid < 1000 quiet
account  required   pam_permit.so
```

Be careful when updating the `password-auth` and `system-auth` files. The order in which modules are listed in a stack is significant!

12. Save your changes and close the file. Then repeat steps 9 to 11 with the file `/etc/pam.d/system-auth`.

How it works...

Properly configuring the authentication requirements for local accounts is a bit of a fractured experience. First, there's the traditional Unix password files (`/etc/passwd` and `/etc/groups`) and the `shadow-utils` package, which adds shadowing support (`/etc/shadow`). Together, these form the core database for local account credentials. In addition, similar to most other modern Linux systems, CentOS uses PAM, a collection of pluggable authentication modules. The PAM stack is configured by default to lookup account information in the shadow file, but it also provides additional functionality that PAM-aware programs can leverage, such as password-strength checking. As an administrator, you're responsible for configuring these services so that they work properly in tandem and operate within the acceptable security guidelines set by your organization.

In this recipe, we first updated the password aging related controls found in `/etc/logins.def`:

```
PASS_MAX_DAYS    90
PASS_MIN_DAYS    0
PASS_MIN_LEN     8
PASS_WARN_AGE    15
```

`PASS_MAX_DAYS` defines how much time can pass before a password must be changed. By setting the value to `90`, a user must change their password at least once every three months (90 days). `PASS_MIN_DAYS` specifies how many days a user must wait to change a new password. Since this value is 0, a user can change their password any time they want-even several times a day if they like. `PASS_WARN_AGE` defines how many days in advance a user will be notified of their password's pending expiration as `PASS_MAX_DAYS` approaches.

 `PASS_MIN_LEN` is supposed to set the minimum password length, but you'll find PAM's password complexity requirements supersede this, making the setting pretty much worthless.

Utilities such as `useradd` use these settings as the defaults when creating entries in the password and shadow files. They aren't applied retroactively to existing users so we need to use `chage` to update their accounts:

```
chage --maxdays 90 --mindays 0 --warndays 15 tboronczyk
```

`chage` can set the minimum and maximum age of a user's password and the notification window for pending expirations, but note the absence of a minimum length requirement.

We can also use `chage` to make a user's password expire immediately so that they must specify a new one the next time they log in. To do so, we provide the `--lastdays` argument with a value of 0:

```
chage --lastdays 0 tboronczyk
```

If you have more than a handful of accounts, you may want to automate using `chage` with some basic shell scripting. Here's a series of commands piped together that update all of the existing user accounts in an automated fashion:

```
getent shadow | awk -F : 'substr($2, 0, 1) == "$" { print
$1 }' | xargs -n 1 chage --maxdays 90 --mindays 0
--warndays 15
```

This works by retrieving the contents of the shadow file and using `awk` to split each record using : as the field separator. `awk` looks at the value in the second field (the encrypted password) to see if it begins with $, indicating the account has a password, to filter out disabled accounts and system accounts without a password. The username from each matching record is then piped to `xargs` which then feeds the names one at a time to `chage`.

As the PAM module `pam_pwquality` checks the complexity of passwords, we specify our password complexity requirements in the module's configuration file, `/etc/security/pwquality.conf`. It gauges the quality of a password using a credit system where each character credits a point towards the password's total score. This score then must meet or exceed the value we gave for `minlen`.

The page at `http://wpollock.com/AUnix2/PAM-Help.htm` has a good explanation of how `pam_pwquality` calculates a password's complexity. It explains the algorithm as follows:

- Add one for each character in the password regardless of the type of the character
- Add one to that for each lowercase letter used, up to a maximum of `lcredit`
- Add one to that for each uppercase letter used, up to a maximum of `ucredit`
- Add one to that for each digit used, up to a maximum of `dcredit`
- Add one to that for each symbol used, up to a maximum of `ocredit`

The page also presents a few complexity calculations for different passwords and is worth reading.

Then we updated the `password-auth` and `system-auth` files to lock a user's account after three unsuccessful login attempts. Different authentication stacks need to be configured because different login methods will invoke a different authentication stack (that is, a logging in over SSH as opposed to logging in locally):

```
auth     required      pam_env.so
auth     required      pam_faillock.so preauth silent audit deny=3
unlock_time=600
auth     sufficient    pam_unix.so nullok try_first_pass
auth     [default=die] pam_faillock.so authfail audit deny=3
unlock_time=600
auth     requisite     pam_succeed_if.so uid >= 1000 quiet_success
auth     required      pam_deny.so
account  required      pam_unix.so
account  required      pam_faillock.so
account  sufficient    pam_localuser.com
account  sufficient    pam_succeed_if.so uid < 1000 quiet
account  required      pam_permit.so
```

The `pam_faillock` module is added at multiple positions in the authentication stack. The first appearance in the `auth` block performs a precheck (`preauth`) to see if the account is already locked out The second appearance tallies the failed attempt (`authfail`). The argument specified by `deny` is the number of failed attempts permitted before locking the account. `unlock_time` specifies how much time the module should wait (in seconds) before unlocking the account so that another login attempt can be made. As the example specifies 600 seconds, a user will have to wait 10 minutes for the lockout to expire. The module's appearance in the `account` block denies authentication to the locked account.

The `faillock` command is used to view the number of failed login attempts and to unlock an account. To see the failed attempts, invoke the command using the `--user` argument to specify the account's username:

```
faillock --user tboronczyk
```

To manually unlock the account before `unlock_time` has elapsed, invoke the command with the `--reset` argument:

```
faillock --user tboronczyk --reset
```

See also

Refer to the following resources for more information on how user accounts are authenticated and how to enforce password restrictions:

- The `chage` **man page** (`man 1 chage`)
- The shadow file man page (`man 5 shadow`)
- The `pam_faillock` **man page** (`man 8 pam_faillock`)
- Linux Documentation Project: Putting the Shadow suite to use (`http://tldp.org /HOWTO/Shadow-Password-HOWTO-7.html`)
- The Linux-PAM System Administrator's Guide (`http://www.linux-pam.org/Li nux-PAM-html/Linux-PAM_SAG.html`)
- RHEL Security Guide: Password Security (`https://access.redhat.com/docume ntation/en-US/Red_Hat_Enterprise_Linux/7/html-single/Security_Guide/ index.html#sec-Password_Security`)

Setting default permissions for new files and directories

Linux's permissions system governs whether a user can enter a directory or read, write, or execute a file. By setting the permission bits on files and directories, access can be granted or revoked to different users and groups of users. However, it's possible for a user to create a file and expect others in their group to access it, but the initial file permissions prevents this. To help avoid this situation, this recipe teaches you how to set the default permissions for new files and directories by specifying a mask value.

Getting ready

This recipe requires a CentOS system and administrative access, either provided by logging in with the `root` account or by using `sudo`.

How to do it...

Follow these steps to specify the default permissions for new files and directories:

1. To set the mask value globally, open the `/etc/profile` file:

   ```
   vi /etc/profile
   ```

2. At the end of the file, add the following directive (adjusting the value as desired). When finished, save and close the file:

   ```
   umask 0007
   ```

3. To override the global mask and set the mask on a per-user basis, open the user's `~/.bashrc` file:

   ```
   vi /home/tboronczyk/.bashrc
   ```

4. At the end of the file, add the following (again adjusting the value as necessary). Then save and close the file:

   ```
   umask 0007
   ```

5. To temporarily set the mask only for the duration of your session, execute the `umask` command at the command prompt:

   ```
   umask 0007
   ```

 You can execute `umask` at the command prompt without providing a mask value to see what your current mask value is.

How it works...

This recipe presents three ways a mask value can be set, which is responsible for determining what permissions are set on newly created files and directories. However, to understand how the mask works, you need to understand the traditional read, write, and execute permission system.

Directories and files in the Linux file system are owned by a user and group, and they are assigned a set of permissions that describe who can access it. When a user tries to access a resource, the system compares its ownership information with requesting user and determines if the requested access should be granted according to the permissions.

The three permissions are read, write, and execute. Since access to each can be only one of the two values (allowed or disallowed), and because such binary options can be represented with 1 for yes and 0 for no, a sequence of 1's and 0's can be viewed as a bit pattern where each permission is given a different position in the sequence. The following figure shows how a list of binary yes's and no's can be converted to a human-friendly value:

	Read	Write	eXecute	converted
tboronczyk	Y	Y	Y	111 = 7
	1	1	1	
mbutterfield	Y	Y	N	110 = 6
	1	1	0	
jbhuse	Y	N	N	100 = 4
	1	0	0	

Binary values represent whether a user has permission to access a resource

From the file or directory's perspective, there are three types of users. The user is either the file's owner, a member of the owning group, or neither (everyone else).

The resource is given a set of permissions for each type of users, as shown in the following figure:

	Owner			Group			All (everyone else)			permissions			
	Read	Write	eXecute	Read	Write	eXecute	Read	Write	eXecute	Owner	Group	All	
danger.sh	Y	Y	Y	Y	Y	Y	Y	Y	Y	111 (7)	111 (7)	111 (7)	777
	1	1	1	1	1	1	1	1	1				
script.sh	Y	Y	Y	Y	N	Y	Y	N	Y	117 (7)	101 (5)	101 (5)	755
	1	1	1	1	0	1	1	0	1				
group.txt	Y	Y	N	Y	Y	N	N	N	N	110 (6)	110 (6)	000 (0)	660
	1	1	0	1	1	0	0	0	0				

The full permission set of a file or directory includes the three types of users

This is the logic behind the traditional Unix permission system, but don't worry if this seems intimidating at first. Determining the permissions for a class of users is really just a matter of addition. Start with 0 for no access at all. To allow read access, add 4. For write access, add 2. For execute, add 1. These values come from viewing the value of the permission in the bit string as a binary number, but they are easy enough to memorize. Thus, to allow all access, we add 4 + 2 + 1 which equals 7. To allow only read and execute access, 4 + 1 equals 5. The more you work with permissions, the more you'll come to recognize certain combinations automatically.

When a file is created, the system begins with 666 as a default value, giving read and write access to all three classes of users. Directories start with 777 since the executable permission on a directory is what allows a user to traverse into it. The system then subtracts the creating user's umask value and the result determines what permissions will be assigned to the resource when it's created.

Suppose we create a new directory and our umask value is 0027. The system subtracts 7 from the all other users' field and 2 from the group's field. 7 - 7 is , and 7 - 2 is 5, so the default permission for a new directory is 750.

Because we start with one bit less in the default value for files, it's possible to end up with a negative permission number. If umask masks out all of the permissions using the value 7, but the starting value is 666 for files, 6 - 7 gives −1. It doesn't make sense to go beyond 0 so the system treats it as 0. So, a mask of 0027 gives us 650 for the file's permissions.

The /etc/profile and ~/.bashrc files are executed whenever a user logs in to configure their session's environment. Calling umask in profile has the effect of setting the mask for all users. .bashrc is executed after profile and is user specific; so, its call to umask overrides the previously set value, setting the mask for that specific user.

See also

Refer to the following resources for more information about umask:

- Wikipedia: Umask (`http://unix.stackexchange.com/questions/1275/why-are-666-the-default-file-creation-permissions`)
- Why are 666 the default file creation permissions? (`https://en.wikipedia.org/wiki/Umask`)
- Controlling file permissions with umask (`http://linuxzoo.net/page/sec_umask.html`)

Running binaries as a different user

Every program on CentOS runs within the environment of a user account regardless of whether the program is executed by a user or run as an automated system process. However, sometimes we want the program to run with different restrictions and access those rights the account is allowed. For example, a user should be able to use the `passwd` command to reset their password. The command needs write access to `/etc/passwd` but we don't want the user running the command to have such access. This recipe teaches you how setting a program's SUID and SGID permission bits allows it to execute within the environment of a different user.

Getting ready

This recipe requires a CentOS system. Administrative privileges are also required, either by logging in with the `root` account or by the use of `sudo`.

How to do it...

Follow these steps to allow a program to execute as a different user:

1. Identify the file's owner and group details using the `ls` command. The third field in its output lists the owner and the fourth field lists the group:

   ```
   ls -l myscript.sh
   ```

   ```
   [tboronczyk@benito ~]$ ls -l /var/lib
   total 8
   drwxr-xr-x. 2 root     root       52 Jul  9 23:22 alternatives
   drwx------. 3 root     root       17 Jul  9 23:24 authconfig
   drwxr-xr-x. 2 root     root        6 Mar  5  2015 dbus
   drwxr-xr-x. 2 root     root        6 Jul 10 00:55 dhclient
   drwxr-xr-x. 2 root     root        6 Jun  9  2014 dnsmasq
   drwxr-xr-x. 2 root     root        6 Jun  9  2014 games
   drwxr-xr-x. 2 root     root        6 Mar  5  2015 initramfs
   -rw-r--r--. 1 root     root        0 Jun  9  2014 logrotate.status
   drwxr-xr-x. 2 root     root       36 Jul  9 23:25 misc
   drwxr-xr-x. 2 root     root     4096 Jul 10 00:56 NetworkManager
   drwxr-xr-x. 2 root     root        6 Jun  9  2014 os-prober
   drwxr-xr-x. 2 root     root       26 Jul  9 23:22 plymouth
   drwxr-x---. 3 root     polkitd    27 Jul  9 23:22 polkit-1
   drwx------. 2 postfix  root       24 Jul  9 23:25 postfix
   drwxr-xr-x. 2 root     root       25 Jul  9 23:23 rhsm
   drwxr-xr-x. 2 root     root     4096 Jul  9 23:24 rpm
   drwxr-xr-x. 2 root     root        6 Jun  9  2014 rpm-state
   drwx------. 2 root     root       28 Jul  9 23:26 rsyslog
   drwxr-xr-x. 4 root     root       33 Jul  9 23:22 stateless
   drwxr-xr-x. 4 root     root       53 Jul  9 23:22 systemd
   drwx------. 2 tss      tss         6 Jun  9  2014 tpm
   drwxr-xr-x. 6 root     root       75 Jul  9 23:24 yum
   [tboronczyk@benito ~]$
   ```

   The -l option displays the file listing in long-form which includes ownership information

2. If necessary, change the file's ownership using `chown` so that the owner is the one whose environment you want the script to execute in:

   ```
   chown newuser:newgroup myscript.sh
   ```

3. Set the SUID bit to allow the program to run as if it were invoked by its owner:

   ```
   chmod u+s myscript.sh
   ```

4. Set the SGID bit to allow the program to run as if it were invoked by a member of its group:

   ```
   chmod g+s myscript.sh
   ```

How it works...

When a file's SUID and SGID bits are set, the program runs within the environment of its owner or group instead of the user who invoked it. This is usually done with administrative programs that an unprivileged user should have access to but the program itself requires administrative permissions to function properly.

The bits are set using `chown` with u set to target the SUID bit. A script with the SUID bit set will execute with the privileges its owner has. g is set to target the SGID bit which allows the script to execute with the privileges of a member of its group. Intuitively, + sets the bit and – removes the bit, later allowing the program to execute in the invoking user's environment.

```
chmod u-s myscript.sh
chmod g-s myscript.sh
```

SUID and SGID may be set numerically as well-the value for SUID is 4 and the value for SGID is 2. These can be summed together and appear as the left-most digit in the numeric permission value. For example, the following sets the SUID bit, the read, write, and execute bits for the file's owner; read, write, and execute bits for group members; and read and execute bits for everyone else:

```
chmod 4775 myscript.sh
```

However, the numeric approach requires you to specify all of the file's permissions. If you need to do that and want to set the SUID or SGID bits at the same time, it's not a problem. Otherwise, it's probably more convenient to use + or – to add or subtract the indented bits.

Setting bits using mnemonic characters with `chmod` also works with the standard permissions. u, g, and a target the desired bits for its owner (u for user), group (g for group), and everybody else (a for all). The characters for read access is r, write w, and execute x. Here are a few examples using mnemonic characters:

- Allow the file's owner to execute the file:

```
chmod o+x myscript.sh
```

- Allow a group member to read the file:

```
chmod g+r myfile.txt
```

- Prevent everyone who is not the owner or a member of the group from writing to the file:

```
chmod a-w readonly.txt
```

See also

Refer to the following resource for more information about chmod and setting the SUID and SGID bits.

- The chmod man page (https://linux.die.net/man/1/chmod)
- How to set the SetUID and SetGID bit for files in Linux and Unix (http://linuxg .net/how-to-set-the-setuid-and-setgid-bit-for-files-in-linux-and-uni x/)
- Wikipedia: Setuid (https://en.wikipedia.org/wiki/Setuid)

Working with SELinux for greater security

This recipe shows you the basics of working with Security-Enhanced Linux (SELinux), a kernel extension that adds an extra layer of security to your CentOS installation. Because it runs at the kernel level, SELinux can control access beyond the reach of the traditional filesystem permissions, including restricting running processes and other resources.

Unfortunately, some administrators disable SELinux because admittedly it can be a source of frustration. They're comfortable with the user/group/all and read/write/execute approach and suddenly find themselves at a loss when SELinux blocks something that seems as it should be available. However, the extra layer of security that SELinux provides is worth the effort of investigating such problems and adjusting its policies if necessary.

Getting ready

This recipe requires a CentOS system. Administrative privileges are also required, either by logging in with the root account or through the use of sudo. The demonstrated commands come from the policycoreutils-python package, so be sure to install the package first using the yum install policycoreutils-python command.

How to do it...

This collection of commands will introduce you to working with SELinux in various contexts, which are as follows:

- Use `sestatus` to verify whether SELinux is enabled and to see what policy is loaded:

```
[tboronczyk@benito ~]$ sestatus
SELinux status:                 enabled
SELinuxfs mount:                /sys/fs/selinux
SELinux root directory:         /etc/selinux
Loaded policy name:             targeted
Current mode:                   enforcing
Mode from config file:          enforcing
Policy MLS status:              enabled
Policy deny_unknown status:     allowed
Max kernel policy version:      28
[tboronczyk@benito ~]$
```

SELinux is enabled on this system and currently enforcing the targeted policy

- Use `id -Z` to see which SELinux account, role, and domain your account is mapped to.
- Use `ls -Z` to see the security context of a file or directory:

```
[tboronczyk@benito ~]$ id -Z
unconfined_u:unconfined_r:unconfined_t:s0-s0:c0.c1023
[tboronczyk@benito ~]$ ls -Z /var/lib
drwxr-xr-x. root    root    system_u:object_r:rpm_var_lib_t:s0 alternatives
drwx------. root    root    system_u:object_r:authconfig_var_lib_t:s0 authconfig
drwxr-xr-x. root    root    system_u:object_r:system_dbusd_var_lib_t:s0 dbus
drwxr-xr-x. root    root    system_u:object_r:dhcpc_state_t:s0 dhclient
drwxr-xr-x. root    root    system_u:object_r:dnsmasq_lease_t:s0 dnsmasq
drwxr-xr-x. root    root    system_u:object_r:games_data_t:s0 games
drwxr-xr-x. root    root    system_u:object_r:var_lib_t:s0    initramfs
-rw-r--r--. root    root    system_u:object_r:logrotate_var_lib_t:s0 logrotate.status
drwxr-xr-x. root    root    system_u:object_r:var_lib_t:s0    misc
drwxr-xr-x. root    root    system_u:object_r:NetworkManager_var_lib_t:s0 NetworkManager
drwxr-xr-x. root    root    system_u:object_r:bootloader_var_lib_t:s0 os-prober
drwxr-xr-x. root    root    system_u:object_r:plymouthd_var_lib_t:s0 plymouth
drwx-x---. root     polkitd system_u:object_r:policykit_var_lib_t:s0 polkit-1
drwx------. postfix root    system_u:object_r:postfix_data_t:s0 postfix
drwxr-xr-x. root    root    system_u:object_r:rhsmcertd_var_lib_t:s0 rhsm
drwxr-xr-x. root    root    system_u:object_r:rpm_var_lib_t:s0 rpm
drwxr-xr-x. root    root    system_u:object_r:var_lib_t:s0    rpm-state
drwx------. root    root    system_u:object_r:syslogd_var_lib_t:s0 rsyslog
drwxr-xr-x. root    root    system_u:object_r:var_lib_t:s0    stateless
drwxr-xr-x. root    root    system_u:object_r:init_var_lib_t:s0 systemd
drwx------. tss     tss     system_u:object_r:tcsd_var_lib_t:s0 tpm
drwxr-xr-x. root    root    system_u:object_r:rpm_var_lib_t:s0 yum
[tboronczyk@benito ~]$
```

Both id and ls can display security context related information

- Use `semodule -l` to review the list of loaded policy modules in the current policy. The output can be quite lengthy and you may find it beneficial to paginate it using `less` or `more`:

```
semodule -l | less
```

- Use `semodule -d` and provide a module's name to disable a specific policy module:

```
semodule -d mysql
```

You can verify that the module is disabled by reviewing the list of policy modules with `semodule -l` again. The word `disabled` should appear to the right of the module name.

- Use `semodule -e` to enable a specific policy module:

```
semodule -e mysql
```

- Use `semanage boolean` to selectively enable or disable features of an active module. The `-l` argument outputs list of available features with their current and default values:

```
semanage boolean -l | less
```

- Use −m followed by −−on or −−off and the feature name to affect the desired feature:

```
semanage boolean -m --on deny_ptrace
```

```
[tboronczyk@benito ~]$ semanage boolean -l | less

SELinux boolean                          State  Default Description

ftp_home_dir                             (off  ,  off) Allow ftp to home dir
smartmon_3ware                           (off  ,  off) Allow smartmon to 3ware
mpd_enable_homedirs                      (off  ,  off) Allow mpd to enable homedirs
xdm_sysadm_login                         (off  ,  off) Allow xdm to sysadm login
xen_use_nfs                              (off  ,  off) Allow xen to use nfs
mozilla_read_content                     (off  ,  off) Allow mozilla to read content
ssh_chroot_rw_homedirs                   (off  ,  off) Allow ssh to chroot rw homedirs
mount_anyfile                            (on   ,   on) Allow mount to anyfile
cron_userdomain_transition               (on   ,   on) Allow cron to userdomain transition
icecast_use_any_tcp_ports                (off  ,  off) Allow icecast to use any tcp ports
openvpn_can_network_connect              (on   ,   on) Allow openvpn to can network connect
zoneminder_anon_write                    (off  ,  off) Allow zoneminder to anon write
minidlna_read_generic_user_content (off  ,  off)  Allow minidlna to read generic user content
spamassassin_can_network                 (off  ,  off) Allow spamassassin to can network
gluster_anon_write                       (off  ,  off) Allow gluster to anon write
deny_ptrace                              (off  ,  off) Allow deny to ptrace
selinuxuser_execmod                      (on   ,   on) Allow selinuxuser to execmod
httpd_can_network_relay                  (off  ,  off) Allow httpd to can network relay
openvpn_enable_homedirs                  (on   ,   on) Allow openvpn to enable homedirs
glance_use_execmem                       (off  ,  off) Allow glance to use execmem
telepathy_tcp_connect_generic_network_ports (on   ,   on)  Allow telepathy to tcp connect generic network ports
httpd_can_connect_mythtv                 (off  ,  off) Allow httpd to can connect mythtv
unconfined_mozilla_plugin_transition (on   ,   on)  Allow unconfined to mozilla plugin transition
saslauthd_read_shadow                    (off  ,  off) Allow saslauthd to read shadow
tor_bind_all_unreserved_ports            (off  ,  off) Allow tor to bind all unreserved ports
httpd_can_network_connect_db             (off  ,  off) Allow httpd to can network connect db
use_ecryptfs_home_dirs                   (off  ,  off) Allow use to ecryptfs home dirs
postgresql_can_rsync                     (off  ,  off) Allow postgresql tp can rsync
polipo_connect_all_unreserved            (off  ,  off) Allow polipo to connect all unreserved
httpd_use_gpg                            (off  ,  off) Allow httpd to use gpg
xserver_clients_write_xshm               (off  ,  off) Allow xserver to clients write xshm
httpd_dbus_sssd                          (off  ,  off) Allow httpd to dbus sssd
selinuxuser_udp_server                   (off  ,  off) Allow selinuxuser to udp server
httpd_enable_cgi                         (on   ,   on) Allow httpd to enable cgi
virt_rw_qemu_ga_data                     (off  ,  off) Allow virt to rw qemu ga data
httpd_verify_dns                         (off  ,  off) Allow httpd to verify dns
ftpd_use_cifs                            (off  ,  off) Allow ftpd to use cifs
staff_use_svirt                          (off  ,  off) Allow staff to use svirt
:
```

semanage boolean -l shows which features of a policy module can be toggled on and off

How it works...

SELinux views the system in terms of objects, subjects, domains, and types. An object is any resource whether it's a file, directory, network port, memory space, and so on. A subject is anything that acts on an object, such as a user or a running program. A domain is the environment in which the subject operates, or in other words the collection of resources available to the subject. Types are simply categories that identify the purpose of an object. Within this framework, SELinux's security policies organize objects into roles and roles into domains.

Domains are granted or denied access to types. A user is allowed to open a specific file, for example, because they belong to a role in a domain that has permission to open that type of object. To decide whether a user has the ability to do something, SELinux maps the system's user accounts to one of the users (and roles and domains) in its own database. By default, accounts map to SELinux's unconfined_u user which is assigned the unconfined_r role and operates in the unconfined_t domain.

This recipe showed us that id -Z can be used to retrieve the user, role, and domain that our user account maps to and ls -Z retrieves a file's security labeling. Of course, the values displayed by the commands are different depending on the file. For example, the binary file /bin/cp executes as the system_u user, is a member of the object_r role, and is in the bin_t domain.

The sestatus command outputs basic status information about SELinux, such as whether it's enabled, enforcing its policies, and how it's enforcing them. SELinux can run in enforcing mode, in which it actively enforces its policies, or in permissive mode, in which it will not prevent any actions but will log a message if an action would have been prevented by the policy. You can set SELinux to permissive mode with setenforce 0.

The semodule command is used to manage policy modules. For the sake of keeping everything organized, a policy is a collection of modules and each module is concerned with a specific program or activity. There are dedicated modules for the most common applications, such as MySQL, Apache HTTP server, and SSHd, which describe which domains have access to which types. This recipe showed us how we can enable or disable these modules using the -e and -d arguments to semodule:

```
semodule -d mysql
semodule -e mysql
```

Finally, the recipe presented the semanage command, which manages various aspects of SELinux. We saw its boolean subcommand, using it to list the specific protections we can toggle on or off.

It probably goes without saying that while SELinux does a great job in protecting your system by adding an extra layer of access controls, fully understanding it and writing custom policies is a serious undertaking. Entire books have been written on this subject and there is a plethora of resources available online. The SELinux Users and Administrator's Guide that is part of the Red Hat Enterprise Linux 7 documentation and a three-part series introducing the basic concepts of SELinux by DigitalOcean are great starting points, and I've listed their URLs here. I also recommend the book *SELinux by Example: Using Security Enhanced Linux* by David Caplan, Karl MacMillan, and Frank Mayer.

See also

Refer to the following resources for more information on working with and better understanding SELinux:

- Wikipedia: Security-Enhanced Linux (`https://en.wikipedia.org/wiki/Security-Enhanced_Linux`)
- SELinux Project Wiki (`http://selinuxproject.org/page/Main_Page`)
- RHEL7 SELinux User's and Administrator's Guide (`https://access.redhat.com/documentation/en-US/Red_Hat_Enterprise_Linux/7/html/SELinux_Users_and_Administrators_Guide/part_I-SELinux.html`)
- CentOS Wiki: SELinux (`http://wiki.centos.org/HowTos/SELinux`)
- An Introduction to SELinux on CentOS 7 (`http://www.digitalocean.com/community/tutorials/an-introduction-to-selinux-on-centos-7-part-1-basic-concepts`)

4

Software Installation Management

This chapter contains the following recipes:

- Registering the EPEL and Remi repositories
- Prioritizing repositories using the Priorities plugin
- Automating software updates with `yum-cron`
- Verifying installed RPM packages
- Compiling a program from source

Introduction

This chapter presents recipes for managing the installation of software on your CentOS system. You'll learn how to add new package repositories to provide a wider selection of software than what's found in the main CentOS repositories, and also how to prioritize the repositories to control those from which a package is installed. You'll also learn how to automate software updates to keep up with the latest security patches and bug fixes, and how to verify the installed packages to make sure a malicious user hasn't tampered with your software. Finally, you'll learn a skill that's slowly fading but is essential if you want to modify the open source software on your system: how to compile software from source.

Registering the EPEL and Remi repositories

A clean CentOS installation will have the main supported repositories enabled, from which we can install a wide variety of software. We can also register third-party repositories to make additional (or newer) software available to us. This recipe teaches you how to add two such repositories, specifically the popular **Extra Packages for Enterprise Linux (EPEL)** and Remi repositories.

Getting ready

This recipe requires a CentOS system with a working network connection. Administrative privileges are also required, either by logging in with the root account or through the use of sudo.

How to do it...

To register the EPEL repository, install the epel-release package:

```
yum install epel-release
```

To register and enable the REMI repository, follow these steps:

1. Download the repository's configuration package:

```
curl -O http://rpms.famillecollet.com/enterprise/remi-release-7.rpm
```

2. Install the downloaded package:

```
yum install remi-release-7.rpm
```

3. Delete the file since it's no longer needed:

```
rm remi-release-7.rpm
```

4. Open the Remi repository's configuration file:

```
vi /etc/yum.repos.d/remi.repo
```

5. Locate the `enabled` option in the `[remi]` section and change it's value to `1` to enable it:

   enabled=1

6. Save your changes and close the file.

How it works...

The EPEL repository hosts software packages that complement those in the official CentOS repositories. It can be automatically configured by installing the `epel-release` package available in the official repositories:

   yum install epel-release

Remi is a popular third-party repository providing newer versions of software found in the official repositories. We downloaded the configuration package for the repository from the project's server using `curl`:

   curl -O http://rpms.famillecollet.com/enterprise/remi-release-7.rpm

We used the `-O` argument (an uppercase letter O, not zero) so that the file will be saved to disk, otherwise its contents would be dumped to the screen. The recipe didn't identify a specific directory you should download the file to. You can download it to your `home` directory, or even `/tmp` if you like, since the file isn't needed after the package is installed.

After the package is downloaded, we can install it using `yum`:

   yum install remi-release-7.rpm

Many times there are alternative ways to accomplish the same task. For instance, the `rpm` command can also be used to install the package after it is downloaded:

rpm -iv remi-release-7.rpm

The `-i` argument installs the package and `-v` instructs `rpm` to be verbose in its output so we can see it's activities.

The `remi-release` package installs the configurations for three Remi repositories: the Remi, Safe Remi, and Remi's PHP 7 repositories. Safe Remi is enabled by default because its packages are considered safe to use with the official CentOS-Base repository. However, the Remi repository is disabled so we need to edit `/etc/yum.repos.d/remi.repo`:

```
# Repository: http://rpms.remirepo.net/
# Blog:       http://blog.remirepo.net/
# Forum:      http://forum.remirepo.net/

[remi]
name=Remi's RPM repository for Enterprise Linux 7 - $basearch
#baseurl=http://rpms.remirepo.net/enterprise/7/remi/$basearch/
mirrorlist=http://rpms.remirepo.net/enterprise/7/remi/mirror
enabled=1
gpgcheck=1
gpgkey=file:///etc/pki/rpm-gpg/RPM-GPG-KEY-remi

[remi-php55]
name=Remi's PHP 5.5 RPM repository for Enterprise Linux 7 - $basearch
#baseurl=http://rpms.remirepo.net/enterprise/7/php55/$basearch/
mirrorlist=http://rpms.remirepo.net/enterprise/7/php55/mirror
# NOTICE: common dependencies are in "remi-safe"
enabled=0
gpgcheck=1
gpgkey=file:///etc/pki/rpm-gpg/RPM-GPG-KEY-remi

[remi-php56]
name=Remi's PHP 5.6 RPM repository for Enterprise Linux 7 - $basearch
#baseurl=http://rpms.remirepo.net/enterprise/7/php56/$basearch/
"/etc/yum.repos.d/remi.repo" 67L, 2340C written
```

The Remi repository is enabled by updating its configuration file

REMI is popular for providing newer releases of PHP. If you want to upgrade your existing PHP installation with a version found in Remi you can enable the desired section in `remi.repo` or in `remi-php70.repo`.

After you've installed the EPEL repository and installed and enabled the Remi repository, you can ask yum to list the available repositories. The EPEL and Remi repositories should appear in its output:

```
yum repolist
```

```
[root@benito ~]# yum repolist
Loaded plugins: fastestmirror
epel/x86_64/metalink                                    |  12 kB   00:00
epel                                                    | 4.3 kB   00:00
remi                                                    | 2.9 kB   00:00
remi-safe                                              | 2.9 kB   00:00
(1/5): epel/x86_64/group_gz                            | 170 kB   00:03
(2/5): epel/x86_64/updateinfo                          | 590 kB   00:06
(3/5): remi-safe/primary_db                            | 485 kB   00:08
(4/5): remi/primary_db                                 | 1.4 MB   00:26
(5/5): epel/x86_64/primary_db                          | 4.3 MB   00:37
Loading mirror speeds from cached hostfile
 * base: mirrors.greenmountainaccess.net
 * epel: fedora.mirrors.pair.com
 * extras: mirror.team-cymru.org
 * remi: mirror.innosol.asia
 * remi-safe: mirror.innosol.asia
 * updates: mirror.spro.net
repo id             repo name                                          status
base/7/x86_64       CentOS-7 - Base                                    9,007
epel/x86_64         Extra Packages for Enterprise Linux 7 - x86_64    10,402
extras/7/x86_64     CentOS-7 - Extras                                    375
remi                Remi's RPM repository for Enterprise Linux 7 - x86_64   3,280
remi-safe           Safe Remi's RPM repository for Enterprise Linux 7 - x86_   1,043
updates/7/x86_64    CentOS-7 - Updates                                 2,231
repolist: 26,338
[root@benito ~]#
```

The EPEL and Remi repositories are enabled and ready to go!

Remi uses the same package names as those found in the official CentOS repositories. Like Remi, the IUS repository provides newer versions of software found in the official repositories, but uses different package names. Some managed service providers recommend using IUS over Remi because they update servers nightly and the differing package names help prevent unplanned upgrades. If you're contracted with such a provider and not using the Priorities plugin (discussed in the next recipe), be sure to heed their advice. More information on IUS can be found at their website, https://ius.io/.

See also

For more information on the EPEL and Remi repositories, refer to the following resources:

- Fedora Project: EPEL (http://fedoraproject.org/wiki/EPEL)
- Remi's RPM repository (http://rpms.famillecollet.com/)
- Install EPEL and additional repositories on CentOS and Red Hat (http://www.rackspace.com/knowledge_center/article/install-epel-and-additional-repositories-on-centos-and-red-hat)

Prioritizing repositories using the Priorities plugin

Although package managers make installing and updating software an almost trivial task, there can still be some pain points if we're not careful. For example, we can configure multiple repositories, including third-party repositories not maintained by CentOS, and the version of a package in one repository can conflict with the same in another. This recipe uses the Priorities plugin to prioritize the repositories we use to help avoid such pitfalls.

Getting ready

This recipe requires a CentOS system with a working network connection. Administrative privileges are also required, either by logging in with the root account or through the use of sudo.

How to do it...

Follow these steps to prioritize which repositories yum downloads software from:

1. Open the /etc/yum.conf file with your text editor. Locate the plugins option and verify that its value is set to 1 to enable plugin support. Update the value if necessary:

   ```
   plugins = 1
   ```

2. Install the yum-plugin-priorities package:

   ```
   yum install yum-plugin-priorities
   ```

3. To set a repository's priority, open its respective configuration file found under /etc/yum.repos.d. Add the priority option as a new entry within each desired section:

   ```
   priority=10
   ```

4. When you're finished, save and close the repository's configuration file.

```
# CentOS-Base.repo
#
# The mirror system uses the connecting IP address of the client and the
# update status of each mirror to pick mirrors that are updated to and
# geographically close to the client.  You should use this for CentOS updates
# unless you are manually picking other mirrors.
#
# If the mirrorlist= does not work for you, as a fall back you can try the
# remarked out baseurl= line instead.
#
#

[base]
name=CentOS-$releasever - Base
mirrorlist=http://mirrorlist.centos.org/?release=$releasever&arch=$basearch&repo
=os&infra=$infra
#baseurl=http://mirror.centos.org/centos/$releasever/os/$basearch/
gpgcheck=1
gpgkey=file:///etc/pki/rpm-gpg/RPM-GPG-KEY-CentOS-7
priority=10

#released updates
[updates]
"/etc/yum.repos.d/CentOS-Base.repo" 45L, 1676C written
```

The CentOS-Base repository is given a relatively high priority for base packages

How it works...

In this recipe, we installed the Priorities plugin and prioritized our repositories by updating their configuration files. By prioritizing one repository over another, we can more easily control the packages and software versions installed on our system.

First, we checked to make sure Yum's plugin support is enabled. We opened its configuration file at /etc/yum.conf and verified the value of the plugins option:

```
plugins = 1
```

Next, we installed the yum-plugin-priorities package:

```
yum install yum-plugin-priorities
```

Priorities comes with its own minimal configuration file at /etc/yum/plugins/priorities.conf. There, the enabled option let's us toggle whether the plugin is active or not. This means we can prioritize the repositories as we like, but temporarily disable prioritization for any reason without removing and then re-adding priority values in the repositories' configuration files:

```
enabled = 1
```

The last step is to edit the repositories' configuration files found in the `/etc/yum.repos.d` directory. Each repository has its own file, for example, the CentOS-Base repository's file is `/etc/yum.repos.d/CentOS-Base.repo`, which configures details about connections and security keys for each channel. To prioritize our repositories, we simply open the desired files and add a new line for the `priority` option in the desired sections:

```
priority = 10
```

Priorities are assigned as a number in the range of 1 to 99, where 1 is the highest priority and 99 is the lowest priority. Any repository or channel we don't explicitly set a priority for will default to priority 99. Repositories that are meant to work together (like EPEL and Remi) can be assigned the same priority.

 Don't use consecutive priority numbers, like 1, 2, 3…. Setting priorities as multiples of 5 or 10, for example 5, 10, 15… or 10, 20, 30… allows you to later add additional repositories without re-prioritizing existing ones.

When priorities are assigned and enabled and when we try to install or update a package which is found in multiple repositories, the package will be retrieved from whichever repository that has the highest priority. In this way, we can control if a third-party repository can replace important base packages, or if updates from supported CentOS repositories can replace third-party packages on a highly-customized system.

See also

Refer to the CentOS Wiki's `yum-plugin-priorities` article for more information on the Priorities plugin at `https://wiki.centos.org/PackageManagement/Yum/Priorities`.

Automating software updates with yum-cron

We know the importance of staying on top of any security alerts and applying important updates, but it can be a tedious and time-consuming task to make sure all of the software on your CentOS system is updated, especially when you're managing more than one server. This recipe shows you how to automate the update process ensuring your system stays up to date without the need for daily interaction.

Getting ready

This recipe requires a CentOS system with a working network connection. Administrative privileges are also required, either by logging in with the `root` account or through the use of `sudo`.

How to do it...

To automate software updates using `yum-cron`, perform the following steps:

1. Install the `yum-cron` package:

   ```
   yum install yum yum-cron
   ```

2. Start and enable the service:

   ```
   systemctl start yum-cron
   systemctl enable yum-cron
   ```

3. Perform a system update to ensure everything is up to date before `yum-cron` takes over:

   ```
   yum update
   ```

How it works...

Our first action step was to install the `yum-cron` package, but you'll notice that the invocation also updates Yum itself. Although we only have to specify `yum-cron`, including `yum` works around a particular versioning bug (you can read the bug report at `https://bug zilla.redhat.com/show_bug.cgi?id=1293713`):

```
yum install yum yum-cron
```

The package installs the `yum-cron` command and a daily cron job to trigger it and a `systemctl` unit used to enable and disable updating. Starting the service with `systemctl` results in the creation of a special lock file. Cron runs the daily cron job every day to invoke `yum-cron`, which checks whether the lock file exists. If the file exists, then it knows it should check for updates. Otherwise, it knows daily updating is disabled (the service is stopped) and does nothing.

The `yum-cron.config` configuration file in `/etc/yum` can be used to modify the general behavior of `yum-cron`. The most important option is `update_cmd` because it lets us specify what type of update to perform. It's possible for `yum-cron` to perform different update strategies, and if you want to perform a more targeted update beyond the default then you can change the value of the `update_cmd` option.

Servers that fill different roles may require different update strategies; for example, you might want to apply only critical security updates on a production server and leave the other software installed at their specific versions. Comments in the configuration file list what values are valid for `update_cmd` and what they mean. `default` performs a general system-wide update, whereas a value such as `security` only applies security-related updates:

```
update_cmd = security
```

Also of interest in `yum-cron.conf` is the `emit_via` option. The `stdio` value means any logging messages that may be generated by `yum-cron` will be passed through a standard output. Usually, this is captured by cron and written to `/var/log/cron`. Cron can be configured to e-mail the output, but you can also specifically configure `yum-cron` to e-mail the messages. If you want the output sent to you by `yum-cron`, change the value of `emit_via` to `email` and the value of `email_to` to your e-mail address:

```
emit_via = email
email_to = tboronczyk@example.com
```

```
[commands]
#   What kind of update to use:
# default                                   = yum upgrade
# security                                  = yum --security upgrade
# security-severity:Critical                = yum --sec-severity=Critical upgrade
# minimal                                   = yum --bugfix update-minimal
# minimal-security                          = yum --security update-minimal
# minimal-security-severity:Critical =   --sec-severity=Critical update-minimal
update_cmd = security

# Whether a message should be emitted when updates are available,
# were downloaded, or applied.
update_messages = yes

# Whether updates should be downloaded when they are available.
download_updates = yes

# Whether updates should be applied when they are available.  Note
# that download_updates must also be yes for the update to be applied.
apply_updates = no

# Maximum amout of time to randomly sleep, in minutes.  The program
# will sleep for a random amount of time between 0 and random_sleep
# minutes before running.  This is useful for e.g. staggering the
# times that multiple systems will access update servers.  If
# random_sleep is 0 or negative, the program will run immediately.
# 6*60 = 360
random_sleep = 360

[emitters]
# Name to use for this system in messages that are emitted.  If
# system_name is None, the hostname will be used.
system_name = None

# How to send messages.  Valid options are stdio and email.  If
# emit_via includes stdio, messages will be sent to stdout; this is useful
# to have cron send the messages.  If emit_via includes email, this
# program will send email itself according to the configured options.
# If emit_via is None or left blank, no messages will be sent.
emit_via = email

# The width, in characters, that messages that are emitted should be
# formatted to.
ouput_width = 80

[email]
# The address to send email messages from.
email_from = root@localhost

# List of addresses to send messages to.
email_to = tboronczyk@example.com

"/etc/yum/yum-cron.conf" 77L, 2550C written
```

yum-cron's configuration file lets us specify a specific update policy and notification options

See also

Refer to the following resources for more information on automating software updates:

- Configure automatic updates (`http://www.certdepot.net/rhel7-configure-automatic-updates`)
- Enabling automatic updates in CentOS 7 and RHEL 7 (`http://linuxaria.com/howto/enabling-automatic-updates-in-centos-7-and-rhel-7`)

Verifying installed RPM packages

It's been said the safest system is one that's *"powered off, cast in a block of concrete, and sealed in a lead-lined room with armed guards."* (Gene Spafford) Your CentOS system is probably concrete-free, which means it's at the risk of attack. This recipe shows you how to audit your system using `rpm` to make sure its installed software hasn't been compromised by an attacker.

Getting ready

This recipe requires a CentOS system with a working network connection. Administrative privileges are also required, either by logging in with the `root` account or through the use of `sudo`.

How to do it...

It is important to first make a backup of the RPM database at `/var/lib/rpm`. There are many ways to do this, but for the sake of this example, we'll make an ISO image of the directory which you can then archive or burn to disc:

1. Install the `genisoimage` and `wodim` packages for the necessary tools to create ISO images and to burn them to disc:

    ```
    yum install genisoimage wodim
    ```

2. Create the ISO image with `genisoimage`:

```
genisoimage -o rpm-db-bckup.iso -R -v /var/lib/rpm
```

If desired, burn the image with `wodim`:

```
wodim -v dev=/dev/cdrom rpm-db-bckup.iso
```

You can delete the ISO file after burning it to disc if you have no plans to use it in the future.

When the time comes to verify your system, follow these steps:

1. Make the backup database available. If you've burned the ISO file to disc, and assuming that it's located at `/dev/cdrom`, use `mount` like this:

```
mount /media /dev/cdrom
```

2. If the backup is an ISO file, use `mount` like this:

```
mount -o loop rpm-db-bckup.iso /media
```

3. Verify the integrity of the installed `rpm` package against the backup copy of the database. `rpm` returns a list of the files that are different from the original package, so a successful audit should have no output:

```
rpm -V --dbpath=/media rpm
```

4. Verify the integrity of all of the packages installed on the system:

```
rpm -Va --dbpath=/media
```

How it works...

An attacker can alter files and replace programs with malicious copies on your system. Luckily, we can identify these changes using `rpm` to verify the integrity of files installed from a package. But to do this, we also need a database that we can trust. The integrity of the database used to compare file details is important because a smart attacker may also think to make changes there as well. It's important to make a read-only backup of the database regularly, perhaps before and after every time you install a new package or install updates. Then you can compare the state of the system's software against a trusted backup and be fully confident with the results.

You can back up to any medium you wish: a removable USB thumb drive, a writable CD or DVD disc, remote storage, or even a high-capacity tape cartridge. The important thing is that it's trustworthy. The recipe demonstrated making a backup of the /var/lib/rpm database as an ISO file, which can be burned to disc or copied around as-is and mounted read-only when needed.

```
genisoimage -o rpm-db-bckup.iso -R -v /var/lib/rpm
```

Long-time Linux users may remember the mkisofs and cdrecord programs. genisoimage and cdrecord are clones, and the former still exists in CentOS in the form of symlinks pointing to genisoimage and cdrecord.

The -o argument gives the name of the ISO file that will be created. -R creates the indexes necessary to preserve the length and casing of the filenames in our image, and -v indicates that genisoimage should be verbose so that we can see its progress. When it's finished, we'll have the rpm-db-backup.iso file.

rpm-db-bckup.iso is a suitable name if you're going to burn the file to disc and delete it. If you plan on archiving the ISO file instead, you'll want to consider including a timestamp in the name of when the backup was taken so that you can keep things organized. For example, the following command uses date to include the date and time in the filename:

```
genisoimage -o rpm-db-bckup-$(date +"%Y-%m-%d_%H%M").iso
-R -v /var/lib/rpm
```

Next, the recipe showed how to use wodim to burn the ISO to disc:

```
wodim -v dev=/dev/cdrom rpm-db-bckup.iso
```

The -v argument puts wodim in verbose mode and the dev argument identifies the CD/DVD drive. The recipe assumed that /dev/cdrom is the appropriate device and you may need to modify the command depending on your system's configuration.

To make the trusted database available, we mounted the disc or ISO file. To mount the disc, we would place the disc in the drive and issue the following command (/dev/cdrom is the device and /media is the mount point its filesystem will be made available on):

```
mount /dev/cdrom /media
```

To mount an ISO file, we issue the following command instead:

```
mount -o loop rpm-db-bckup.iso /media
```

After the trusted database was made available, we used `rpm` with the `-V` option, which verifies an installed package. By default, `rpm` uses the files in `/var/lib/rpm` as the database, so we used the `--dbpath` option to override this and instead point to our trusted copy:

```
rpm -V -dbpath=/media rpm
```

While we can provide one or more package names to check, the `-a` option will verify all of the packages installed on the system:

```
rpm -Va --dbpath=/media
```

`rpm` runs through a series of tests, checking the size of files and their permissions, and reports those that fail one or more tests. No output means the files installed on your system are exactly as they were when they were first installed by the package(s). Otherwise, `rpm` displays a dot for those tests that pass and one of the following mnemonic indicators to show which tests fail:

- S: The size of the file has changed
- M: The file's permissions have changed
- 5: The MD5 checksum of the file does not match the expected checksum
- L: The symlink has changed
- D: The device has changed
- U: The user owner of the file has changed
- G: The owning group of the file has changed
- T: The file's timestamp has changed

`rpm` will also report if a file is missing.

However, not all discrepancies are bad. It's up to us to know what changes are acceptable or not. Changes to a configuration file, for example, may be acceptable, but changes to a binary utility are certainly an indication of trouble. rpm differentiates configuration files by listing c next to the test results, which helps us differentiate them from other types of files:

```
[root@benito ~]# rpm -Va --dbpath=/media
S.5....T.   c /etc/chrony.conf
S.5....T.   c /etc/sysconfig/authconfig
.......T.     /lib/modules/3.10.0-229.el7.x86_64/modules.devname
.......T.     /lib/modules/3.10.0-229.el7.x86_64/modules.softdep
....L....   c /etc/pam.d/fingerprint-auth
....L....   c /etc/pam.d/password-auth
....L....   c /etc/pam.d/postlogin
....L....   c /etc/pam.d/smartcard-auth
....L....   c /etc/pam.d/system-auth
[root@benito ~]#
```

Differences are reported when verifying the integrity of this system's packages

See also

Refer to the following resources for more information on verifying the integrity of installed software:

- The rpm manual page (man 8 rpm)
- Verifying files with Red Hat's RPM (http://www.sans.org/security-resources/idfaq/rpm.php)
- wodim cannot open SCSI drive (http://www.linuxquestions.org/questions/linux-software-2/wodim-cdrecord-cannot-open-scsi-drive-4175544944/)

Compiling a program from source

Modern-day package managers make it easy to install software; with just a single command, we can install a program and its dependencies from any of our configured repositories. Yet an important value in the Linux community and free software movement is the ability to modify your software as you see fit (perhaps you want to fix a bug or add a new feature). For software written in a compiled language, such as C, this often means modifying the program's source code and compiling the code into an executable binary. This recipe walks you through compiling and installing the GNU Hello program.

Getting ready

This recipe requires a CentOS system with a working network connection. An unprivileged user account capable of escalating its privileges using sudo should also be available.

How to do it...

Perform the following steps to compile and install the program from the source code:

1. Using sudo to elevate your account's privileges, install the gcc package:

   ```
   sudo yum install gcc
   ```

2. Download the GNU Hello source code:

   ```
   curl ftp://ftp.gnu.org/gnu/hello/hello-2.10.tar.gz | tar - zx
   ```

3. Enter the project's directory:

   ```
   cd hello-2.10
   ```

4. Run the configure script using the --help argument to view the project's build options. The output can be quite lengthy and you may find it beneficial to paginate the content using less:

   ```
   ./configure --help | less
   ```

5. Run the configure script again, this time specifying any desired build options to generate a Makefile file:

   ```
   ./configure --prefix=/usr/local
   ```

6. Invoke make which uses Makefile as a guide to compile the project:

   ```
   make
   ```

7. Using sudo to again escalate your privileges, install the program and its supporting files:

   ```
   sudo make install
   ```

8. Now, we can run the hello program to display a friendly greeting:

   ```
   hello
   ```

How it works...

This recipe taught you the canonical `configure`, `make`, and `make install` route of compiling and installing software from the source code.

The minimal CentOS installation does not include a C compiler (a program that translates source code written in the C programming language into a binary, machine-executable format), so the first thing we did was install the GNU Compiler Collection. Because the package will be installed system-wide, elevated privileges were needed for `yum`:

```
sudo yum install gcc
```

Since the GNU Hello project is written in C and includes a pregenerated `configure` script, `gcc` is all we need. There may be other projects though for which you'll need additional software, such as `autoconf`, to generate a `configure` scripts, or compiler support for other languages like Fortran, C++, Objective-C, and Go. For a more capable build environment, consider installing the `Development Tools` package group:

```
sudo yum groupinstall "Development Tools"
```

Next, we downloaded a copy of the project's source code from its FTP server. The code is distributed as a compressed archive which we retrieved using `curl`. We omitted the `-O` argument that we used in previous recipes but piped the output directly to `tar` to decompress it. This results in the creation of a directory named `hello-2.10` that contains the project's source code:

```
curl ftp://ftp.gnu.org/gnu/hello/hello-2.10.tar.gz | tar -zx
```

Quite often, a project will include several informative text files, so feel free to look around at the directory's content. Some common files are:

- README: This gives a general overview of the project (name, version, description, and so on)
- CHANGELOG: This lists the changes made in each release
- INSTALL: This contains installation instructions
- LICENCE: This contains license information governing the use and distribution of the project's code

If the project uses the GNU Autotools build system (which GNU Hello uses), we can expect to find a `configure` script in the collection of source files. The job of `configure` is to scan our system's build environment to ensure that any necessary tools and dependencies are available and to generate the `Makefile` file. `Makefile` will contain instructions that compile and install the program, and any options we pass to `configure` ultimately find their way into `Makefile`.

To see what options are available to us, we first ran `configure` with `--help`:

```
./configure --help | less
```

Some of the options may be unique to the project while others are more general, having to do with setting paths and such as used in later parts of the build process. Some important general options are as follows:

- `--prefix`: The base hierarchy in which the program and its files will be installed
- `--disable-FEATURE`: This compiles the program without enabling the target feature that would otherwise be enabled
- `--enable-FEATURE`: This compiles the program with the optional target feature enabled
- `--with-PACKAGE`: This links to a specific library needed for some feature

The second time we ran `configure`, we did so providing the `--prefix` option:

```
./configure --prefix=/usr/local
```

The prefix value of `/usr/local` means that this directory will be prefixed to the various paths where the different files will be installed to. For example, when we install the program, the compiled `hello` file is copied to `PREFIX/bin`, which is `/usr/local/bin`, the project's manual page will be installed under `PREFIX/share/man`, which is `/usr/local/share/man`, and so on.

 This recipe installs GNU Hello as a system-wide accessible program. But don't forget, you can use the `--prefix` option to compile and install files to personal directories too:

```
./configure --prefix=/home/tboronczyk/.personal
```

Once `configure` generated `Makefile`, we executed those statements with `make` to compile the project:

```
make
```

By default, `make` looks for a file named `Makefile` in the current directory to run. If for whatever reason the target script is named differently, we can tell `make` which file to use with its `-f` option:

```
make -f ./Makefile
```

Also, `Makefile` files often contain several sets of instructions or targets. Some common targets are as follows:

- `all`: Compiles the program
- `check`: Runs any test suites that accompany the project to verify its proper functioning
- `clean`: Deletes any intermediate files created during the compilation process
- `distclean`: Deletes the files created during the configuration process or compilation process, leaving only those files in the original distribution
- `dist`: Creates an archive to distribute the program
- `install`: Installs the compiled program and any other necessary files to their final home on the system
- `uninstall`: Deletes files that were installed by `install`

The default target if none are provided is `all`.

Ideally, we don't want to compile software as `root` because it's possible for a `Makefile` to create arbitrary files in any location, something which can be taken advantage of by an attacker. Executing the file as a standard user blocks this attack vector simply because the unprivileged account doesn't have write-access to sensitive directories. This is why we used `sudo` only for the `install` target when we moved the program and its files to the directories under `/usr/local`.

See also

Refer to the following resources for more information on building software:

- GNU Hello (`http://www.gnu.org/software/hello`)
- RHEL7 Developer Guide (`https://access.redhat.com/documentation/en-US/Red_Hat_Enterprise_Linux/7/html/Developer_Guide/index.html`)
- Autotools Mythbuster (`http://autotools.io/`)
- CentOS Wiki: Set up an RPM Build Environment (`http://wiki.centos.org/HowTos/SetupRpmBuildEnvironment`)

5
Managing Filesystems and Storage

This chapter contains the following recipes:

- Viewing the size of files and available storage
- Setting storage limits for users and groups
- Creating a RAM disk
- Creating a RAID
- Replacing a device in a RAID
- Creating a new LVM volume
- Removing an existing LVM volume
- Adding storage and growing an LVM volume
- Working with LVM snapshots

Introduction

The recipes in this chapter focus on leveraging your CentOS system's storage to maintain availability, increase reliability, and to keep your data safe against inevitable disk failures. You'll learn how to determine how much space your files take up and how much storage is still available. Then, you'll see how to put limits in place to ensure that users use the system's storage resources equitably. We'll also create a RAM disk, a memory-based low latency storage for frequently accessed data. Then you'll learn how to create and manage RAID arrays to provide reliable storage, and how to work with LVM volumes to allocate logical drives from storage pools to better utilize your system's total storage capacity.

Viewing the size of files and available storage

Programs and services can behave unexpectedly or stop working entirely when storage space runs tight, so it's important to know how much space is available on our system. This recipe introduces a handful of commands used to determine how large your files and directories are and how much storage is used and is available.

Getting ready

This recipe requires a working CentOS system. Administrative privileges may be needed depending on the permissions of the directories and files you want to inspect.

How to do it...

- To display the storage capacity of a mounted filesystem, use the df command:

  ```
  df -h /
  ```

- To view the size of a file, use the ls command:

  ```
  ls -sh file.txt
  ```

- To determine the size of a directory (the sum of sizes of all of its files), use the du command:

  ```
  du -sh ~
  ```

How it works...

The df command returns information about how much free space is available on a mounted filesystem. The preceding example asked for details about the root filesystem.

```
df -h /
```

The -h argument formats the information in a human-readable format, listing the values as megabytes, gigabytes, and so on, as opposed to block counts. When invoked without any arguments, df displays its information in 512-byte block counts for all mounted filesystems. We can specify one or more mount points with this command, in which case df reports only on those filesystems.

```
[root@benito /]# df -h
Filesystem                  Size  Used Avail Use% Mounted on
/dev/mapper/centos-root      50G  787M   50G   2% /
devtmpfs                    236M     0  236M   0% /dev
tmpfs                       245M     0  245M   0% /dev/shm
tmpfs                       245M  4.4M  241M   2% /run
tmpfs                       245M     0  245M   0% /sys/fs/cgroup
/dev/master/centos-home     449G   33M  449G   1% /home
/dev/sda1                   497M  134M  364M  27% /boot
[root@benito /]#
```

Values presented as megabytes and gigabytes are more informative than when given in block counts

The output's first column, labeled Filesystem, and the last, labeled Mounted on, identifies the filesystem and mount point it's been made available on, respectively. The Size column shows the total amount of space the filesystem provides. The Used column shows how much of that space is occupied and the Avail column shows how much is still available. Use% shows how much space is occupied as a percentage.

While df gives us a high-level view of our overall storage usage, to view the size of individual files we can use ls. The command supports a large number of arguments that show meta information for files and directories, such as their ownership details, create time, and size.

This recipe used the -s argument to return the file's size and -h to again display the value in a human-readable format:

```
ls -hs filename.txt
```

If you use ls to show the size of a directory, it will likely report 4.0 K regardless of which directory you choose. This is because directories aren't really containers holding files like we usually imagine; a directory is really a special file that contains an index listing the files that are within it. This index occupies a block's worth of storage. ls reports the amount of space the directory occupies as a file, not the sum of the sizes of its files.

To view the total size of all of the files in a directory, which is usually what we want when talking about directory size, we need to use the du command:

```
du -hs ~
```

The −s argument prints only the value for the current directory and −h formats the value in a human-readable format. Without any arguments, du also displays 512-byte block counts for all files and directories within the current directory. However, directories are treated as containers so the values reflect the block count of all of their contained files. We can also list one or more files or directories, in which case du reports back only on those targets. By targeting all of the files/directories within a directory and piping the output through sort, we can use du to identify targets that consume the most storage:

```
du -hs ./* | sort -hr
```

sort's −h argument organizes the human-readable numbers correctly (for example, 4.0K is less than 3M even though 3 is less than 4 in a numerical sort) and −r reverses the order to display the largest entries first:

```
[tboronczyk@benito ~]$ du -hs ./* | sort -hr
1.8G      ./Documents
673M      ./Music
451M      ./Dropbox
6.4M      ./Git
1.7M      ./php-7.0.3.tar.gz2
4.0K      ./notes.txt
4.0K      ./vendor.txt
[tboronczyk@benito ~]$
```

Sorting can help identify what consumes the most storage

See also

For more information on the commands mentioned in this recipe, refer to their respective man pages:

- The df manual page (man 1 df)
- The du manual page (man 1 du)
- The ls manual page (man 1 ls)

Setting storage limits for users and groups

Imposing limits on the amount of storage a user can consume is an effective way to manage resources and ensure they are made available to everyone fairly, especially in a multiuser environment. This recipe shows you how to enable quotas and set limits by users and groups.

Getting ready

This recipe requires a CentOS system with administrative privileges provided by logging in with the root account or using sudo. It assumes /home mounts its own filesystem.

How to do it...

Follow these steps to set up quotas and specify storage limits:

1. Open the /etc/fstab file for editing:

   ```
   vi /etc/fstab
   ```

2. To enable user quotas, which enforce usage limits based on user accounts, add uquota to the mount options for /home. For group quotas, add gquota. Both uquota and gquota can be given together to enable both:

   ```
   /dev/mapper/centos-home /home xfs defaults,uquota,gquota 0  0
   ```

3. Save your changes and close the file.
4. Reboot the system:

   ```
   shutdown -r +5 'Reboot required for system maintenance'
   ```

5. When the system reboots, launch the xfs_quota shell in expert mode:

   ```
   xfs_quota -x /home
   ```

6. Set limits for a user account using the `limit` command:

   ```
   limit bsoft=5g bhard=6g tboronczyk
   ```

7. Use the `quota` command to verify that the user's limits have been set:

   ```
   quota -h tboronczyk
   ```

8. Set limits for a group using `limit -g`:

   ```
   limit -g bsoft=20g bhard=21g users
   ```

9. Use `quota -g` to verify that the group's limits have been set:

   ```
   quota -gh users
   ```

10. Type `quit` or press *Ctrl + D* to exit the shell:

    ```
    quit
    ```

How it works...

Quotas are not enabled by default and must be enabled explicitly in the filesystem's mount options; so, we updated `/etc/fstab` and added the `uquota` and/or `gquota` option for `/home`:

```
/dev/mapper/centos-home /home xfs defaults,uquota,gquota 0 0
```

We should never unmount a filesystem that's in use because we don't want to risk corrupting or losing data. So, it's important that no one else is logged in when we remount `/home`. If you're logged in as `root` and you're certain you're the only user logged in, you can remount the filesystem with `umount` immediately followed by `mount`. But if others are logged on, it's best to perform a reboot as the recipe suggests. When the system reboots, it will have automatically mounted `/home` and the quota options will be in effect:

```
shutdown -r +5 'Reboot required for server maintenance'
```

Next, we ran `xfs_quota` as an interactive shell to enter commands to manage our quotas. We used the `-x` argument to start the shell in expert mode (the commands we need to manage quotas are only available in expert mode) and gave the filesystem's mount point on which we're going to set quotas:

```
xfs_quota -x /home
```

 The traditional quota utilities can be used to manage basic quotas, but `xfs_quota` lets us take advantage of the additional quota functionality unique to XFS. For example, using `xfs_quota` we can also manage project quotas.

The two commands with the most interest for us are `limit` and `quota`. `limit` is used to set the quota limits and `quota` is used to report the quota information.

We can set four limits with `limit`. They are as follows:

- `isoft`: This sets a soft limit on the number of inodes used
- `ihard`: This sets a hard limit on the number of inodes used
- `bsoft`: This sets a soft limit on the number of blocks used
- `bhard`: This sets a hard limit on the number of blocks used

An inode is a data structure used by filesystems to track files and directories. Each file and directory are represented by an inode, so setting a limit on the number of inodes a user can have essentially limits the number of files/directories they can have.

Blocks represent the physical storage, and setting a quota on the number of blocks for a user limits the amount of storage space their files can consume. The typical block size is 512 bytes, meaning two blocks are used to store 1 KB of data. The recipe's examples set a soft block limit of 5 GB for the user account and a hard limit of 6 GB. The suffixes k, m, and g are used to specify values as kilobytes, megabytes, and gigabytes, respectively:

```
limit bsoft=5g bhard=5500m tboronczyk
```

 Commands can be run in `xfs_quota` without entering the interactive shell by using `-c`:
```
xfs_quota -x -c 'limit -u bsoft=5g tboronczyk' /home
```

A hard limit specifies a value that the user absolutely cannot surpass. For example, a user with a hard limit of 100 inodes and having 99 files will only be able to create one more file. An attempt to create a file beyond that will be met with an error.

On the other hand, a soft limit defines a limit a user can surpass for a small amount of time. Once the limit is exceeded, the user enters a grace period. A user with a soft block limit of 5 GB will be able to consume more than 5 GB of storage, but only for a certain amount of time. If they're still violating the limit by the end of the grace period, the soft limit will be treated as a hard limit and they won't be able to save any more data.

The grace period is 7 days by default. We can change this with the `timer` command, using `-i` to change the inodes timer and `-b` to change the block timer:

```
timer -b 3d tboronczyk
```

To review the current quotas, the `quota` command is used. `-h` presents the values in human-readable values:

```
quota -h tboronczyk
```

The default output shows the filesystem and its mount point and the user's block quota details: the number of blocks consumed (under the **Blocks** header), soft limit (**Quota**), hard limit (**Limit**), and the elapsed time of a soft-limit violation's grace period (**Warn/Time**). `-i` will retrieve the same information for inode quotas, and `-b` and `-i` can be used together to display both sets of information at the same time:

```
quota -bih tboronczyk
```

```
xfs_quota> quota -bih tboronczyk
Disk quotas for User tboronczyk (1000)
Filesystem   Blocks  Quota  Limit Warn/Time    Files Quota Limit Warn/Time   Mounted on
/dev/mapper/centos-home
               16K      5G   5.4G  00 [------]      5  1000  1.5k  00 [------] /home
xfs_quota>
```

Block and inode quotas can be displayed at the same time

The `limit` and `quota` commands all default to working with a user's quota, although we can explicitly manage a user's quota using the `-u` argument. To manage a group's quota, we use `-g`:

```
quota -gh users
```

As mentioned earlier, `xfs_quota` also allows us to manage project quotas. These are essentially limits placed on specific directories that are enforced regardless of user or group ownership. To use project quotas, use the `pquota` mount option:

```
/dev/mapper/centos-home /home xfs defaults,uquota,pquota 0 0
```

 Project quotas and group quotas cannot be used together; `mount` will fail to mount the filesystem if both `pquota` and `gquota` are given. Depending on the filesystem, this may prevent your system from booting.

Next, create the file `/etc/projid`. Each line is an entry made up of an arbitrary project name and a unique ID number separated by a colon:

```
echo "my_project:42" >> /etc/projid
```

Then, create the file `/etc/projects`. Its entries are made up of the project ID, a separating colon, and the project's directory. Together, the `projects` and `projid` files define the relationship between the project's name and its directory:

```
echo "42:/home/dev/project" >> /etc/projects
```

With the two configuration files in place, the final step is to initialize the project's quota tracking in `xfs_quota` using `project -c`:

```
project -c my_project
```

With the initial setup steps complete, you can use the `limit` and `quota` commands to manage the project's quotas using the `-p` argument:

```
limit -p bsoft=10g bhard=11g my_project
```

See also

Refer to the following resources for more information on working with quotas:

- The `xfs_quota` manual page (`man 8 xfs_quota`)
- Enable User and Group Disk Quota on CentOS 7 (http://www.linuxtechi.com/enable-user-group-disk-quota-on-centos-7-rhel-7/)

Creating a RAM disk

This recipe teaches you how to take advantage of RAM's low latency using a RAM disk, a section of memory made available as if it were a standard storage device. RAM disks often store volatile data that is constantly read and updated in memory. For example, on desktop systems they're used for storing a browser's cache to speed up web surfing. In server environments, RAM disks can store cache data for high-load proxy services to reduce latency.

Getting ready

This recipe requires a CentOS system with administrative privileges provided by logging in with the `root` account or using `sudo`.

How to do it...

Perform the following steps to create and use a RAM disk:

1. Check whether there is sufficient memory available for the RAM disk using `free` command (a practical RAM disk will need to be smaller than the amount of free memory):

   ```
   free -h
   ```

2. Use `mount` to mount a `tmpfs` filesystem at the desired mount point, giving the target size as a mount option:

   ```
   mount -t tmpfs -o size=512M tmpfs /mnt
   ```

3. When the RAM disk is no longer needed, unmount the filesystem:

   ```
   umount /mnt
   ```

How it works...

Whenever we access data on a hard drive, its motors must first spin up the storage platters and position the magnetic head at the correct location. These mechanical actions make access painfully slow compared to accessing data already resident in system memory (RAM). Exact measurements depend on the individual system and its hardware, but disk access takes somewhere in the neighborhood of 10 milliseconds or 10,000,000 nanoseconds. Memory access only takes about 200 nanoseconds, so it's safe to say accessing RAM is at least 10,000 times faster than disk even as a low estimate.

Before creating the RAM disk, you should first review the amount of free memory available on your system using the `free` command:

```
free -h
```

`free` command responds with how much memory is available and how much memory is in use. The `-h` argument formats the output in a human-readable format (listing the values in megabytes and gigabytes instead of bytes). We can see numbers for RAM, swap disks, and any special buffers used by the kernel, but we're really interested in the amount of used and free memory listed by the `Mem` and `Swap` entries. A low amount of free memory and a high amount of used swap is an indication that we probably won't have sufficient memory for a practical RAM disk:

```
[root@benito ~]# free -h
              total        used        free      shared  buff/cache   available
Mem:           741M         92M        430M        4.9M        245M        518M
Swap:          1.5G          0B        1.5G
[root@benito ~]#
```

With only 1 GB of RAM, this system has resources to support only a relatively small RAM disk

Next, we used `mount` to make the desired amount of memory available at the given mount point. The recipe used `/mnt`, but you're free to use whatever mount point you see fit:

```
mount -t tmpfs -o size=512M tmpfs /mnt
```

The invocation specifies `tmpfs` as the mount device and `/mnt` as the mount point. `-t` specifies the underlying filesystem, in this case, `tmpfs` and `-o` specifies our mount options for the filesystem. A list of possible options for the `tmpfs` filesystem can be found in the `mount` man page, but the most important option is `size`, which sets the desired size of the filesystem.

 It's possible to specify a value for `size` that's greater than the amount of available RAM but most of the time this isn't desirable. The extra data is marshaled to swap once RAM is exhausted and this will increase latency, negating the benefits of using a RAM disk in the first place.

Remember, RAM disks serve as low latency temporary storage for volatile data. Because its data is stored in memory, the contents of the disk are lost when either the system shuts down or the disk is unmounted. Never store persistent data to your RAM disk.

See also

Refer to the following resources for more information about RAM disks:

- The `mount` manual page (`man 8 mount`)
- How to create a RAM disk in Linux (`http://www.jamescoyle.net/how-to/943-create-a-ram-disk-in-linux`)
- What is `/dev/shm` and its practical usage? (`http://www.cyberciti.biz/tips/what-is-devshm-and-its-practical-usage.html`)

Creating a RAID

In this recipe, you'll learn how to configure a redundant array of disks (RAID). Configuring an array of disks to provide redundant storage is an excellent way to protect your data from drive failures. For example, if your data resides on a single disk and that drive fails, then the data is lost. You'll have to replace the drive and restore the data from your latest backup. But if two disks are in a RAID-1 configuration, your data is mirrored and can still be accessed from the working drive when the other fails. The failure doesn't impact access to the data and you can replace the faulty drive at a more convenient time.

Getting ready

This recipe requires a working CentOS system and elevated privileges. It assumes that at least two new disks have been installed (identified as /dev/sdb and /dev/sdc) and we will partition and configure them.

How to do it...

Perform the following steps to create a RAID:

1. Use lsblk to identify the new storage devices.
2. Launch cfdisk to partition the first drive:

   cfdisk -z /dev/sdb

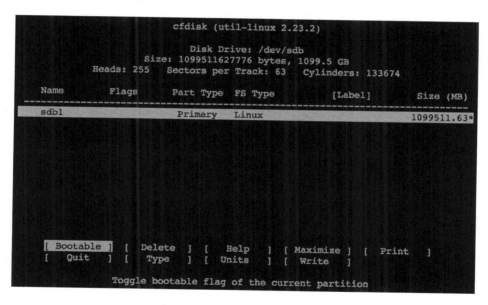

cfdisk presents a user-friendly interface for partitioning storage devices

3. To create a single partition that occupies the entire disk, use the left and right arrow keys to select New and press *Enter*. Then select Primary and accept the default size.

4. Select Write and confirm the action by typing yes when prompted. Select Quit to exit cfdisk.

5. Repeat steps 1 to 4 to partition the second drive.

6. Install the mdadm package:

```
yum install mdadm
```

7. Use mdadm -C to create a new array using the two partitions. The following example creates a RAID-1 (mirroring) configuration:

```
mdadm -C md0 -l 1 -n 2 /dev/sdb1 /dev/sdc1
```

8. Use the -D option to examine the RAID:

```
mdadm -D /dev/md/md0
```

9. Format the RAID using the XFS filesystem with mkfs.xfs:

```
mkfs.xfs /dev/md/md0
```

10. Mount the RAID for use:

```
mount /dev/md/md0 /mnt
```

How it works...

There are many ways to configure disks to work together, especially when it comes to things like data mirroring, striping, and parity checking. Some configurations are implemented at the hardware level and others can be implemented using software. This recipe used mdadm to set up multiple disks in a RAID configuration, specifically RAID-1.

The Storage Networking Industry Association has standardized several different RAID configurations. Some of the more common configurations are as follows:

- **RAID-0**: Data is distributed evenly across two or more disks. This configuration offers no redundancy, and the failure of a single disk in the array will result in data loss. However, it offers increased performance since data can be read and written to different disks simultaneously.

- **RAID-1**: Data is duplicated between disks. Write activity is slower because the same data must be written to each disk, but this configuration offers excellent redundancy; the data remains accessible as long as there is at least one functioning disk.

- **RAID-5**: Blocks of data and parity information are split between two or more disks. If a member of the array fails, parity information on another disk can be used to reconstruct the missing data. Write performance is slower, but read performance is increased since data can be read simultaneously from different disks. This configuration can withstand the failure of a single disk, although the failure of a second disk will result in data loss.
- **RAID-6**: This configuration is similar to RAID-5, but maintains an extra parity block. The array can withstand two disk failures before data is lost.

There are other standard configurations as well (RAID-2, RAID-3, and so on), and even non-standard configurations, but these are rarely used in practice. As with everything in life, there are trade-offs between the different RAID configurations, and selecting the right configuration for you will depend on how you want to balance redundancy, fault-tolerance, and latency.

lsblk prints information for the block devices (storage disks) attached to our CentOS system, and it should be relatively easy to identify the names of the new devices simply by looking at the drive sizes and lack of partitions. This recipe assumes that the new devices are /dev/sdb and /dev/sdc; you'll need to use whatever is appropriate for your system when invoking the cfdisk and mdadm commands:

```
[root@benito ~]# lsblk
NAME              MAJ:MIN RM    SIZE RO TYPE MOUNTPOINT
sda                   8:0   0    500G  0 disk
├─sda1                8:1   0    500M  0 part /boot
└─sda2                8:2   0  499.5G  0 part
  ├─centos-swap     253:0   0     1G   0 lvm  [SWAP]
  ├─centos-root     253:1   0     50G  0 lvm  /
  └─centos-home     253:2   0  448.5G  0 lvm  /home
sdb                  8:16   0     1T   0 disk
sdc                  8:32   0     1T   0 disk
sdb                  8:48   0    500G  0 disk
sde                  8:64   0    500G  0 disk
sr0                  11:0   1   1024M  0 rom
[root@benito ~]#
```

Several unconfigured drives are installed on the system

A new primary partition is created on each disk that occupies its entire capacity. The recipe uses cfdisk, a program that offers a console-based graphical interface to manipulate partitions. However, there are other partitioning utilities installed in CentOS that you can use instead if you're comfortable with them, such as fdisk, sfdisk, and parted.

Once the disks are partitioned, we're ready to configure the RAID. The `mdadm` program used to set up and administer RAIDs is installed using `yum`:

```
yum install mdadm
```

`mdadm -C` creates a new RAID configuration and requires a name to identify it. `md0` is used in the recipe which results in creating the device `/dev/md/md0`. The other arguments describe the desired configuration:

```
mdadm -C md0 -l 1 -n 2 /dev/sdb1 /dev/sdc1
```

The `-l` (a lower-case L) option specifies the standard RAID level, in this case 1 (the number 1) represents RAID-1. If you wanted to set up RAID-5 instead, you'd use `-l 5`. The `-n` option specifies the number of partitions the RAID will use, and then we list the partitions. The recipe configures two partitions, `/dev/sdb1` and `/dev/sdc1`.

`mdadm -D` displays information for a given array that's useful in examining the configuration and verifying its health. The output lists details such as the RAID level, available storage size, which partitions make up the array, whether any partitions/devices are failing, resync status, and other useful information:

```
mdadm -D /dev/md/md0
```

```
[root@benito ~]# mdadm -D /dev/md/md0
/dev/md/md0:
          Version : 1.2
    Creation Time : Sat Aug  6 00:16:38 2016
       Raid Level : raid1
       Array Size : 1073610688 (1023.87 GiB 1099.38 GB)
    Used Dev Size : 1073610688 (1023.87 GiB 1099.38 GB)
     Raid Devices : 2
    Total Devices : 2
      Persistence : Superblock is persistent

    Intent Bitmap : Internal

      Update Time : Sat Aug  6 00:17:09 2016
            State : clean, resyncing
   Active Devices : 2
  Working Devices : 2
   Failed Devices : 0
    Spare Devices : 0

    Resync Status : 0% complete

             Name : benito.localdomain:md0 (local to host benito.localdomain)
             UUID : 1f8e5917:4490939c:7d5bb981:90a0dc7f
           Events : 6

   Number   Major   Minor   RaidDevice State
      0       8       17        0      active sync   /dev/sdb1
      1       8       33        1      active sync   /dev/sdc1
```

mdadm displays the status of the new RAID configuration

`mdadm -E` retrieves information for one or more partitions that make up the array:

mdadm -E /dev/sdb1 /dev/sdc1

Next, the storage space is formatted with an XFS filesystem using the `mkfs.xfs` command:

mkfs.xfs /dev/md/md0

Finally, the RAID-backed storage space is ready for use. The recipe demonstrates mounting it manually with the `mount` command, although you can also add an entry to `/etc/fstab` for the filesystem to be mounted automatically whenever the system boots up.

See also

For more information on setting up RAIDs, refer to the following resources:

- The `cfdisk` manual page (`man 8 cfdisk`)
- The `mdadm` manual page (`man 8 mdadm`)
- The `mkfs.xfs` manual page (`man 8 mkfs.xfs`)
- Linux RAID Wiki: Linux RAID (`https://raid.wiki.kernel.org/index.php/Linux_Raid`)
- Mdadm Cheat Sheet (`http://www.ducea.com/29/3/8/mdadm-cheat-sheet/`)
- Introduction to RAID (`http://www.tecmint.com/understanding-raid-setup-in-linux/`)
- Standard RAID levels (`https://en.wikipedia.org/wiki/Standard_RAID_levels`)

Replacing a device in a RAID

When an array member fails, it's important to replace it as soon as possible because the failure of additional drives increases the chance of data loss. This recipe teaches you how to properly replace a bad drive and rebuild the array.

Getting ready

This recipe requires a CentOS system with administrative privileges provided by logging in with the `root` account or using `sudo`. It assumes that a RAID-1 configuration has been set up as described in the previous recipe and the drive that will be replaced is /dev/sdb.

How to do it...

Follow these steps to replace a failed disk in a RAID:

1. Mark the failed partition as faulty with `mdadm` using the `-f` option:

   ```
   mdadm /dev/md/md0 -f /dev/sdb1
   ```

2. Remove the partition from the RAID's configuration with `-r`:

   ```
   mdadm /dev/md/md0 -r /dev/sdb1
   ```

3. Physically replace the faulty disk.
4. Partition the new drive with `cfdisk`:

   ```
   cfdisk -z /dev/sdb
   ```

5. Use the `-a` option to add the partition to the RAID:

   ```
   mdadm /dev/md/md0 -a /dev/sdb1
   ```

How it works...

It's important to replace bad members as soon you become aware of the failure because, depending on the fault tolerance of your configuration, the failure of a second device may result in full data loss.

A member must be marked faulty before we can safely remove it, so the first step is to fail the partition. To do this, we used `mdadm`. The `-f` argument specifies the partition we want failed:

```
mdadm /dev/md/md0 -f /dev/sdb1
```

Then, to remove the partition from the RAID, we used the −r argument:

```
mdadm /dev/md/md0 -r /dev/sdb1
```

Now that the device is no longer in use, we can replace the physical drive. Whether the drive can be hot-swapped while the system is running or if a system shutdown is necessary depends on your hardware.

Once the replacement partition was ready, we added it to the RAID with the −a argument. The RAID will begin to rebuild itself, distributing data and parity information to the new partition, as soon as the partition is added:

```
mdadm /dev/md/md0 -a /dev/sdb1
```

The last recipe showed how the −D (and −E) argument of mdadm is used to retrieve status information about the RAID. You can review the output to monitor the rebuild's progress, but a more concise report is available via /proc/mdstat. The contents show the speed at which the rebuild is being processed and estimate the time it will take for it to complete. Using watch to repeatedly display /proc/mdstat, you can create a make-shift dashboard to monitor the process:

```
watch -n 10 -x cat /proc/mdstat
```

```
Every 10.0s: cat /proc/mdstat                                    Sat Aug 6 02:13:40 2016

Personalities : [raid1]
md127 : active raid1 sdb1[0] sdc1[1]
      1073610688 blocks super 1.2 [2/1] [_U]
      [=>...................]  recovery =  5.7% (62161792/1073610688) finish=83.4min speed=201883K/sec
      bitmap: 8/8 pages [32KB], 65536KB chunk

unused devices: <none>
```

The estimated time for this RAID's rebuild to complete is about an hour and a half

See also

Refer to the following resources for more information on replacing failed drives in a RAID:

- The mdadm manual page (man 8 mdadm)
- Replacing a failed hard drive in a software RAID (https://www.howtoforge.com /replacing_hard_disks_in_a_raid1_array)
- Five tips to speed up RAID re-building and re-syncing (http://www.cyberciti. biz/tips/linux-raid-increase-resync-rebuild-speed.html)

Creating a new LVM volume

Logical Volume Manager (LVM) abstracts data storage away from the physical hardware, which lets us configure the partitions on one or more physical drives to act as one logical device. We also have the freedom to later add or remove physical partitions and grow or shrink the logical device. This recipe show's you how to create a new LVM group and a logical device from the group's storage.

Getting ready

This recipe requires a working CentOS system and elevated privileges. It assumes that at least two new disks have been installed (identified as /dev/sdb and /dev/sdc) and we will partition and configure them.

How to do it...

Perform these steps to set up a new LVM group and create a volume:

1. Use lsblk to identify the new storage devices.

 You can set up LVM with RAID storage as well. Skip to step 5 and replace the partitions with RAID devices (for example, /dev/md/md0) in the given commands.

2. Launch cfdisk to partition the first drive and create a single partition that occupies the entire disk:

   cfdisk -z /dev/sdb

3. Repeat step 2 to partition the second drive.
4. Use pvcreate to register the new partitions as physical volumes:

   pvcreate /dev/sdb1 /dev/sdc1

5. Verify that the physical volumes are listed in the output of pvs:

   pvs

6. Using `vgcreate`, group the physical volumes to form a volume group:

```
vgcreate vg0 /dev/sdb1 /dev/sdc1
```

7. Verify that the group is listed in the output of `vgs`:

```
vgs
```

8. Using `lvcreate`, create a logical volume from the storage pool provided by the volume group:

```
lvcreate -n myvol -L 500G vg0
```

9. Format the volume using the XFS filesystem:

```
mkfs.xfs /dev/vg0/myvol
```

10. Mount the volume for use:

```
mount /dev/vg0/myvol /mnt
```

How it works...

LVM is another approach to configure multiple storage units to work together, focusing on pooling their resources together in a flexible way. These units can be disk partitions, as well as RAID arrays, and so the generic term *volume* is used.

The recipe starts with the assumption that we have two new disks as our storage volumes and provides steps for identifying the devices and partitioning them using `lsblk` and `cfdisk`. It uses `/dev/sdb` and `/dev/sdc` as the devices, but you should use whatever is appropriate for your system. Once the disks are partitioned, we're ready to register the partitions as physical volumes with `pvcreate`. The term *physical volume* describes storage available as a physical partition or RAID.

```
pvcreate /dev/sdb1 /dev/sdc1
```

Next, the physical volumes are grouped as a volume group using `vgcreate`. The recipe created a volume group name `vg0` using the `sdb1` and `sdc2` partitions.

```
vgcrate vg0 /dev/sdb1 /dev/sdc1
```

The desired name for the volume group is passed first to `vgcreate`, followed by the physical volumes we want to group together. If `sdb1` and `sdc1` both have a capacity of 1 TB each, their storage is combined and the volume group will have 2 TB. If we were to later add a 500 GB volume to the group, the group's storage capacity would increase to 2.5 TB.

The `pvs` and `vgs` commands return basic information about physical volumes or volume groups, respectively, and the recipe uses them to verify that each registration was successful. `pvs` reports the physical volumes that are registered and which group they are assigned to, any attributes, and their storage capacity. `vgs` lists the groups, the number of physical volumes that make up each group's pool, the number of logical volumes using storage from the group, and the groups' capacities.

```
[root@benito ~]# pvs
PV         VG      Fmt   Attr PSize      PFree
/dev/sda2  centos  lvm2  a--    499.51g    64.00m
/dev/sdb1  vg0     lvm2  a--   1024.00g   524.00g
/dev/sdc1  vg0     lvm2  a--   1024.00g  1024.00g
[root@benito ~]# vgs
VG      #PV #LV #SN Attr   VSize    VFree
centos    1   3   0 wz--n- 499.51g 64.00m
vg0       2   1   0 wz--n-   2.00t  1.51t
[root@benito ~]#
```

pvs and vgs are used to review the status of physical volumes and volume groups

A new logical volume is created from the pooled storage of the volume group using the `lvcreate` command:

```
lvcreate -n myvol -L 500G vg0
```

The `-n` option provides the name for the logical volume and `-L` provides the amount of storage to allocate the volume from the pool. The final argument is the name of the volume group used to support the volume. The values given in the recipe's example creates a volume named `myvol` with a capacity of 500 GB backed by the `vg0` group. Logical volumes are organized under `/dev` by group, so the volume is available as `/dev/vg0/myvol`.

Finally, the volume is formatted with the XFS filesystem using `mkfs.xfs`:

```
mkfs.xfs /dev/vg0/myvol
```

The logical volume is now ready for use and can be mounted manually with `mount` and/or an entry can be made in `/etc/fstab` to mount the volume automatically at system boot time.

See also

For more information on getting started with LVM, refer to the following resources:

- The `lvcreate` manual page (`man 8 lvcreate`)
- The `pvcreate` manual page (`man 8 pvcreate`)
- The `vgcreate` manual page (`man 8 vgcreate`)
- Linux Partition HOWTO (`http://tldp.org/HOWTO/Partition/index.html`)
- LVM made easy (`http://www.tuxradar.com/content/lvm-made-easy`)
- Manage LVM volumes with System Storage Manager (`http://xmodulo.com/manage-lvm-volumes-centos-rhel-7-system-storage-manager.html`)

Removing an existing LVM volume

The flexibility of LVM allows us to allocate the pooled storage of physical volumes however we see fit. This recipe shows us how to delete a logical volume and free its storage back to the volume group for use by other logical volumes.

Getting ready

This recipe requires a CentOS system with administrative privileges provided by logging in with the `root` account or using `sudo`. It assumes that a logical volume has been created as described in the preceding recipe.

How to do it...

Perform the following steps to remove an LVM volume:

1. Unmount the filesystem with `umount`:

   ```
   umount /mnt
   ```

2. Open `/etc/fstab` and verify that there isn't an entry to automatically mount the filesystem. If there is, remove the entry, save your changes, and close the file.

3. Use `lvremove` to delete the logical volume:

    `lvremove vg0/myvol`

4. Review the output of `vgs` to verify the removal.

How it works...

Deleting a volume frees its storage back to the volume group, which can then be used to create new logical volumes or support growing an existing volume. This recipe taught you how to destroy a logical volume using the `lvremove` command.

Because a volume can't be freed if it's in use, the first step is to make sure that its filesystem is unmounted. If the filesystem is mounted automatically, its entry in `/etc/fstab` should also be removed.

Next, `lvremove` is invoked with the name of the logical volume to free it:

`lvremove vg0/myvol`

You can delete all of the volumes from a pool by providing just the pool name:

`lvremove vg0`

The recipe suggests checking the output of `vgs` to verify that the logical volume was removed. In the output, the number of logical volumes under the `#LV` column should have decreased and the amount of free space under the `VFree` column increased appropriately.

See also

Refer to the following resources for more information on removing a volume:

*   The `lvremove` manual page (`man 8 lvremove`)
*   The `vgs` manual page (`man 8 vgs`)

Adding storage and growing an LVM volume

The size of logical volumes doesn't need to be fixed and we're free to allocate more storage for one from its volume group. This recipe teaches us how to add more storage to the group and then grow the size of the logical volume to take advantage of it.

Getting ready

This recipe requires a CentOS system with administrative privileges provided by logging in with the root account or using sudo. It assumes that a new disk has been installed and partitioned (identified as /dev/sdd1) and a logical group and volume have been configured as described in previous recipes.

How to do it...

Follow these steps to add storage and increase the size of an LVM volume:

1. Register the new partition as a physical volume:

   pvcreate /dev/sdd1

2. Review the output of pvs to confirm that the volume was registered:

   pvs

3. Use vgextend to add the physical volume to the desired volume group:

   vgextend vg0 /dev/sdd1

4. Review the output of vgs to confirm that the volume was added to the group:

   vgs

5. Use lvextend to increase the size of the desired logical volume:

   lvextend vg0/myvol —L+500G

6. Review the output of lvs to confirm the new capacity:

   lvs

7. Expand the filesystem with `xfs_grow` to use the new capacity:

```
xfs_grow -d /mnt
```

An XFS filesystem must be mounted to expand its size; if it's not already mounted, you'll need to do so before executing `xfs_grow`.

8. Confirm the new size of the filesystem using `df`:

```
df -h /mnt
```

How it works...

The recipe assumed that a new partition has been prepared, which was then registered as a physical volume using the `pvcreate` command. Then the physical volume was assigned to the `vg0` volume group using `vgextend`, increasing the group's available storage:

```
vgextend vg0 /dev/sdd1
```

`lvextend` was invoked to grow the size of a logical volume, `vg0/myvol`:

```
lvextend vg0/myvol -L+500G
```

The `-L` argument specifies the amount of storage to allocate from the pool. It's value can be an absolute value, for example, `-L 500G`, in which case the volume will be resized to have that much capacity. A relative value can also be used to increase the volume's current capacity by some amount. The recipe used `-L+500G` to grow the size of the logical volume by an additional 500 GB.

You will receive an error if you provide a value for `-L` less than the logical volume's current capacity because `lvextend` only increases the capacity of a volume. The `lvreduce` command is used to reduce the size of logical volumes:

```
lvreduce vg0/myvol -L 500GB
```

Given a straight value, `-L` specifies the total capacity for the volume. In the preceding command, the capacity for `vg0/myvol` is reduced to `500GB`. Given a relative value, for example `-L-500GB`, `lvreduce` reduces the volume's capacity by the specified amount.

When finished, the logical volume's capacity can be confirmed by inspecting the output of the `lvs` command. The command reports the logical volumes that exist and to which group they are assigned, their attributes, storage capacity, and other statistics.

```
[root@benito ~]# vgs
VG      #PV #LV #SN Attr   VSize   VFree
centos   1   3   0 wz--n- 499.51g 64.00m
vg0      3   1   0 wz--n-   2.49t  2.00t
[root@benito ~]# lvextend vg0/myvol -L+500G
Size of logical volume vg0/myvol changed from 500.00 GiB (128000 extents) to 1000.00 GiB (256000 extents).
Logical volume myvol successfully resized
[root@benito ~]# vgs
LV     VG      Attr      LSize    Pool Origin Data%  Meta%  Move Log Cpy%Sync Convert
home   centos  wi ao     118.15g
root   centos  -wi-ao---- 50.00g
swap   centos  -wi-ao----  1.00g
myvol  vg0     -wi-a---- 1000.00g
[root@benito ~]#
```

The capacity of the logical volume has increased but the filesystem needs to be resized to use it

Finally, the filesystem needs to be expanded to make use of the additional space available to it with `xfs_growfs`. Filesystems must be mounted for the utility to work, and the recipe assumes that it's mounted at `/mnt`. The `-d` argument instructs `xfs_grow` to increase the size of the filesystem as much as possible (the entire size of the volume).

```
xfs_growfs -d /mnt
```

Alternatively, you can give a specific size with `-D`. Its value is given in block counts, so some math will be required to grow the filesystem to the desired size. For example, let's say you have a 1 TB filesystem and the block size is 4,096 bytes (the default). The block count will be 268,435,456 blocks. If you want to grow the filesystem an additional 500 GB, the target block count will be `399507456`:

```
xfs_growfs -D 399507456 /mnt
```

To make life a little easier, here's a table that presents block counts for common sizes:

Size	Blocks
100MB	25,600
512MB	131,072
1GB	263,144
5GB	1,210,720
10GB	2,621,440
50GB	12,107,200
100GB	26,214,400
500GB	131,072,000
1TB	268,435,456
2TB	536,870,912

These block counts can be used with xfs_growfs to grow an XFS filesystem

While it's possible to reduce the size of a logical volume, it's only possible to grow an XFS filesystem. If you want to reduce the size of an XFS-supported volume you'll have to move its data to a safe location, remove and recreate the logical volume with a smaller size, and later move the data back.

See also

Refer to the following resources for more information on growing an LVM volume:

- The `xfs_growfs` manual page (`man 8 xfs_growfs`)
- Linux guide to the XFS filesystem (`http://landoflinux.com/linux_xfs_files ystem_introduction.html`)
- Extend/Reduce LVM's in Linux (`http://www.tecmint.com/extend-and-reduce -lvms-in-linux/`)
- How to grow an XFS-formatted disk (`http://superuser.com/questions/192/h ow-to-grow-xfs-formated-disk/11486#11486`)

Working with LVM snapshots

A logical volume, also called a linear volume, is just one type of volume we can create; LVM also lets us create snapshot volumes. A snapshot volume is associated with a logical volume and keeps track of changes made to the logical volume's data. We can then merge the snapshot back into the logical volume to roll back the data. This recipe will show you how to do just that.

Getting ready

This recipe requires a CentOS system with administrative privileges provided by logging in with the `root` account or using `sudo`. It assumes that a logical volume has been configured and sufficient storage exists in its volume group for the snapshot.

How to do it...

The following commands show you how to work with LVM snapshots. Before you begin, you should verify that there is sufficient storage available in the volume group to support the snapshot using `vgs`.

1. Use `lvcreate -s` to create a snapshot volume:

   ```
   lvcreate -s -L 100M -n myvolsnap vg0/myvol
   ```

2. A snapshot volume may be deleted using `lvremove`:

   ```
   lvremove vg0/myvolsnap
   ```

3. A snapshot volume may be mounted and accessed with `mount`:

   ```
   mount -o ro /dev/vg0/myvolsnap /mnt
   ```

4. To restore a logical volume to the state it was in when the snapshot was made, make sure neither are mounted and use `lvconvert`:

   ```
   lvconvert -v --merge vg0/myvolsnap
   ```

How it works...

This recipe presented commands to create a snapshot volume which then tracks the changes made to a logical volume and to merge the snapshot back into the logical volume.

Snapshots are created using the `lvcreate` command with the `-s` flag. `-n` gives the name for the snapshot and `-L` specifies how much storage will be allocated for it from the volume group. The final argument is the logical volume the snapshot is created from:

```
lvcreate -s -L 100M -n myvolsnap vg0/myvol
```

The values given in the example create a snapshot of `vg0/myvol` named `myvolsnap` with a capacity of 100 MB. Storage for the snapshot volume is allocated from the same group as its logical volume so that there should be sufficient storage to support the snapshot. Luckily, snapshot volumes don't copy all of the data from the original volume. Instead, they use a copy-on-write strategy where only the differences are recorded to the snapshot when the data is modified.

If the deltas exceed the snapshot volume's capacity, LVM won't be able to continue to record changes and the snapshot will no longer be valid. For this reason, you should periodically monitor the snapshot's storage usage and either resize the snapshot or discard the snapshot and create a new one with a larger capacity if necessary. As with other volumes, `lvremove` is used to delete snapshot volumes:

```
lvremove vg0/myvolsnap
```

A snapshot can also be mounted and accessed like other logical volumes. LVM transparently reads unmodified data from the original logical volume so that the data appears as a full copy. Depending on the your reasons for creating a snapshot, you may want to use the `ro` mount option to mount the volume read-only to prevent inadvertent changes from being introduced:

```
mount -o ro /dev/vg0/myvolsnap /mnt
```

`lvconvert` is used to change a volume's type and other characteristics. You should unmount both the logical and snapshot volumes before calling `lvconvert` so that the merge process can begin immediately. Otherwise, LVM will schedule the process to begin after both have been unmounted and either the logical or snapshot volume is mounted again.

To revert the logical volume's data, we target its snapshot volume and use the `--merge` option:

```
lvconvert -v --merge vg0/myvolsnap
```

Merging the snapshot volume's data to its logical volume rolls back the changes to the logical volume's data, basically restoring it to the state it was in at the time the snapshot was created. When finished, the snapshot is automatically deleted. `-v` puts `lvconvert` into verbose mode, which is useful to monitor its progress and to know when the merge is complete and the snapshot has been deleted.

See also

Refer to the following resources for more information on working with snapshots:

- The `lvconvert` manual page (`man 8 lvconvert`)
- How to take a snapshot logical volume and restore (`http://www.tecmint.com/take-snapshot-of-logical-volume-and-restore-in-lvm/`)
- How to take volume snapshots (`http://www.unixarena.com/213/8/linux-lvm-how-to-take-volume-snapshot.html`)

6

Allowing Remote Access

This chapter contains the following recipes:

- Running commands remotely through SSH
- Configuring a more secure SSH login
- Securely connecting to SSH without a password
- Restricting SSH access by user or group
- Protecting SSH with Fail2ban
- Confining sessions to a chroot jail
- Configuring TigerVNC
- Tunneling VNC connections through SSH

Introduction

The recipes in this chapter will help you provide remote access to your CentOS system in a security-conscious way. You'll learn how to execute commands on a remote system through SSH, configure the OpenSSH SSH server to increase security surrounding remote logins, and use key-based authentication to connect. You'll also learn how to allow or deny access to different users, configure Fail2ban to automatically block suspected IP addresses to protect your server from brute force attacks better, and restrict users to a chroot jail once they've logged in. The concluding recipes show you how to provide remote access to a complete desktop environment using VNC, and how to secure that access by tunneling VNC traffic through an SSH tunnel.

Running commands remotely through SSH

This recipe shows you how to execute one-shot commands on a remote system through **Secure Shell (SSH)**. Having the ability to run commands without establishing a full interactive session can be convenient because you can avoid running a second terminal; everything can be done directly from the same command line.

Getting ready

This recipe requires a remote system running the OpenSSH server and a local computer with the OpenSSH SSH client installed (both should be installed by default on CentOS). The examples assume that the remote system is configured with the IP address 192.168.56.100. Also, you will need a user account available on the remote system.

How to do it...

The following examples show you how to run commands on a remote system from your local system through SSH:

- To execute a command remotely, use `ssh` and specify the hostname or IP address of the target system followed by the command and its arguments:

  ```
  ssh 192.168.56.100 uname -a
  ```

- To execute the command as a different user, provide a username with the remote system's address:

  ```
  ssh tboronczyk@192.168.56.100 id -un
  ```

- If the remote command requires `sudo`, supply `ssh` with the `-t` argument:

  ```
  ssh -t 192.168.56.100 sudo mount /mnt
  ```

- Use the `-X` argument to forward the remote system's X11 display to execute a graphical program:

  ```
  ssh -X 192.168.56.100 gnome-calculator
  ```

- Use quotes when you execute a complex command, for example, a series of commands or when using I/O redirection. This avoids ambiguity between the local and remote shells:

```
ssh 192.168.56.100 "tar tvzf archive.tgz > contents.txt"
```

- You can pipe input from the local system to remote commands that read from stdin:

```
cat foo.txt | ssh 192.168.56.100 "cat > foo.txt"
```

How it works...

`ssh` is used mainly to log in to a remote system and access an interactive shell because it's possible that many people don't know that commands can be executed remotely without a shell. This recipe presented several examples that illustrate how you can use `ssh` to run remote commands, each of which follow this general invocation pattern:

```
ssh [options] [user@]host command
```

Anything provided after the remote host is accepted as the command to execute remotely by `ssh` as demonstrated in the following two examples. The first invokes `uname` to print information about the remote system such as the kernel, processor, and operating system, and the second runs `id` to display the username of the current effective user ID:

```
ssh 192.168.56.100 uname -a
ssh tboronczyk@192.168.56.100 id -un
```

`ssh` doesn't launch an interactive shell when running these commands as there's no reason for it to allocate a tty/pseudo-terminal; it acts as the shell itself and routes input and output between the remote and local systems. However, some commands require a terminal to function properly. For example, `sudo` uses the terminal to ensure the user's password isn't printed on the screen as they type it. Without a terminal, `sudo` refuses to run and reports back that `you must have a tty to run sudo`. We can provide the `-t` argument when executing such commands to force `ssh` to allocate a remote terminal resource:

```
ssh -t 192.168.56.100 sudo mount /mnt
```

The -X argument forwards the X11 display and allows us to run graphical programs. The program appears as if it were running in our local desktop environment, although in reality it's running on the remote system:

```
ssh -X 192.168.56.100 "gnome-calculator"
```

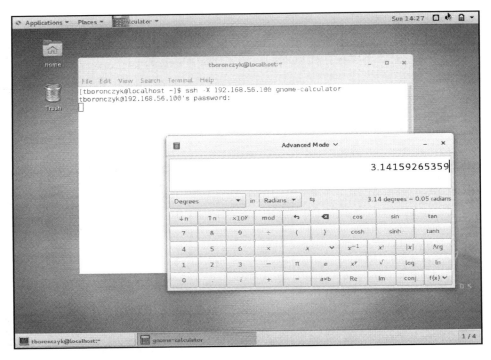

Graphical applications can be run using X11 forwarding

To make sure an invocation is interpreted how you intend, you may need to quote commands. This is especially true when using I/O redirection or when you are running multiple commands. To see why, consider the following example:

```
ssh 192.168.56.100 "tar tvzf archive.tgz > contents.txt"
```

tar outputs a list of files in the archive which is then redirected to create the contents.txt file. Everything happens remotely—tar runs on the remote system and the new file is created on the remote system.

Now, here's the same invocation but without quoting:

```
ssh 192.168.56.100 tar tvzf archive.tgz > contents.txt
```

`tar` still executes remotely, but the local shell interprets the redirect and `contents.txt` is created on the local system.

I/O redirection is possible in both directions. That is, we can pipe input from the local system to the remote system's stdin:

```
cat foo.txt | ssh 192.168.56.100 "cat > foo.txt"
```

In this example, `foo.txt` is read by `cat` and the contents are piped to the remote system. There, a remotely running instance of `cat` will be waiting to read the input. When it detects the end of the transmission, `cat` outputs what it received, which is then redirected to create `foo.txt` on the remote system. In essence, we've just made a copy of `foo.txt` from the local system to the remote system.

See also

Refer to the following resources for more information on running commands remotely through SSH:

- The `ssh` manual page (`man 1 ssh`)
- Piping with SSH (`http://linux.icydog.net/ssh/piping.php`)
- Commandlinefu.com SSH commands (`http://www.commandlinefu.com/commands/matching/ssh/c3No/sort-by-votes`)

Configuring a more secure SSH login

SSH is considered a secure alternative to older protocols, such as Telnet, rsh, and rlogin, because it encrypts the connection between the client and server. This encryption protects the traffic from any ne'er-do-wells who may be eavesdropping on the network. However, your system can still fall victim to the denial of service attacks or a malicious user who takes advantage of an idle session that was carelessly left unattended. This recipe takes the first steps in hardening SSH by updating the server's configuration to increase security surrounding remote logins.

Getting ready

This recipe requires a CentOS system running the OpenSSH server. Administrative privileges are also required, either by logging in with the `root` account or through the use of `sudo`.

How to do it...

Follow these steps to increase the security of your SSH logins:

1. Open the SSH server's configuration file with your text editor:

   ```
   vi /etc/ssh/sshd_config
   ```

2. Locate the `LoginGraceTime` option. Uncomment it and change its value to 30 seconds to limit the amount of time users are given to provide their credentials:

   ```
   LoginGraceTime 30
   ```

3. Find and uncomment the `PrintLastLog` option and change its value to `yes` to show the user the time and location of their last login:

   ```
   PrintLastLog yes
   ```

4. Uncomment the `Banner` option and set its value to `/etc/banner` to display a login warning to users:

   ```
   Banner /etc/banner
   ```

5. Save your changes and close the configuration file.

6. Create the `/etc/banner` file with the following (or similar) verbiage:

   ```
   This computer system is for authorized use only. All  activity is
   logged and monitored. Users accessing this  system without
   authority, or in excess of their authority,  may be subject to
   criminal, civil, and administrative  action. Continuing to use
   this system indicates your consent to these terms and conditions
   of use.
   ```

7. Restart the SSH server for the configuration changes to take effect:

   ```
   systemctl restart sshd.service
   ```

8. To automatically log out sessions after 10 minutes of inactivity, create the `/etc/profile.d/timeout.sh` file with the following:

```
export TMOUT=600
```

How it works...

The first option we adjusted in the SSH server's configuration file was `LoginGraceTime`, to determine how long a user is allowed to enter their username and password. By default, the connection attempt times out if the user doesn't provide their credentials within two minutes. We reduced this time to 30 seconds, but you can set a more appropriate value if you find this not to be long enough:

```
LoginGraceTime 30
```

Then, setting the `PrintLastLog` option's value to `yes` causes the time and location of the user's last log in to be displayed. This is helpful because an unknown time or location can alert a user if their account has been compromised and is being used for unauthorized access:

```
PrintLastLog yes
```

Next, we configured a login banner. A strongly-worded warning isn't likely to deter a malicious user, but many organizations require them to be prominently displayed when a user logs in for legal reasons. Such messages are considered to be sufficient notification in some jurisdictions to inform users that their actions are monitored and they should have no expectations of privacy for what they do on the system. This gives the organization better legal standing to prosecute any abuse.

To display the warning before the login prompt, we set `Banner` with the path to a file containing our message. Then we created the file with the desired text:

```
Banner /etc/banner
```

The user is presented with a banner message before logging in to the remote system nroff can be used to justify the banner's text:

```
(echo -e ".ll 75\n.pl 0\n.nh"; cat) | nroff > /etc/banner
```

cat reads text from stdin (press *Ctrl* + *D* when you're finished) and both the echo'd instructions and the text are piped to nroff for formatting.

.ll tells nroff to set the line length at 75 characters. It's a good idea to use a value less than 80 because the traditional terminal displays 80 characters per line.

.pl sets the page length, and setting it prevents nroff from adding additional whitespace after the text in an attempt to fill the length of some imaginary printed page.

.nh prevents nroff from hyphenating words at the end of a line.

If you want to display the banner after the user logs in instead of before, you can use the message of the day file instead. In this case, uncomment the PrintMotd option and set its value to yes and then save your text in /etc/motd.

Finally, we created the /etc/profile.d/timeout.sh file to set the TMOUT environment variable. Setting TMOUT under /etc/profile.d applies it globally to all users when they log in. To target individual users instead, or if you want to override the global value for specific users, you can place the export in their ~/.bash_profile file:

```
export TMOUT=600
```

Now with the variable set, bash automatically closes the user's session if it's been inactive for the specified amount of time with the message timed out waiting for input: auto-logout. The value is given in seconds, with the recipe's example closing idle sessions after 10 minutes.

See also

Refer to the following resources for more information on tightening security on SSH logins:

- The sshd_config manual page (man 5 sshd_config)
- RHEL 7 System Administrator's Guide: OpenSSH (https://access.redhat.com/documentation/en-US/Red_Hat_Enterprise_Linux/7/html/System_Administrators_Guide/ch-OpenSSH.html)

- CentOS Wiki: Securing OpenSSH (https://wiki.centos.org/HowTos/Network/SecuringSSH)
- Should I use a login banner? (http://serverfault.com/questions/24376/should-i-use-a-login-banner-and-if-so-what-should-it-say)

Securely connecting to SSH without a password

This recipe teaches you how to generate a key pair and set up key-based authentication for SSH sessions, allowing you to secretly connect to a remote system without using a password. Key-based authentication is considered more secure than using a password because a weak password can be easy to guess and a strong password can be easy to forget and more likely to be written down. In either case, an attacker has a fairly good chance of discovering a user's password. With key-based authentication, a user must supply the correct private key file, which is practically impossible to crack or spoof.

Getting ready

This recipe requires a remote system running the OpenSSH server and a local computer with the OpenSSH SSH client installed. Its examples assume that the remote system is configured with the IP address 192.168.56.100. Also, you will need an available user account on the remote system.

How to do it...

Follow these steps to set up key-based authentication for SSH sessions:

1. On the local computer, use the ssh-keygen command to create a pair of authentication keys. Accept the default path/filename for the keys and leave the passphrase empty:

   ```
   ssh-keygen -b 3072 -C "Timothy Boronczyk"
   ```

2. Create the .ssh directory if it doesn't already exist in your remote home directory:

   ```
   ssh 192.168.56.100 "mkdir -m 700 .ssh"
   ```

3. Append the contents of `id_rsa.pub` to `.ssh/authorized_keys` on the remote system:

```
cat .ssh/id_rsa.pub | ssh 192.168.56.100 "cat >>
.ssh/authorized_keys"
```

4. Secure the `authorized_keys` file's permissions:

```
ssh 192.168.56.100 "chmod 640 .ssh/authorized_keys"
```

5. Verify that you can connect to the remote system without providing a password:

```
ssh 192.168.56.100
```

6. Repeat steps 2 through 5 for any additional remote systems you want to log in to using key-based authentication.

How it works...

Key-based authentication is considered more secure than using passwords because it's nearly impractical to crack a suitable encryption key while brute forcing a password is trivial. This recipe used the OpenSSH suite's `ssh-keygen` program to generate a new pair of keys, which we then used to authenticate our SSH session:

```
ssh-keygen -b 3072 -C "Timothy Boronczyk"
```

-C embeds a brief comment in the key which is useful for identifying the owner or purpose of a key and -b sets the number of bits used for the key's modulus. The more bits used, the larger the number that can be represented, which means greater resistance to cracking attacks. If -b isn't provided, the default value is 2,048 bits. Based on the estimates of the rate at which computing power increases, 2,048 is generally thought to be suitable until around the year 2030 (researchers developed a successful attack against 1,024-bit keys in 2010). A 3,072-bit key is considered suitable beyond 2030.

We accepted the suggested `~/.ssh/id_rsa` value as the name of the output file when prompted (this is where `ssh` looks for our private identity key by default when we connect to a remote server). We also didn't provide a passphrase. If we were to give one, then the key would be encrypted and we'd need to provide the password to decrypt the key every time we wanted to use it.

When `ssh-keygen` is finished, the private key `id_rsa` and the public key `id_rsa.pub` can be found in the `.ssh` directory:

```
[tboronczyk@localhost ~]$ ssh-keygen -b 3072 -C "Timothy Boronczyk"
Generating public/private rsa key pair.
Enter file in which to save the key (/home/tboronczyk/.ssh/id_rsa):
Enter passphrase (empty for no passphrase):
Enter same passphrase again:
Your identification has been saved in /home/tboronczyk/.ssh/id_rsa.
Your public key has been saved in /home/tboronczyk/.ssh/id_rsa.pub.
The key fingerprint is:
e5:65:7e:3c:76:bc:20:12:d4:55:b9:ed:60:12:8b:42 Timothy Boronczyk
The key's randomart image is:
+--[ RSA 3072]-----+
|       .. .....   |
|      E  ..  .    |
|     . ...oo   o  |
|     .oo+o.oo.    |
|     So...+=oo    |
|      . .o.oo     |
|           .      |
|                  |
|                  |
+-----------------+
[tboronczyk@localhost ~]$
```

The pair of keys is generated for password-less authentication

Then, we created the `.ssh` directory in our home directory on the remote system. You can execute the `mkdir` command while being logged in to the remote system, otherwise you can execute the command remotely through SSH:

```
ssh 192.168.56.100 "mkdir -m 700 .ssh"
```

Next, we added the public key to `.ssh/authorized_keys` on the remote system:

```
cat .ssh/id_rsa.pub | ssh 192.168.56.100 "cat >>  .ssh/authorized_keys"
```

Because proper permissions help ensure the security of your keys, `ssh` won't consider them safe to use if the permissions are too lax. The permissions on the `.ssh` directory should be read, write, and execute permissions only for the owner (`700`), read permissions for the owner and group, and write permissions for the owner (`640`) on `authorized_keys`. A simple `chmod` call ensures that everything is correct:

```
ssh 192.168.56.100 "chmod 640 .ssh/authorized_keys"
```

When we connect, `ssh` sees the `id_rsa` file and sends our private key as part of the connection request. The server checks for the corresponding public key in the `authorized_keys` file, and if everything matches up then we're authorized and logged in.

See also

Refer to the following resources for more information on using key-based authentication with OpenSSH:

- RHEL 7 System Administrator's Guide: OpenSSH (`https://access.redhat.com /documentation/en-US/Red_Hat_Enterprise_Linux/7/html/System_Administ rators_Guide/ch-OpenSSH.html`)
- SSH password versus key authentication (`http://security.stackexchange.co m/questions/33381/ssh-password-vs-key-authentication`)

Restricting SSH access by user or group

Depending on the role of your system and which user accounts are configured on it, you may not want all of its registered users to have access through SSH. This recipe shows you how to configure the SSH server to restrict remote user access by explicitly granting or denying the users access.

Getting ready

This recipe requires a CentOS system running the OpenSSH server. Administrative privileges are also required, either by logging in with the `root` account or through the use of `sudo`.

How to do it...

Follow these steps to restrict users' SSH access:

1. Open the SSH server's configuration file with your text editor:

   ```
   vi /etc/ssh/sshd_config
   ```

2. Find the `PermitEmptyPasswords` option. Uncomment it and set its value to `no` to disallow accounts with empty passwords:

    PermitEmptyPasswords no

3. To disallow remote access with the `root` account, locate and uncomment the `PermitRootLogin` option and set its value to `no`:

    PermitRootLogin no

4. Deny remote access for specific user accounts by adding an entry for `DenyUsers`. The option's value should be a space-separated list of usernames you want to deny:

    DenyUsers bbarrera jbhuse mbutterfield

5. Deny remote access for users who are members of a specific group by adding an entry for `DenyGroups`:

    DenyGroups users noremote

6. Add an `AllowUsers` entry to deny access to everyone except those in the list of permitted users:

    AllowUsers abell tboronczyk

7. Add an `AllowGroups` entry to deny access to everyone except those in the list of permitted groups:

    AllowGroups itadmin remote

8. Save your changes and close the file.
9. Restart the SSH server for the changes to take effect:

    systemctl restart sshd.service

How it works...

First, we uncommented `PermitEmptyPasswords` and set its value to `no`. This prevents user accounts that don't have a password from being used to log in over SSH:

PermitEmptyPasswords no

Passwords are the first level of defense in protecting ourselves from malicious attacks using compromised user accounts. Without a strong password, anyone can log in simply by knowing the username. This is a scary thought because usernames can be easily guessed and sometimes are even publicly available in the form of e-mail addresses and so on.

Next, we uncommented the `PermitRootLogin` option and set its value to `no`. This prevents `root` from establishing an SSH session directly:

```
PermitRootLogin no
```

Such restrictions were of critical importance when protocols such as Telnet were used because the username and password were often sent across the network in plain text—an attacker could easily monitor the network traffic and capture the password. However, even though SSH makes this concern moot by encrypting its traffic, the password is still vulnerable from brute force cracking attacks. For this reason, it's wise to require users to authenticate using their unprivileged account first and then use `su` or `sudo` to elevate their privileges when necessary (refer to `Chapter 3`, *User and Permission Management*).

The recipe then presented the `DenyUsers`, `DenyGroups`, `AllowUsers`, and `AllowGroups` options as a way to restrict SSH access on a larger scale.

The `DenyUsers` option prohibits specific users from logging in. While other user accounts will be able to access the system remotely, the users listed under `DenyUsers` will see the message `Permission Denied`. The recipe's example denies access to the users `bbarrera`, `jbhuse`, and `mbutterfield`:

```
DenyUsers bbarrera jbhuse mbutterfield
```

The `DenyGroups` option works similarly, but denies users based on their group membership; the following example denies access to anyone who's a member of the `users` group or the `noremote` group:

```
DenyGroups users noremote
```

The denial options are useful for blacklisting a small number of users. To block all users except for a select few, we use the allow options. `AllowUsers` denies access to everyone except those specified. `AllowGroups` is its counterpart allowing only those users who are members of the specified group:

```
AllowUsers abell tboronczyk
AllowGroups itadmin remote
```

The options can also have values that use * and ? as wildcards. * matches zero or more characters and ? matches a single character. For example, the following denies all users:

```
DenyUsers *
```

 AllowUsers and AllowGroups deny all users/groups except the ones they list. Be careful if you depend on SSH to administer your servers because it's very easy to block yourself with these. Before logging out of your current SSH session, check that you can successfully log in using a second terminal. If there's a problem, you'll still be logged in with the first session and will able to fix the issue.

See also

Refer to the following for more information on restricting remote SSH access:

- The sshd_config manual page (man 5 sshd_config)
- RHEL 7 System Administrator's Guide: OpenSSH (https://access.redhat.com /documentation/en-US/Red_Hat_Enterprise_Linux/7/html/System_Administ rators_Guide/ch-OpenSSH.html)
- SSH how to deny all users except for one? (http://www.linuxquestions.org/qu estions/linux-security-4/howto-sshd-deny-all-users-except-for-one-36 8752/)

Protecting SSH with Fail2ban

A determined attacker may try to brute force a user's password to gain access or attempt repeated logins to consume network and system resources as part of a denial of service attack. Fail2ban can help protect you from such attacks by monitoring a server's log files, identifying suspicious activity, and automatically banning the IP addresses responsible for the activity. This recipe teaches you how to install Fail2ban to safeguard your system.

Getting ready

This recipe requires a CentOS system running the OpenSSH server. Administrative privileges are also required, either by logging in with the `root` account or through the use of `sudo`. The `fail2ban` package is hosted by the EPEL repository; if the repository is not already registered, refer to the *Registering the EPEL and Remi repositories* recipe in `Chapter 4, Software Installation Management`.

How to do it...

Follow these steps to protect your system with Fail2ban:

1. Install the `fail2ban` package:

   ```
   yum install fail2ban
   ```

2. Create the jail configuration file `/etc/fail2ban/jail.local` using the following contents:

   ```
   [sshd]
   enabled=true
   bantime=86400
   maxretry=5
   ```

3. Start the Fail2ban service and enable its automatic start-up when the system boots:

   ```
   systemctl start fail2ban.service
   systemctl enable fail2ban.service
   ```

4. To view the `sshd` jail's status, use `fail2ban-client` with the `status` command:

   ```
   fail2ban-client status sshd
   ```

How it works...

You've learned how to install Fail2ban and configure automated IP blocking after several failed login attempts. You also learned how to manually ban and unban addresses using `fail2ban-client`.

A Fail2ban jail configuration brings together filter and action definitions to perform an activity whenever certain patterns are observed in a server's log file. Filters specify the pattern definitions for identifying interesting log entries, for example, repeated authentication failures. Actions, on the other hand, define the commands that run when a filter is matched. Fail2ban is shipped with several predefined filters for common servers such as Apache, MySQL, Sendmail, and SSH, and several predefined actions such as managing iptable entries to block and unblock IP addresses, sending e-mail notifications, and triggering DNS updates.

There are several jails defined in `/etc/fail2ban/jail.conf`. To activate the `sshd` jail, we created the `jail.local` file with entries that override and extend the default jail definition:

```
[sshd]
enabled=true
bantime=86400
maxretry=5
```

Intuitively, the `enabled` option enables or disables the jail. `maxretry`, which we set to 5, is the number of failed login attempts permitted before Fail2ban enacts the ban. `bantime` sets how long the ban will last, which we set to `86400` seconds. With this configuration, users are allowed up to 5 failed attempts before their IP address is banned for 24 hours.

The existing definition from `jail.conf` already identifies the default port and the log file location. If you're running SSH on a nonstandard port, you can override the original definition's setting using `port`. The location of the SSH's log file can be overridden with `logfile`.

`fail2ban-client` is used to interact with the Fail2ban service. Its `status` command outputs information about the service's current state, and if `status` is followed by a jail name then status information about the jail is returned instead. Perhaps of particular interest in the jail's status is a list of IP addresses that have been banned:

```
fail2ban-client status sshd
```

```
[root@benito ~]# fail2ban-client status sshd
Status for the jail: sshd
|- Filter
|  |- Currently failed: 1
|  |- Total failed:      18
|  `- File list:         /var/log/secure
`- Actions
   |- Currently banned: 2
   |- Total banned:     5
   `- Banned IP list:   10.25.30.107 192.168.56.12
[root@benito ~]#
```

The jail's status output presents the list of banned addresses

The client also has `get` and `set` commands to inspect and update various properties of the running service. For example, `get sshd bantime` returns the configured ban duration. `set sshd bantime` temporarily updates the duration until the service is restarted.

You can manually ban an IP address by setting the jail's `banip` property:

```
fail2ban-client set sshd banip 10.25.30.107
```

To manually unban an address, set `unbanip`:

```
fail2ban-client set sshd unbanip 10.25.30.107
```

Being able to manually unban addresses is important in case a legitimate address is banned for some reason. If there are addresses that should never be blocked, perhaps a test integration server executing failed logins on purpose, or perhaps an administrator's computer, you can identify them using the `ignoreip` option in your `jail.local` configuration file and Fail2ban will avoid banning those addresses:

```
ignoreip=10.25.30.107
```

See also

Refer to the following resources for more information on Fail2ban:

- The `fail2ban-client` manual page (`man 1 fail2ban-client`)
- Fail2ban Wiki (`http://www.fail2ban.org/wiki/index.php/Main_Page`)
- Permanently ban repeat offenders with Fail2ban (`http://stuffphilwrites.com/213/3/permanently-ban-repeat-offenders-fail2ban/`)
- Monitoring the Fail2ban log (`http://www.the-art-of-web.com/system/fail2ban-log/`)

Confining sessions to a chroot jail

This recipe teaches you how to set up a chroot jail. A chroot call changes the user's view of the filesystem hierarchy by setting a particular path as the root; for the user, the path appears as / and they are unable to traverse beyond it. This creates a sandbox or jail, confining the user to a small branch of the real hierarchy. Chroot jails are commonly used for security purposes, for example, user containment and honeypots and also for application testing and in recovery procedures.

Getting ready

This recipe requires a CentOS system running the OpenSSH server. Administrative privileges are also required, either by logging in with the root account or through the use of sudo.

How to do it...

Follow these steps to configure a chroot jail and confine users to it:

1. Download the cpchroot script needed to copy commands and their dependencies into the chroot environment:

   ```
   curl -Lo ~/cpchroot tinyurl.com/zyzozdp
   ```

2. Make the script executable using chmod:

   ```
   chmod +x ~/cpchroot
   ```

3. Create the /jail directory and its subdirectories to mimic a root filesystem:

   ```
   mkdir -p /jail/{dev,home,usr/{bin,lib,lib64,share}}
   cd /jail
   ln -s usr/bin bin
   ln -s usr/lib lib
   ln -s usr/lib64 lib64
   ```

4. Execute the chroot script to copy the desired programs and commands:

   ```
   ~/cpchroot /jail bash cat cp find grep less ls
   mkdir mv pwd rm rmdir
   ```

5. Copy the terminfo database:

   ```
   cp -R /usr/share/terminfo /jail/usr/share
   ```

6. Create the special device files under /jail/dev using mknod:

   ```
   cd /jail/dev
   mknod null c 1 3
   mknod zero c 1 5
   mknod random c 1 8
   ```

7. Create a group for chroot'd users:

```
groupadd sandbox
```

8. Open the `/etc/ssh/sshd_config` file with your text editor and add the following to the end of the file:

```
Match Group sandbox
    ChrootDirectory /jail
```

9. Save your changes and close the configuration file.
10. Restart the SSH server for the changes to take effect:

```
systemctl restart sshd.service
```

To create a new chroot'd user, create the user with `useradd` and assign them to the `sandbox` group:

```
useradd -s /bin/bash -m -G sandbox rdiamond
```

Then, move their `home` directory to reside under the chroot `jail`:

```
mv /home/rdiamond /jail/home
```

To chroot an existing user, assign them to the `sandbox` group and move their `home` directory to the `jail`:

```
usermod -G sandbox bbarrera
mv /home/bbarrera /jail/home
```

How it works...

Identifying and copying dependencies is tedious and error-prone if done manually. So, I've written a helper script to automate the process of finding and cloning programs with their dependencies into the jail. Our first steps were to download the script using `curl` and then make it executable using `chmod`:

```
curl -Lo ~/cpchroot tinyurl.com/zyzozdp
chmod +x ~/cpchroot
```

The script is hosted on GitHub, but its direct URL was prohibitively long so I used a URL-shortening service to shorten the address. We need to provide `-L` for `curl` to follow any redirects (the service responds with a redirect to GitHub) and `-o` sets the name of the download, in this case `cpchroot`, in your `home` directory.

If you're having problems because of the URL-shortening service, you can find the direct link by visiting `https://gist.github.com/tboronczyk/d77b1baafd13daab3b`, clicking on the **Raw** button, and then copying the URL that appears in your browser's address bar.

Next, we created the /jail directory containing a directory structure that mimics the root filesystem. When a user logs in and is chroot'd, they and everything they do will be contained to /jail. They will not be able to traverse outside that directory, so we need to replicate the directory layout the programs expect:

```
mkdir -p /jail/{dev,home,usr/{bin,lib,lib64,share}}
cd /jail
ln -s usr/bin bin
ln -s usr/lib lib
ln -s usr/lib64 lib64
```

We used mkdir with the -p option and took advantage of shell expansion to create most of the layout with a single command. CentOS sets up its top-level /bin, /lib, and /lib64 directories as symbolic links to the corresponding directories under /usr, which we duplicated using ln within the /jail directory. The final layout looks like the following one presented:

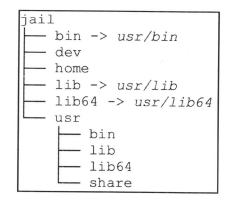

The layout of the sandbox root mimics that of the host's root filesystem

Next, we used the script to copy the desired commands to the jail. The script does the hard work of finding each program's binary and identifies all of the libraries it depends on, and then it copies everything into the appropriate location in the sandboxed filesystem:

```
~/cpchroot /jail bash cat cp find grep less ls mkdir mv pwd rm rmdir
```

Its first argument is the directory acting as our chroot'd root, and then following that is a list of one or more programs we want to make available to the user. The recipe provides a dozen programs as an example, and you should feel free to add or omit some as you see fit. At a minimum, you need a shell (`bash`). I recommend that you include at least `ls` and `pwd` so that the user can navigate.

Then, we copied the `terminfo` database to the `jail`:

```
cp -R /usr/share/terminfo /jail/usr/share/
```

Some programs, such as `screen`, `less`, and `vi`, use the `terminfo` database to make sure their output displays correctly. The database is a collection of files that describe the capabilities of different terminal types, such as the number of lines per screen, how to clear the screen, what colors are supported, and so on. If this information isn't accessible, users will be warned that the `terminal is not fully functional` and the output may be garbled.

To finish making the `jail`, we created the `/dev/null`, `/dev/zero`, and `/dev/random` devices with the `mknod` command:

```
cd /jail/dev/
mknod null c 1 3
mknod zero c 1 5
mknod random c 1 8
```

`mknod` is used to create special files such as character files and block files. These files are special because they can generate data (as is the case with `null` and `zero`) or represent physical devices and receive data. Both `null` and `zero` are character files, as indicated by the letter `c`, since we read from them one character at a time. Block files, on the other hand, operate with several characters at a time. A physical storage disk is often represented as a block device.

We also need to provide a major and minor number when creating a character or block device. These values are predefined and understood by the kernel as to how the device file should behave. 1 and 3 are the major and minor numbers that define a null device. 1 and 5 define the file as a null byte source. You can see the full list of major and minor number assignments in the Linux Allocated Device document listed in this recipe's *See also* section.

After the chroot environment was set up, we turned our attention to configure the SSH server. First, we created the `sandbox` group, which can be assigned to any user we want contained:

```
groupadd sandbox
```

Next, we added a `Match` block to the SSH server's configuration file targeting the new group:

```
Match Group sandbox
    ChrootDirectory /jail
```

`Match` starts a new conditional section in the configuration file that applies only when its condition is matched. In this case, we're matching the user's group to `sandbox`. When the user is a member of the group, the `ChrootDirectory` option is applied and it sets `/jail` as the user's root directory. Now when a user connects, anything they do will be confined to the chroot jail, including actions that happen automatically such as launching an interactive shell (`bash`).

Bash tries to place the user in their `home` directory after signing in. However, if their `home` directory isn't accessible, the user will see the error message `Could not chdir to home directory` and find themselves in the root directory. To avoid this, we moved their `home` directory into the `jail`:

```
mv /home/jbhuse /jail/home/
```

 You might be tempted to specify the `home` directory when creating a new user, as follows:

```
useradd -m -D /jail/home/jbhuse -G sandbox jbhuse
```

Unfortunately, this doesn't work. The `home` directory is created in the desired location, the user is chroot'd, and the path is viewed in relation to `/jail` so that bash looks for `/jail/jail/home/jbhuse`. This is why the recipe demonstrates moving the `home` directory as a second step. The entry in `/etc/passwd` stays, `/home/jbhuse` is interpreted as `/jail/home/jbhuse`, and all is right with the world.

See also

Refer to the following for more information on setting up chroot environments:

- The `sshd_config` manual page (`man 5 sshd_config`)
- How to Configure SFTP with Chroot (`http://www.unixmen.com/configure-sftp-chroot-rhel-centos-7`)

- Safely identify dependencies for chrooting (`http://zaemis.blogspot.com/216/2/safely-identify-dependencies-for-chroot.html`)
- Linux allocated devices (`https://www.kernel.org/doc/Documentation/devices.txt`)

Configuring TigerVNC

Virtual Network Computing (VNC) works by capturing the display's frame buffer and making it available across the network. This recipe shows you how to install TigerVNC and configure it to provide remote users access to their graphical desktop environment as if they were physically in front of the system.

Getting ready

This recipe requires two systems, a CentOS system to host the VNC server (remote system) and a local computer with a VNC client to connect to it. It assumes that the remote system is running the OpenSSH SSH server and a graphical desktop environment such as GNOME or KDE. Administrative privileges are required on the remote server, either by logging in with the `root` account or through the use of `sudo`. The local computer is expected to have a VNC client installed.

How to do it...

Follow these steps to install and configure TigerVNC:

1. On the remote system, install the TigerVNC server package:

   ```
   yum install tigervnc-server
   ```

2. Copy the example unit file provided with the package to `/etc/systemd/system`, adjusting its name to include the username of the person using VNC:

   ```
   cp /usr/lib/systemd/system/vncserver@.service
   /etc/systemd/system/vncserver-tboronczyk@.service
   ```

3. Open the new unit file with your text editor:

```
vi /etc/systemd/system/vncserver-tboronczyk@.service
```

4. Replace the <USER> placeholder that appears in the [Service] section's ExecStart and PIDFile entries:

```
ExecStart=/usr/sbin/runuser -l tboronczyk -c "/usr/bin/
vncserver %i"
PIDFile=/home/tboronczyk/.vnc/%H%i.pid
```

5. Save your changes and close the file.
6. Repeat steps 2 to 5 for each user who will use VNC to connect to their desktop.
7. Reload systemd's configuration to make it aware of the new unit files:

```
systemctl daemon-reload
```

8. Open ports 5900 through 5903 in the system's firewall to accept incoming VNC requests:

```
firewall-cmd --zone=public --permanent --add-service=vnc- server
firewall-cmd --reload
```

9. The users using VNC should set the password they'll use to authenticate with the VNC server using vncpasswd:

```
vncpasswd
```

10. When a user wants to connect, specify a display number after @ in the unit's name when starting TigerVNC:

```
systemctl start vncserver-tboronczyk@:1.service
```

11. Stop the server when it's not in use:

```
systemctl stop vncserver-tboronczyk@.service
```

How it works...

Along with the VNC server, the tigervnc-server package installs a systemd unit file to start and stop the server. However, there's some configuration we need to attend to before using it because the server runs under the user's account to obtain their desktop.

When TigerVNC starts, it connects to the X server and logs in to the user's desktop just as if the user was sitting in front of the system itself. This means each user needs their own instance of the server running and we need to configure it for each user. We made a copy of the original unit file found under `/usr/lib/systemd/system`, one for each user.

```
cp /usr/lib/systemd/system/vncserver@.service /etc/systemd/system/
vncserver-tboronczyk@.service
```

The name of the copied file contains the username so that we can keep everything organized. They're placed under `/etc/systemd/system` because `systemd` looks in `/etc/systemd` for units before searching `/usr/lib/systemd` (in fact, many entries in `/etc/systemd` are symbolic links to their original files under `/usr/lib/systemd`). So, placing the copies there lets us keep the original intact and safeguards us from loosing our configuration in the event of an upgrade where the original until file is replaced.

```
[root@benito ~]# ls /etc/systemd/system/vncserver-*@.service
/etc/systemd/system/abell@.service
/etc/systemd/system/bbarrera@.service
/etc/systemd/system/jbhuse@.service
/etc/systemd/system/mbutterfield@.service
/etc/systemd/system/ndragneel@.service
/etc/systemd/system/rdiamond@.service
/etc/systemd/system/tboronczyk@.service
[root@benito ~]#
```

This system has VNC access configured for several users

We replaced any occurrence of the `<USER>` placeholder under the `[SERVICE]` section in each configuration file with the appropriate username:

```
ExecStart=/usr/sbin/runuser -l tboronczyk -c "/usr/bin/vncserver %i"
PIDFile=/home/tboronczyk/.vnc/%H%i.pid
```

The command specified in the `ExecStart` entry is invoked when we start the server using `systemctl start`; it uses `runuser` to run TigerVNC under the user's account. The `-l` (lowercase L) argument provides the username and `-c` specifies the command and its arguments that `runuser` will execute. The `PIDFile` entry specifies the directory in which the running process will keep track of its process ID.

Dan Walsh, the author of `runuser`, wrote a blog entry entitled *runuser vs su* detailing the backstory behind the command. You can read it online at h ttp://danwalsh.livejournal.com/55588.html.

The @ symbol appearing in the filename has special significance to systemd. Anything after it and before the file suffix is passed to the commands in the unit file replacing %i. This lets us pass limited information to the server, for example, the display number for TigerVNC to run on. When we start the server as shown in the recipe, :1 is given after @. The value is parsed by systemd and TigerVNC is started on display 1. If we use :2, the server will start on display 2. We can start multiple instances of TigerVNC for different users or even for the same user as long as the display is different for each:

```
systemctl start vncserver-tboronczyk@:1.service
```

Traffic for the display's corresponding port should be allowed by the firewall. Display 0 uses port 5900, display 1 uses port 5901, display 2 uses port 5902, and so on. If you're using FirewallD, the predefined vnc-server service opens ports 5900–5903:

```
firewall-cmd --zone=public --permanent --add-service=vnc-server
```

If you need additional ports or if you don't need to open the entire range, you can open just what you need using --add-port:

```
firewall-cmd --zone=public --permanent --add-port=5901/tcp
```

The user needs to set a VNC password using vncpasswd before they can connect to the display. The password must be at least six characters long, although only the first eight characters are significant. Moreover, the password is stored in the user's ~/.vnc/ directory. In the light of these issues, it's recommended that the user doesn't use the same password as their account password. It's also wise to run the VNC server only when needed since anyone who knows the display number and password can connect to it.

The user also needs a VNC client to connect from their local computer. CentOS users can install the tigervnc package to use TigerVNC's client. Other popular clients are Vinagre for Ubuntu, RealVNC for TightVNC on Windows, and Chicken of the VNC for OS X:

```
yum install tigervnc
```

The IP address or hostname for the remote system and the display (port) that VNC is running are needed to establish the connection. They can be provided in different ways depending on the client, but the standard format accepted by most clients appends the display to the system's address, for example, `192.168.56.100:1`. The user will then be prompted for their password, and if all goes well they'll be connected to the remote display:

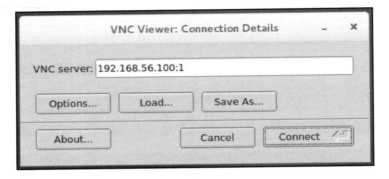

A user prepares to connect to a remote display using VNC

See also

Refer to the following resources for more information on running TigerVNC and how systemd uses @ in filenames:

- TigerVNC (`http://tigervnc.org/`)
- RHEL 7 System Administrator's Guide: TigerVNC (`https://access.redhat.com/documentation/en-US/Red_Hat_Enterprise_Linux/7/html/System_Administrators_Guide/ch-TigerVNC.html`)
- ArchWiki: TigerVNC (`https://wiki.archlinux.org/index.php/TigerVNC`)
- The @ symbol and `systemctl` (`http://superuser.com/questions/393423/the-symbol-and-systemctl-and-vsftpd/393429#393429`)
- Understanding Systemd Units and Unit Files (`https://www.digitalocean.com/community/tutorials/understanding-systemd-units-and-unit-files`)

Tunneling VNC connections through SSH

The previous recipe showed you how to give remote access to the user's desktop through VNC. However, there are clearly some security concerns if the service is running on an untrusted network. Only the display number and password are required to connect, and the password can be relatively easy for a malicious user to crack given that only the first eight characters are significant. Moreover, the traffic is unencrypted and it may be snooped. To help mitigate these risks, this recipe teaches you how to route the VNC connection through an encrypted SSH tunnel.

Getting ready

This recipe requires two systems, a CentOS system hosting the VNC server (remote system) and a local computer with a VNC client to connect to it. It assumes that the remote system is running the OpenSSH SSH server and TigerVNC server and is configured with the IP address 192.168.56.100. It also assumes that you have administrative privileges. The VNC server should be configured as described in the previous recipe. The local computer should have the OpenSSH SSH client (ssh) and a VNC client installed.

How to do it...

Follow these steps to route VNC connections through an encrypted SSH tunnel:

1. On the remote server, open a vncserver@.service configuration file using your text editor:

   ```
   vi /etc/systemd/system/vncserver-tboronczyk@.service
   ```

2. Locate the ExecStart entry and add the -localhost argument to the vncserver command invoked by runuser:

   ```
   ExecStart=/usr/sbin/runuser -l tboronczyk -c "/usr/bin/vncserver
   -localhost %i"
   ```

3. Save your change and close the file.
4. Repeat steps 1 to 3 as necessary for the other users' configuration files.
5. Reload systemd's configuration to make it aware of the updates:

   ```
   systemctl daemon-reload
   ```

6. Start the VNC server:

```
systemctl start vncserver-tboronczyk@:1.service
```

7. On your local system, establish an SSH session to the server with -L to define the tunnel:

```
ssh -L 5901:localhost:5901 192.168.56.100
```

8. Connect to the tunnel's local endpoint (localhost:1) using a VNC client.

How it works...

This recipe showed you how to secure VNC by tunneling its traffic through SSH. We configured the TigerVNC server to only accept connections from its localhost and then set up a tunnel on the local client side to route traffic through an SSH connection. This helps mitigate some of the aforementioned security risks because proper authentication is needed to establish the tunnel and encrypt the VNC traffic.

First, you edited the ExecStart command in the unit files used to start instances of the VNC server. The -localhost argument to vncserver instructs the server to communicate only with the local system; any incoming connections originating from the network will be refused:

```
ExecStart=/usr/sbin/runuser -l tboronczyk -c "/usr/bin/vncserver
-localhost %i"
```

On the client side, the user now needs to establish an SSH tunnel using ssh before they can connect to the remote display:

```
ssh -L 5901:localhost:5901 192.168.56.100
```

The -L argument defines the tunnel as local-port:target-host:target-port. The target host and port represent the final destination in relation to the server ssh is connected to. For example, we know that the recipe is running the user's desktop on display 1 which uses port 5901. We also know that TigerVNC server is running on 192.168.56.100 but configured to listen only to its localhost. This means, we need to connect to localhost:5901 from 192.168.56.100. Thus, localhost:5901 is the target in relation to that system.

Once the user has an established tunnel, they can minimize the session's terminal. (Don't close it!) ssh is connected to the remote system while also listening on the local port (also 5901). On the remote server, ssh has established a second connection to the target host and port. The VNC client will connect to the local port by using the address localhost:1 where the traffic is then routed through the SSH tunnel to the remote server and then forwarded to the final destination.

The remote system acts as a gateway as traffic travels through it from the client's tunnel to the final destination. Keep in mind, unless a tunnel to the target has also been created on the remote server, the second leg of the data's journey is not encrypted. This isn't a concern for this recipe because the remote and target hosts are the same. If your final destination is anything other than localhost, ensure that the network is trusted or create a second tunnel.

 Routing traffic with SSH in this fashion can be done to secure other services as well, for example, NFS, FTP, HTTP, POP3, and SMTP. The overall process is the same: configure the server to listen locally and then establish the tunnel on the client.

See also

Refer to the following resources to learn more about SSH tunneling:

- The ssh manual page (man 1 ssh)
- Securing network traffic with SSH (https://security.berkeley.edu/resources/best-practices-how-articles/securing-network-traffic-ssh-tunnels)
- SSH tunneling made easy (http://www.revsys.com/writings/quicktips/ssh-tunnel.html)

7

Working with Databases

This chapter contains the following recipes:

- Setting up a MySQL database
- Backing up and restoring a MySQL database
- Configuring MySQL replication
- Setting up a MySQL cluster
- Setting up a MongoDB database
- Backing up and restoring a MongoDB database
- Configuring a MongoDB replica set
- Setting up an OpenLDAP directory
- Backing up and restoring an OpenLDAP directory

Introduction

This chapter focuses on three databases. First, you'll learn how to install one of the most widely used relational database servers, MySQL. You'll also learn how to set up master-slave replication to maintain mirror copies of your MySQL databases, and how to stand up a MySQL cluster to provide scalable, high-availability data storage. Next, we'll move to the world of NoSQL databases. You'll learn how to install the popular document-oriented database server MongoDB, and how to configure a MongoDB replica set (replication). Then you'll learn how to set up an LDAP directory server using OpenLDAP. For each of these databases, the chapter also has recipes to show you how to perform basic backup and restore tasks to keep your data safe.

Setting up a MySQL database

This recipe shows you how to perform a basic installation of the popular MySQL database server on CentOS. MySQL is the second most widely used database system today, which is found across many different industries providing data storage for everything from dynamic websites to large-scale data warehouses.

Getting ready

This recipe requires a CentOS system with a working network connection and administrative privileges either using the root account or sudo.

How to do it...

Follow these steps to install MySQL and create a new database:

1. Download the repository configuration package for the Oracle-maintained MySQL repository:

   ```
   curl -LO dev.mysql.com/get/mysql57-community-release-el7-
   7.noarch.rpm
   ```

2. Install the downloaded package:

   ```
   yum install mysql57-community-release-el7-7.noarch.rpm
   ```

3. Now that the MySQL repository is registered, install the mysql-community-server package:

   ```
   yum install mysql-community-server
   ```

4. Start the MySQL server and enable it to start automatically whenever the system reboots:

   ```
   systemctl start mysqld.service
   systemctl enable mysqld.service
   ```

5. Open port 3306 in the system's firewall to allow outside connections to MySQL:

   ```
   firewall-cmd --zone=public --permanent --add-service=mysql
   firewall-cmd --reload
   ```

6. Retrieve the temporary password for MySQL's `root` user from the server's log file:

```
grep "temporary password" /var/log/mysqld.log
```

7. Set a new password for `root` using `mysqladmin`. When the program prompts for the current password, enter the temporary password found in the logs:

```
mysqladmin -u root -p password
```

8. Use `mysql` to connect to the MySQL server using the `root` account:

```
mysql -u root -p
```

9. To create a new database, execute a CREATE DATABASE statement:

```
CREATE DATABASE packt;
```

10. Execute a CREATE USER statement to create a MySQL user account for working with the database:

```
CREATE USER "tboronczyk"@"localhost" IDENTIFIED  BY "P@$$W0rd";
```

11. Execute a GRANT statement to assign the appropriate privileges to the account for the new database:

```
GRANT CREATE, DROP, ALTER, LOCK TABLES, INDEX,  INSERT, UPDATE,
SELECT, DELETE ON packt.* TO "tboronczyk"@"localhost";
```

12. Execute FLUSH PRIVILEGES to instruct MySQL to rebuild its privileges cache:

```
FLUSH PRIVILEGES;
```

13. Exit the MySQL client and return to the terminal:

```
exit
```

How it works...

We began by downloading the package that registers the Oracle-maintained MySQL repository on our system. MySQL is installed from the Oracle repository, because the CentOS repositories install MariaDB instead. After a series of acquisitions between 2008 and 2010, the MySQL codebase and trademark became the property of Oracle. Widespread concern over Oracle's stewardship and the future of MySQL prompted one of the original developers of MySQL to fork the project and start MariaDB. In 2014, the Red Hat and CentOS repositories replaced MySQL as the default database with MariaDB (welcome to the world of open-source politics).

 MariaDB's goal is to remain a free, open-source project under the GNU GPL license and to be an "enhanced, drop-in replacement" for MySQL. For now, differences between the two are negligible to the casual user. But in the world of forked replacements, it's mainly the programming interfaces and communication protocols that remain compatible. Core functionality may remain the same initially, but new features are added independently as time goes on and the products' feature sets begin to diverge. MariaDB acknowledges this with a jump in versioning numbers. MariaDB 5.1 offers the same features as MySQL 5.1, as does MariaDB 5.5 for MySQL 5.5. However, MariaDB doesn't plan to implement all of MySQL 5.6's features and changed their version number to 10.0. For those keeping score at home, the Oracle-maintained repository hosts MySQL 5.7 at the time of this writing. The CentOS repositories currently offer MariaDB 5.5.

The server that hosts the package assumes that people download the file using a web browser and issues a redirect to begin the download. Since we're using `curl`, we supplied the `-L` argument to follow the redirects to reach the actual package:

```
curl -LO dev.mysql.com/get/mysql57-community-release-el7-7.noarch.rpm
```

Next, we installed the downloaded package. Once the repository is registered, we're able to install MySQL with the `mysql-community-server` package. The package installs the server binaries, and the client utilities to work with MySQL are installed as dependencies:

```
yum install mysql57-community-release-el7-7.noarch.rpm
yum install mysql-community-server
```

MySQL maintains its own user accounts and its administrative user is named `root`. Just like CentOS's `root` user, you shouldn't use the account for regular activities; it should be reserved for administrative tasks such as creating new users, granting privileges, and flushing the server's caches. Other less-privileged accounts should be used for everyday activities. To protect the `root` account, its password is randomly generated the first time we start the MySQL server. We needed to search the log file where MySQL recorded the password so that we can set a new password of our own choosing:

```
grep "temporary password" /var/log/mysqld.log
```

Knowing the temporary password, we used `mysqladmin` to change it. The `-u` option gives the username of the MySQL account, `-p` prompts us for the account's password, and `password` is the utility's subcommand used to change passwords. We entered the temporary password when prompted for the original and then we were asked to enter and confirm the new password:

```
mysqladmin -u root -p password
```

 A random default password for `root` is a new behavior starting with MySQL 5.6, which writes the password to `/root/.mysql_secret`, whereas 5.7 writes it to the log file. In older versions, and thus MariaDB since 5.5 is installed by the CentOS repositories, the password is empty. The `validate_password` plugin is also activated in MySQL 5.7. It requires the password to be eight characters or more with at least one number, one upper and one lowercase character, and one special character (that is, punctuation). Consider these requirements when choosing root's new password.

```
[root@benito ~]# systemctl start mysqld.service
[root@benito ~]# systemctl enable mysqld.service
[root@benito ~]# grep "temporary password" /var/log/mysqld.log
2016-06-09T22:24:14.930078Z 1 [Note] A temporary password is generated for root@
benito: 71=(ygh4(Jid
[root@benito ~]# mysqladmin -u root -p password
Enter password:
New password:
Confirm new password:
Warning: Since password will be sent to server in plain text, use ssl connection
 to ensure password safety.
[root@benito ~]#
```

The temporary password is needed to set root's permanent password

There are several clients that we can use to connect to MySQL and interact with our databases. This recipe used `mysql` since it will have been installed by default as a dependency. Again, `-u` identifies the account's username and `-p` prompts us for its password:

```
mysql -u root -p
```

When running in interactive mode, the client displays the prompt `mysql>` at which we submit our SQL statements. After each query, the client displays the server's response, how long the statement took to execute, and if the server reported any errors or warnings.

We issued a CREATE DATABASE statement at the prompt to create the new database named `packt`:

```
CREATE DATABASE packt;
```

Then we created a new user account with CREATE USER to avoid using `root` for our day-to-day work. The account is named `tboronczyk` and is allowed to authenticate from the localhost:

```
CREATE USER "tboronczyk"@"localhost" IDENTIFIED BY "P@$$w0rd";
```

A system's hostname or IP address can replace `localhost` if the account will connect to the server from a different system. MySQL treats each username and hostname pair to be separate accounts though, for example `tboronczyk@localhost` and `tboronczyk@192.168.56.100` are different accounts and can have different privileges assigned to them.

> You can use wildcards in the hostname to create an account that can connect from multiple systems. The `%` wildcard matches zero or more characters, so it can be used to represent any system:
>
> ```
> CREATE USER "tboronczyk"@"%" IDENTIFIED BY "P@$$w0rd";
> ```

New accounts are created without any privileges, so we must assign them by executing a GRANT statement:

```
GRANT CREATE, DROP, ALTER, LOCK TABLES, INSERT, UPDATE, SELECT,
DELETE ON packt.* TO "tboronczyk"@"localhost";
```

The statement assigns the following privileges to the user for all tables (denoted by *) in the packt database:

- CREATE: This allows the user to create databases and tables
- DROP: This allows the user to delete entire tables and databases
- ALTER: This allows the user to change the definition of an existing table
- LOCK TABLES: This allows the user to lock a table for exclusive read or write access
- INDEX: This allows the user to create table indexes
- INSERT: This allows the user to add records to a table
- UPDATE: This allows the user to update records in a table
- SELECT: This allows the user to retrieve records from a table
- DELETE: This allows the user to delete records from a table

A full list of privileges and what they permit a user to do can be found in the official MySQL documentation online at http://dev.mysql.com/doc/refman/5.7/en/grant.html.

Next, we instructed MySQL to rebuild its privileges cache using FLUSH PRIVILEGES:

```
FLUSH PRIVILEGES;
```

When MySQL starts up, it caches the user and permissions information in memory (you'll recall from Chapter 5, *Managing Filesystems and Storage*, that reading from memory is much faster than reading from disk) and then checks the cache every time a user performs an action to verify if they have sufficient privileges. We need to tell MySQL to update its cache whenever we create or delete a user account or grant or revoke an account's privileges, or else our changes will go unnoticed until the next time MySQL starts.

When using mysql to connect to MySQL, you may frequently invoke it with additional options. A common option is -h, which identifies the hostname or IP address of the remote server if MySQL is running on a different system. -e executes a statement directly instead of launching mysql in interactive mode. Also, to work with a specific database, the name can be given either after the rest of the command or you can use -D to specify it. The following example demonstrates all of these by connecting to the MySQL server on 192.168.56.100 and executing a SELECT statement against its sakila database:

```
mysql -u tboronczyk -p -h 192.168.56.100 -D sakila -e "SELECT
last_name, first_name FROM actor"
```

See also

Refer to the following resources for more information on working with MySQL:

- The `mysql` manual page (`man 1 mysql`)
- MySQL 5.7 reference manual (`http://dev.mysql.com/doc/refman/5.7/en`)
- Jump Start MySQL (`http://www.amazon.com/Jump-Start-MySQL-Timothy-Boro nczyk/dp/992461286`)
- MySQL Tutorial (`http://www.mysqltutorial.org/`)

Backing up and restoring a MySQL database

This recipe shows you how to back up your MySQL databases using `mysqldump`. The utility connects to the MySQL server, queries the structure of the database and its data, and outputs the data in the form of SQL statements. The backup can then be used to restore the database or populate a new database with the data.

Getting ready

This recipe requires a running MySQL server and access to either MySQL's `root` user or another user with the necessary privileges to perform the backup.

How to do it...

Follow these steps to make a backup of a MySQL database:

1. Connect to the MySQL database you want to back up:

   ```
   mysql -u root -p packt
   ```

2. Execute a FLUSH TABLES statement to set the database's tables read-only:

   ```
   FLUSH TABLES WITH READ LOCK;
   ```

3. Open a second terminal, leaving the first one active with the `mysql` client still running.

4. In the new terminal, use `mysqldump` to export the table definitions and data:

```
mysqldump -u root -p packt > backup.sql
```

5. Return to the first terminal once the backup is complete and exit `mysql` to unlock the tables.

Because the backup consists of SQL statements, you can recreate the database by importing the statements with `mysql`:

```
mysql -u root -p packt < backup.sql
```

How it works...

The consequences of lost data can range from mild irritation to serious economic repercussions, so it's important to protect yourself with backups. Just think what would happen if your bank lost all of your financial records! The more important your data is to you and the more difficult it is to be recreated if it were to be lost, the more important it is to have backups in case something bad happens.

Prior to making the backup, we connected to the server and executed FLUSH TABLES. The statement forces MySQL to finalize any data updates that may be pending and then sets the tables read-only to prevent modifications to the data while the backup is in progress. This ensures that the data in our backup is consistent:

```
FLUSH TABLES WITH READ LOCK;
```

The tables remain read-only until we release the lock, either by executing an UNLOCK TABLES statement or by terminating the connection to the MySQL server, so we left the current session running and opened a second terminal to perform the backup. While the tables are read-only, any queries that retrieve data will execute, but those that update or insert data will be blocked.

Consider setting up MySQL replication as described in the *Configuring MySQL replication* recipe and then back up the slave's copy of the database to avoid any downtime. Stop replication on the slave, use `mysqldump` to export the data, and then resume replication. The master's tables don't need to be locked and any changes made on the master while replication is suspended will be replicated once the slave comes back online.

Then, we used `mysqldump` to export all of the table definitions and data from the database:

```
mysqldump -u root -p packt > backup.sql
```

Keep yourself organized by including the date in your backup filenames:

```
mysqldump -u root -p packt > backup-$(date +%F).sql
```

`mysqldump` queries the database to retrieve the data, so whichever account we use to perform the backup, it must have the necessary privileges. What exactly those permissions are, ultimately depends on your database's schema. For example, the account needs the SHOW VIEW privilege if your database uses views. The same holds true for the account used to restore the database. You should keep this in mind if you want to use dedicated accounts for your backup and restore activities.

To back up only certain tables, you can list them after the database. For example, the following backs up the `customers` and `addresses` tables:

```
mysqldump -u root -p packt customers addresses > backup.sql
```

There are also several options you can provide to `mysqldump` that affect what it includes in the backup. Here's a list of some of the more commonly used ones:

- `--no-add-drop-table`: This does not include a DROP TABLE statement before any CREATE TABLE statements in the output. Without dropping a table first, the import process may fail on the CREATE TABLE statement when the backup is restored on a system that already has the tables defined.
- `--events`: This exports the definitions for any stored events associated with the database.
- `--hex-blob`: This outputs binary values using the hexadecimal notation. This can help protect against certain byte sequences being incorrectly interpreted, causing a restore to fail.
- `--tables`: This backs up only the specific tables. This is an alternate way of specifying tables instead of listing them after the database name.
- `--routines`: This exports the definitions for any stored procedures associated with the database.
- `--where`: This is a WHERE condition used to return only specific rows. For example, `--tables customers --where "last_name LIKE 'B%'"` will only export rows from the `customers` table for customers whose last name starts with B.

You can find a complete list of options in the online documentation at `http://dev.mysql.c`

om/doc/refman/5.7/en/mysqldump.html.

See also

Refer to the following resources for more information on making backups with mysqldump:

- The mysqldump manual page (man 1 mysqldump)
- MySQL 5.7 Reference Manual: mysqldump (http://dev.mysql.com/doc/refman /5.7/en/mysqldump.html)
- Backup and Restore MySQL Database Using mysqldump (http://www.thegeeks tuff.com/28/9/backup-and-restore-mysql-database-using-mysqldump)

Configuring MySQL replication

This recipe teaches you how to configure MySQL's master-slave replication to maintain mirror copies of your databases in near real time.

To replicate data, the master MySQL server records details about any changes that take place (inserts, updates, and so on) to a file known as the binary log. Each slave server connects to the master's system, reads the information from the log file, and then duplicates the change to maintain their own local copy of the database. Each slave server is responsible for itself, which means we can bring a slave down for maintenance without affecting the availability of the master. Once it comes back online, the slave resumes replication from where it left off.

Replication can be useful in many situations. For example, if a full copy of the database is maintained on a slave, you can swap out the master server with little effort for a failover or disaster-recovery situation. For environments where scalability and performance are a concern, write operations can be performed by the master while intensive read operations can be handled by a collection of read-only slaves behind a load balancer.

Getting ready

This recipe demonstrates how to configure MySQL replication using two systems. The first system is the master MySQL server, which we'll assume has the IP address 192.168.56.100. The second system is the slave server and has the address 192.168.56.101. You'll need administrative access on both systems either using the root account or sudo to complete the configuration.

Both systems should have MySQL installed as discussed by the earlier *Setting up a MySQL database* recipe. If you're setting up replication after one or more databases have already been created on the master, follow the *Backing up and restoring a MySQL database* recipe to back them up and import them to the slave before configuring replication. This ensures that replication starts with all databases in sync.

How to do it...

Follow these steps to configure master-slave replication for MySQL:

1. Use your text editor to open the master MySQL server's configuration file at /etc/my.cnf:

   ```
   vi /etc/my.cnf
   ```

2. In the [mysqld] section, add a new entry for the server-id option and set its value to 1:

   ```
   server-id = 1
   ```

3. Locate the log_bin option and uncomment it:

   ```
   log_bin
   ```

4. Save your changes and close the configuration file.

5. Restart the server so that the changes will take effect:

   ```
   systemctl restart mysqld.service
   ```

6. Connect to the master server using mysql and create a new account for slaves to use. The account requires the REPLICATION SLAVE privilege:

   ```
   CREATE USER "slave"@"192.168.56.101" IDENTIFIED BY "S3CR3t##";
   GRANT REPLICATION SLAVE ON *.* TO "slave"@"192.168.56.101";
   FLUSH PRIVILEGES;
   ```

7. Execute SHOW MASTER STATUS to determine the master's current position in writing to the binary log. Note the values returned for File and Position, as the information will be required to configure the slave:

```
SHOW MASTER STATUS;
```

```
mysql > SHOW MASTER STATUS
+------------------------+----------+--------------+------------------+-------------------+
| File                   | Position | Binlog_Do_DB | Binlog_Ignore_DB | Executed_Gtid_set |
+------------------------+----------+--------------+------------------+-------------------+
| localhost-bin.000003   |     1235 |              |                  |                   |
+------------------------+----------+--------------+------------------+-------------------+
1 row in set (0.00 sec)

mysql >
```

The master's status includes the name of the log file and the server's write position

8. Use your editor to open the slave's configuration file. Add a new entry for the server-id option and set its value to 2:

```
server-id = 2
```

9. Add an entry for the read-only option:

```
read-only
```

10. Save your changes and close the file.
11. Restart the slave for the changes to take effect:

```
systemctl restart mysqld.service
```

12. To configure communication with the master, connect to the slave using mysql, and execute a CHANGE MASTER statement. The values should reflect those returned by SHOW MASTER STATUS in step 7:

```
CHANGE MASTER TO
    MASTER_HOST = "192.168.56.100",
    MASTER_USER = "slave",
    MASTER_PASSWORD = "S3CR3t##",
    MASTER_LOG_FILE = "localhost-bin.000003",
    MASTER_LOG_POS = 1235;
```

13. Start the replication process by executing START SLAVE on the slave system:

```
START SLAVE;
```

14. Execute SHOW SLAVE STATUS to verify replication is running. The values returned for Slave_IO_Running and Slave_SQL_Running should both be Yes:

```
SHOW SLAVE STATUS\G
```

SHOW SLAVE STATUS returns a fair amount of information-listed as a table, column wrapping makes the output impossible to read. Using \G to execute the statement (as opposed to the semicolon) will make mysql display the results vertically which, in this case, is much more readable.

15. To stop replication, execute STOP SLAVE on the slave system.

How it works...

Configuration began in the master's /etc/my.cnf file, where we added the server-id option to give the server a numeric identifier. Each server in the replication setup uses this value to identify itself to the others, so it must be unique across the environment. Then, we uncommented the log_bin option to instruct the server to record the details of each change to the binary log.

```
[mysqld]
server-id = 1

# Remove leading # and set to the amount of RAM for the most important data
# cacne in MySQL. Start at 70% of total RAM for dedicated server, else 10%.
# innodb_buffer_pool_size = 128M
#
# Remove leading # to turn on a very important data integrity option: logging
# changes to the binary log between backups.
log_bin

# Remove leading # to set options mainly useful for reporting servers.
# The server defaults are faster for transactions and fast SELECTs.
# Adjust sizes as needed, experiment to find the optimal values.
# join_buffer_suze = 128M
# sort_buffer_size = 2M
# read_rnd_buffer_size = 2M
datadir=/var/lib/mysql
socket=/var/lib/mysql/mysql.sock

# Disabling symbolic-links is recommended to prevent assorted security risks
symbolic-links=0

log-error=/var/log/mysqld.log
```

The master server's configuration file sets the server identifier and enables logging

Next, we created a dedicated account on the master server and granted it the REPLICATION SLAVE privilege. The slave will use this account to connect to the master and read from the log:

```
CREATE USER "slave"@"192.168.56.101" IDENTIFIED BY "S3CR3t##";
GRANT REPLICATION SLAVE ON *.* TO "slave"@"192.168.56.101";
```

Finally, we executed SHOW MASTER STATUS command. The values of File and Position in the result identify the name of the binary log file and the server's current position in it. As the master writes to the log, the position increases and the suffix attached to the log's filename changes when the log files are rotated. We need to know the current position so we can configure the slave to begin reading/replicating from that point onward.

On the slave, we set the server's unique identifier and added the read-only option in the configuration file. If someone were to make a change in the slave's database that conflicts with an incoming update from the binary log, then replication would break. The read-only option is a safeguard that prevents users from updating the slave databases directly, ensuring all updates come from the master.

Next, we set up the slave's replication process using CHANGE MASTER statement. The CHANGE MASTER statement identifies the master, sets the username and password the slave will use to connect, and identifies the name of the log and the current position to start replicating from:

```
CHANGE MASTER TO
  MASTER_HOST = "192.168.56.100",
  MASTER_USER = "slave",
  MASTER_PASSWORD = "S3CR3t##",
  MASTER_LOG_FILE = "localhost-bin.000003",
  MASTER_LOG_POS = 1235;
```

Replication is started with START SLAVE and stopped with STOP SLAVE. The SHOW SLAVE STATUS returns information about the current state of replication:

```
mysql> SHOW SLAVE STATUS\G
*************************** 1. row ***************************
               Slave_IO_State: Waiting for master to send event
                  Master_Host: 192.168.56.100
                  Master_User: repluser
                  Master_Port: 3306
                Connect_Retry: 60
              Master_Log_File: localhost-bin.000003
          Read_Master_Log_Pos: 1235
               Relay_Log_File: localhost-relay-bin.000002
                Relay_Log_Pos: 806
        Relay_Master_Log_File: localhost-bin.000003
             Slave_IO_Running: Yes
            Slave_SQL_Running: Yes
              Replicate_Do_DB:
          Replicate_Ignore_DB:
           Replicate_Do_Table:
       Replicate_Ignore_Table:
      Replicate_Wild_Do_Table:
  Replicate_Wild_Ignore_Table:
                   Last_Errno: 0
                   Last_Error:
                 Skip_Counter: 0
          Exec_Master_Log_Pos: 968
```

We can check the slave's status to see whether replication is running without any issues

MySQL creates two background processes when replication is running-one communicates with the master (the IO process) and the other executes the SQL statements to maintain the local database (the SQL process). The Slave_IO_Running value shows whether the communication process is running or not, while the value of Slave_SQL_Running reflects whether or not the execution process is running. Both values should be Yes when replication is running.

If there's a problem with replication, the `Last_IO_Error` and `Last_SQL_Error` entries will report any errors thrown for their respective processes. You can also tell how far behind the slave is from the master by comparing the values of the `Master_Log_File` and `Read_Master_Log_Pos` fields with what the `SHOW MASTER STATUS` returns.

The current configuration enables the slave to replicate every database from the master, but we can also restrict replication to certain databases by adding the `replicate-do-db` entries in the slave's `my.cnf` file. Multiple entries may be given, which will have one entry per database:

```
replicate-do-db = packt
replicate-do-db = acme
replicate-do-db = sakila
```

Alternatively, we can use the `replicate-ignore-db` option to replicate everything except specific databases:

```
replicate-ignore-db = mysql
```

Replication can be filtered at the table-level as well, targeting and ignoring specific tables in a database using the `replicate-do-table` and `replicate-ignore-table` options:

```
replicate-do-table = acme.customers
replicate-do-table = acme.addresses
```

See also

Refer to the following resources for more information on replicating MySQL databases:

- MySQL 5.7 Reference Manual: Replication (http://dev.mysql.com/doc/refman/5.7/en/replication.html)
- MySQL Replication on RHEL 7 (https://www.youtube.com/watch?v=kIfRXshR2zc)
- MySQL High Availability Architectures (http://skillachie.com/214/7/25/mysql-high-availability-architectures)
- Replication Tips and Tricks in MySQL (http://www.linux-mag.com/id/1661/)

Standing up a MySQL cluster

This recipe guides you through the process of setting up a MySQL cluster. Clustered databases meet the challenges of scalability and high-availability by partitioning the data across multiple systems and maintaining replicas to avoid single points of failure.

The members of a cluster are referred to as nodes. There are three node types in a MySQL cluster: data nodes, API nodes, and the management node. Data nodes are responsible for storing data. Users and processes then connect to an API node to access the database. The management node manages the cluster as a whole. Although multiple nodes can be installed on the same system, for example, both an API node and a data node may be hosted on the same system. However, hosting multiple data nodes on the same system is obviously not a good idea because it negates MySQL's efforts to distribute the data.

Getting ready

This recipe demonstrates how to deploy a MySQL cluster using four systems. The first system will host the management node and we'll assume that it has the IP address `192.168.56.100`. The second system will host the API node and have the address `192.168.56.101`. The remaining systems will be configured with data nodes and use the addresses `192.168.56.102` and `192.168.56.103`. You'll need administrative access on all four systems either using the `root` account or `sudo`.

How to do it...

Follow these steps to set up a clustered MySQL database:

1. Download the cluster archive from the MySQL website and extract its packages using `tar`:

   ```
   curl -L dev.mysql.com/get/Downloads/MySQL-Cluster-7.4/
   MySQL-Cluster-gpl-7.4.10-1.el7.x86_64.rpm-bundle.tar | tar  x
   ```

2. On each system, install `perl-Data-Dumper` and replace the installed `mariadb-libs` package with the downloaded `MySQL-Cluster-shared` package:

   ```
   yum install perl-Data-Dumper MySQL-Cluster-shared-gpl-*.rpm
   yum erase mariadb-libs
   ```

3. Install the `MySQL-Cluster-server` and `MySQL-Cluster-client` packages on each system:

```
yum install MySQL-Cluster-{server,client}-gpl-*.rpm
```

4. On the system hosting the management node, create the `/var/lib/mysql-cluster` directory:

```
mkdir /var/lib/mysql-cluster
```

5. Create the cluster's configuration file for the management node at `/var/lib/mysql-cluster/config.ini` as follows:

```
[ndbd default]
NoOfReplicas = 2
DataMemory = 100M
IndexMemory = 10M
ServerPort = 2202
[ndb_mgmd]
hostname = 192.168.56.100
[mysqld]
hostname = 192.168.56.101
[ndbd]
hostname = 192.168.56.102
[ndbd]
hostname = 192.168.56.103
```

6. Start the management node:

```
ndb_mgmd -f /var/lib/mysql-cluster/config.ini
```

7. Open port `1186` in the management node system's firewall:

```
firewall-cmd --zone=public --permanent --add-port=1186/tcp
firewall-cmd --reload
```

8. On each data node's system, create the file `/etc/my.cnf` using the following:

```
[mysql_cluster]
ndb-connectstring = 192.168.56.100
```

9. Start each data node:

```
ndbd
```

10. Open port 2202 in the data nodes' systems' firewall:

    ```
    firewall-cmd --zone=public --permanent --add-port=2202/tcp
    firewall-cmd --reload
    ```

11. Create /etc/my.cnf on the system hosting the API node using the following:

    ```
    [mysqld]
    ndbcluster
    default-storage-engine = ndbcluster
    [mysql_cluster]
    ndb-connectstring = 192.168.56.100
    ```

12. Start MySQL server as the API node:

    ```
    mysqld_safe &
    ```

13. Retrieve the root account's temporary password that was created when the MySQL server was installed. It's recorded in /root/.mysql_secret:

    ```
    cat /root/.mysql_secret
    ```

14. Set a new password for the root account using mysqladmin. When prompted for the current password, enter the one identified in the previous step:

    ```
    mysqladmin -u root -p password
    ```

15. Open port 3306 in the API node system's firewall:

    ```
    firewall-cmd --zone=public --permanent --add-service=mysql
    firewall-cmd --reload
    ```

16. Verify the status of the cluster using the ndb_mgm client on the system hosting the management node:

    ```
    ndb_mgm -e SHOW
    ```

How it works...

This recipe taught you how to set up a MySQL clustered database with two data nodes: one API node and one management node. The management node consists of the ndb_mgmd process that provides configuration information to the other nodes and monitors them. On the data nodes, the ndbd process handles the storage, partitioning, and replication of the clustered data. A MySQL server aware of the management node and the data nodes acts as the API node through which users can work with the clustered database.

The packages available in the Oracle-maintained repository are built without support for Network Database (NDB), so we first downloaded an archive from the MySQL website that has packages which will install a version of MySQL that supports NDB/clustering:

```
curl -L dev.mysql.com/get/Downloads/MySQL-Cluster-7.4/MySQL-
Cluster-gpl-7.4.10-1.el7.x86_64.rpm-bundle.tar | tar x
```

MySQL abstracts the details of exactly how data is physically organized and manipulated, delegating this to its various storage engines. Different engines have different abilities. Since the NDB engine is the one that implements clustering, we need a build that supports the engine. Instead of writing curl's output to a file as we've done in other recipes, this time we piped the output directly to tar with the x argument to expand the archive on the fly.

Afterwards, we installed the perl-Data-Dumper package from the CentOS repository and replaced the mariadb-libs package already installed with the just downloaded MySQL-Cluster-shared package on each system:

```
yum install perl-Data-Dumper MySQL-Cluster-shared-gpl-*.rpm
yum erase mariadb-libs
```

The MySQL-Cluster-shared package provides the shared libraries used by other programs to work with MySQL. These libraries replace the MariaDB version installed from the CentOS repositories by default and save us from experiencing library conflicts that would prevent a clean install. Since it's no longer needed afterwards, we uninstalled the mariadb-libs package.

Some of the post-installation steps performed by Yum after it installs the MySQL-Cluster-server package are scripted in Perl and use Perl's Data::Dumper module. This makes the Perl-Data-Dumper package a dependency for the MySQL-Cluster-server package. However, a bug causes Yum to miss this, so we installed the package ourselves so that the MySQL-Cluster-server package's installation will proceed smoothly. It wouldn't prevent the package from installing, but it would have required us to complete some additional configuration steps manually.

With the requirements in place, we then installed the `MySQL-Cluster-server` and `MySQL-Cluster-client` packages on each system:

```
yum install MySQL-Cluster-{server,client}-gpl-*.rpm
```

Configuration for the overall cluster is pretty much centralized with the management node in `/var/lib/mysql-cluster/config.ini`. The file is divided into several sections, the first being `[ndb default]`, which provides the default configuration values that should be used for the cluster. The values here apply to each node of the cluster unless overridden by a more specific directive in the respective node's configuration section:

```
[ndbd default]
NoOfReplicas = 2
DataMemory = 100M
IndexMemory = 10M
ServerPort = 2202
```

The `NoOfReplicas` option sets the number of replicas in the cluster. Its value may be set to 1 or 2, although 2 is the recommended value. Recall that not only a clustered database is partitioned across the data nodes but it is also replicated; each node hosts a partition typically *1/n* the size of the database (where *n* is the number of data nodes) and also a replica of the other nodes. The cluster can still function if a system goes offline because its data is still available in the replica. A value of 1 for `NoOfReplicas` means that there would be only one copy of the database (no replica) and the availability of the database depends on all data nodes being up.

The data nodes hold their working copy of the database in RAM to reduce latency while periodically syncing the data to disk. The `DataMemory` option specifies how much RAM should be reserved for the data by the nodes and `IndexMemory` specifies how much memory should be reserved for primary keys and unique indexes. Whatever values you provide, be sure that sufficient resources are available to avoid RAM swapping.

The `ServerPort` option specifies the port number the nodes will use to communicate with one another. By default, MySQL would dynamically allocate ports to make it easier to run multiple nodes on the same system, but since this recipe runs each node on its own host system and we need to know the port to allow traffic through the firewall, we specified the port ourselves.

The subsequent sections in the configuration use the `hostname` option to specify the addresses at which the management node (via the `[ndb_mgmtd]` section), the API node (the `[mysqld]` section), and the data nodes (the `[ndbd]` section) are running. As made evident by the multiple `[ndbd]` sections, multiple sections of the same type will appear if there is more than one node of that type running in the cluster:

```
[ndb_mgmd]
hostname = 192.168.56.100
[mysqld]
hostname = 192.168.56.101
[ndbd]
hostname = 192.168.56.102
[ndbd]
hostname = 192.168.56.103
```

On the remaining systems, `/etc/my.cnf` is created as the configuration file used by the data nodes and the API node. Each includes a `[mysql_cluster]` section, which gives the `ndb-connectstring` option:

```
[mysql_cluster]
ndb-connectstring = 192.168.56.100
```

The `ndb-connectstring` option specifies the address of the system that hosts the management node. As the data and API nodes come online, they communicate with the manager to receive their configuration information. If your cluster has more than one management node, the additional nodes can be listed in the connection string separated by commas:

```
ndb-connectstring = "192.168.56.100,192.168.56.105,192.168.56.106"
```

Additionally, the API node's configuration includes the `[mysqld]` section. It includes the `ndbcluster` option to enable the NDB engine and the `default-storage-engine` option instructing MySQL to use NDB to manage all new tables unless otherwise specified in the table's CREATE TABLE statement:

```
[mysqld]
ndbcluster
default-storage-engine = ndbcluster
```

When a user or process creates a new table with the CREATE TABLE statement, they can specify which of MySQL's storage engines should be used to manage its data with the ENGINE directive, for example:

```
CREATE TABLE users (
    id INTEGER UNSIGNED NOT NULL PRIMARY KEY,
    first_name VARCHAR(50) NOT NULL DEFAULT '',
    last_name VARCHAR(50) NOT NULL DEFAULT ''
)
ENGINE = NDBCluster;
```

The default engine is InnoDB engine. However, only data in NDB-managed tables make their way to the cluster. If a table is managed by another engine, the data resides locally on the API node and is not available to other nodes in the cluster. To prevent unexpected problems and any confusion this can cause, we changed the default engine so that tables will use the NDB engine when the ENGINE directive isn't provided.

The order in which nodes are started when bringing up the MySQL cluster is important, since one node may depend on the others. The management node is started first, followed by the data nodes, and then the API node.

The password for MySQL's root account on the API node is randomly generated the first time the server is started, and it is written to the /root/.mysql_secret file, just as we used mysqladmin to change it in the *Setting up a MySQL database* recipe:

```
cat /root/.mysql_secret
mysqladmin -u root -p password
```

The SHOW command sent to the ndb_mgm client on the management node's system allows us to view the status of the cluster and ensure everything is up and running as it should be. The client can be invoked in interactive mode, or commands can be passed to it directly using the -e argument:

```
ndb_mgm -e SHOW
```

```
[root@benito ~]# ndb_mgm -e SHOW
Connected to Management Server at: 192.168.56.100:1186
Cluster Configuration
---------------------
[ndbd(NDB)]     2 node(s)
id=3    @192.168.56.102  (mysql-5.6.28 ndb-7.4.10, Nodegroup: 0, *)
id=4    @192.168.56.103  (mysql-5.6.28 ndb-7.4.10, Nodegroup: 0)

[ndb_mgmd(MGM)] 1 node(s)
id=1    @192.168.56.100  (mysql-5.6.28 ndb-7.4.10)

[mysqld(API)]   1 node(s)
id=2    @192.168.56.101  (mysql-5.6.28 ndb-7.4.10)

[root@benito ~]#
```

The status of the MySQL cluster can be viewed using the ndb_mgm client

See also

Refer to the following resources for more information on working with MySQL clusters:

- MySQL Reference Manual: MySQL Cluster Core Concepts (http://dev.mysql.com/doc/refman/5.7/en/mysql-cluster-basics.html)
- MySQL Reference Manual: MySQL Cluster Installation (http://dev.mysql.com/doc/refman/5.7/en/mysql-cluster-installation.html)
- MySQL Reference Manual: MySQL Cluster Nodes, Node Groups, Replicas, and Partitions (http://dev.mysql.com/doc/refman/5.7/en/mysql-cluster-nodes-groups.html)
- MySQL Reference Manual: Online Backup of MySQL Cluster (http://dev.mysql.com/doc/refman/5.7/en/mysql-cluster-backup.html)
- Set Up a MySQL Cluster the Easy Way (http://youtube.com/watch?v=64jtbkuPtvc)
- *High Availability MySQL Cookbook* by Alex Davies (https://www.packtpub.com/big-data-and-business-intelligence/high-availability-mysql-cookbook)

Setting up a MongoDB database

Although relational databases have dominated the world of data storage, there have always been other systems that specialize in alternative ways of working with data, for example document and object-oriented databases, key-value databases, and hierarchical databases. The popularity of these alternative databases has experienced a resurgence thanks to the recent *NoSQL* and *Big Data* movements. This recipe teaches you how to install MongoDB, a modern document-oriented database system.

Getting ready

This recipe requires a CentOS system with a working network connection and administrative privileges by either using the root account or sudo. It also assumes you have registered the EPEL repository (see the *Registering the EPEL and Remi repositories* recipe in Chapter 4, *Software Installation Management*).

How to do it...

Follow these steps to install MongoDB and create a new database:

1. Install the mongodb-server and mongodb packages from the EPEL repository:

   ```
   yum install mongodb-server mongodb
   ```

2. Open /etc/mongod.conf with your text editor:

   ```
   vi /etc/mongod.conf
   ```

3. Locate the auth entry and uncomment it, making sure its value is true:

   ```
   # Run with/without security
   auth = true
   ```

4. Locate the bind-ip option and comment it out:

   ```
   # Comma separated list of ip addresses to listen on
   # bind_ip = 127.0.0.1
   ```

5. Save your changes to the configuration file and close it.

6. Start the MongoDB server and enable it to start automatically whenever the system reboots:

```
systemctl start mongod.service
systemctl enable mongod.service
```

7. Open port 27017 in the system's firewall:

```
firewall-cmd --zone=public --permanent --add-port=27017/tcp
firewall-cmd --reload
```

7. Connect to the MongoDB server with mongo:

```
mongo
```

8. Set admin as the active database:

```
use admin
```

9. Execute createUser() to create a new user for managing user accounts:

```
db.createUser({
  user: "admin",
  pwd: "P@$$W0rd",
  roles: [{ role: "userAdminAnyDatabase", db: "admin" }]
})
```

10. Authenticate yourself using the newly created admin account:

```
db.auth({ user: "admin", pwd: "P@$$W0rd" })
```

11. Set packt as the active database:

```
use packt
```

12. Create a user account for working with the database:

```
db.createUser({
  user: "tboronczyk",
  pwd: "S3CR3t##",
  roles: [{ role: "readWrite", db: "packt" }]
})
```

13. Exit the client and return to the terminal:

```
exit
```

How it works...

MongoDB is the most popular in its class of databases and is used by many high-profile companies, including eBay, Craigslist, SAP, and Yandex. The necessary packages are available in the EPEL repository; `mongodb-server` contains the MongoDB server application and the `mongodb` package contains the client and other utilities for working with the server and databases:

```
yum install mongodb-server mongodb
```

MongoDB runs without security enabled by default and anyone may perform any action against any database. To prevent this, we enabled security by uncommenting the `auth` option in MongoDB's configuration file (`/etc/mongod.conf`). Once security is enabled, users must authenticate themselves before they can work with a database, and the server verifies that the account has the right to perform the requested action:

```
auth = true
```

The current configuration permits MongoDB to listen for connections only on the loop-back interface (`127.0.0.1`), so we also commented out the `bind_ip` option:

```
# bind_ip = 127.0.0.1
```

Left unbound, MongoDB will be accessible via all of the system's addresses. Alternatively, if the system has multiple addresses (perhaps the system has multiple interfaces or you've implemented the *Binding multiple addresses to a single Ethernet device* recipe in `Chapter 2`, *Networking*) and you want MongoDB to respond on only one of them, you can leave the option active with the desired IP address as its value.

After updating the configuration file, we started the server and opened MongoDB's default port in the system's firewall to allow remote connections:

```
firewall-cmd --zone=public --permanent --add-port=27017/tcp
firewall-cmd --reload
```

Next, we used the `mongo` client to establish a connection to the MongoDB server running on the localhost:

```
mongo
```

We set `admin` as the active database and executed the `createUser()` method to create an administrator account dedicated to managing MongoDB's database users:

```
use admin
db.createUser({
  user: "admin",
  pwd: "P@$$W0rd",
  roles: [{ role: "userAdminAnyDatabase", db: "admin" }]
})
```

The `createUser()` method accepts a document with properties listing the new account's username (`user`), password (`pwd`), and roles (`roles`) and adds it to the `system.users` collection in the active database (`admin`). User accounts are stored at the database level and the database storing a user's details is known as that user's authentication database. Users may work with other databases, but they must authenticate against their authentication database first. Even if their usernames are the same, accounts created in different databases are considered separate and may have different permissions.

The `roles` property is an array of objects, each listing a role that the user is a member of when they work with the given database. In the case of `admin`, the user is a member of the `userAdminAnyDatabase` role. MongoDB's permission system is based on role-based access control (RBAC). The focus of RBAC is on users and what roles they play as opposed to granting individual permissions to each account. Permissions are assigned to a role and then user accounts are given membership in the role inheriting its permissions.

`userAdminAnyDatabase` is a built-in role configured with the necessary permissions to create and delete user accounts, assign membership in a role, and manage user passwords for any database. MongoDB ships with several predefined roles besides `userAdminAnyDatabase`. They include the following:

- `dbAdmin`: These users are responsible for administering the database
- `userAdmin`: These users are responsible for administering other users
- `read`: These are users that only read documents from the database
- `readWrite`: These are users who read documents and also need write access to insert/modify them
- `dbOwner`: These are users who own the database (combines the `dbAdmin`, `userAdmin`, and `readWrite` roles)

There are also the `backup` and `restore` roles for users responsible for performing database backups, roles for managing MongoDB clusters, and additional global versions of some of the aforementioned roles, such as `readAnyDatabase`, for users who need read-access to all of MongoDB's databases. A complete list of roles can be found in the official documentation online at `https://docs.mongodb.com/manual/reference/built-in-roles/`.

> The principles of least privilege encourage us to avoid over-using the global roles; it's better to create users that work with their own databases. If an account needs to work with a database outside its authentication database, multiple roles can be assigned as follows:
>
> ```
> db.createUser({
>   user: "tboronczyk",
>   pwd: "S3CR3t##",
>   roles: [
>     { role: "read", db: "admin" },
>     { role: "readWrite", db: "packt" },
>     { role: "readWrite", db: "acme" }
>   ]
> })
> ```

Next, we used the new `admin` user to create a new user for the `packt` database (and to create the `packt` database itself as a side effect):

```
db.auth("admin", "P@$$W0rd")
use packt
db.createUser({
  user: "tboronczyk",
  pwd: "S3CR3t##",
  roles: [{ role: "readWrite", db: "packt" }]
})
```

Databases and collections are implicitly created by MongoDB when the first document is inserted, and since MongoDB stores new users in the active database, setting `packt` as the active database and creating a user is enough to trigger its creation.

The `auth()` method assumes that the active database is the authentication database for the provided credentials. In this instance, authentication is successful because `admin` was already the active database; attempting to authenticate as `admin` after switching to `packt` would fail. However, the identity persists after authentication until the next time we call `auth()` or we exit the client. So, even though we switched databases, we're still operating within the roles and privileges of the `admin` database's `admin` user.

Although the recipe connected to the server with a bare `mongo` invocation, the active database can be specified on the command line. `mongo` also offers several options, for example, to connect to a MongoDB server running on a different system and provide authentication credentials. `--host` identifies the remote hostname or IP address where MongoDB is running, and the `--username` and `--password` options allow you to provide your account's authentication details:

```
mongo --host 192.168.56.100 --username tboronczyk --password "" packt
```

If the database is given in the invocation when `--username` and `--password` are used as well, MongoDB assumes that the database is the account's authentication database. If the account belongs to another database, its authentication database can be given using the `--authenticationDatabase` option:

```
mongo --authenticationDatabase admin --username admin --password
"" packt
```

The `--password` option expects a value, but MongoDB will prompt you for a password when its value is empty. I suggest that you use an empty string ("") for the value, as I have done here, to force the password prompt.

 Never enter a password as part of a command's invocation for security reasons. The password may appear in the output of `ps` while the command is running and will also appear in your shell's history.

See also

Refer to the following resources for more information on working with MongoDB:

- The MongoDB manual (http://docs.mongodb.org/manual)
- MongoDB Manual: Role-Based Access Control (http://docs.mongodb.org/manual/core/authorization)
- MongoDB Tutorial for Beginners (http://www.youtube.com/watch?v=W-WihPoEbR4)
- Wikipedia: Role-based access control (https://en.wikipedia.org/wiki/Role-based_access_control)

Backing up and restoring a MongoDB database

This recipe teaches you how to back up a MongoDB database using the `mongodump` utility and restore it using `mongorestore`.

Getting ready

This recipe requires a running MongoDB server and access to a user account with membership in the `userAdmin` role.

How to do it...

Follow these steps to back up a MongoDB database:

1. Connect to MongoDB as a user with membership in the `userAdmin` role:

   ```
   mongo --username admin --password "" admin
   ```

2. Create an account with membership in the `backup` and `restore` roles to be used for creating and restoring backups:

   ```
   db.createUser({
     user: "backupusr",
     pwd: "B@CK&4th",
     roles: [
       { role: "backup", db: "admin" },
       { role: "restore", db: "admin" }
     ]
   })
   ```

3. Use `mongodump` on the command-line to export a MongoDB database:

   ```
   mongodump --authenticationDatabase admin --username  backupusr
   --password "" --db packt
   ```

4. To restore a database from the backup made by `mongodump`, use the `mongorestore` program:

   ```
   mongorestore --authenticationDatabase admin --username  backupusr
   --password "" --drop --db packt dump/packt
   ```

How it works...

The account used to make a backup must have the privileges assigned to the `backup` role and the restore account must have those assigned to the `restore` role. So, we connected to the MongoDB server and created an account with membership in both roles prior to using the utilities:

```
db.createUser({
  user: "backupusr",
  pwd: "B@CK&4th",
  roles: [
    { role: "backup", db: "admin" },
    { role: "restore", db: "admin" }
  ]
})
```

The new account is then used with `mongodump` to back up our database:

```
mongodump --authenticationDatabase admin --username backupusr
--password "" --db packt
```

The preceding invocation exports everything in the `packt` database as specified by the `--db` argument. If `--db` is not given, `mongodump` exports all of the available databases except for the server's `local` database. It's possible to export just a specific collection from the database using the `--collection` argument:

```
mongodump --db packt --collection authors
```

By default, `mongodump` creates a local directory named `dump` to organize the exported data. Within `dump` exists a directory for each exported database and within that are two files for each collection. The first file is a BSON file, a binary JSON-like format used because it offers a richer set of data types than JSON does. For example, JSON doesn't define a date type. Whereas JSON offers only a single numeric type, BSON supports 32 and 64-bit integers and doubles. The second file is a metadata JSON file that stores details about the collection, such as any collection options or index definitions.

mongodump will overwrite any existing files if the dump directory already exists. To avoid problems, you can specify a different location with the --out argument:

```
mongodump --db packt --out dump-$(date +%F)
```

```
[tboronczyk@benito ~]$ ls -lR ./dump
./dump:
total 4
drwxr-xr-x. 2 tboronczyk tboronczyk 4096 Aug 13 21:31 packt

./dump/packt:
total 396
-rw-r--r--. 1 tboronczyk tboronczyk   9459 Aug 13 21:28 authors.bson
-rw-r--r--. 1 tboronczyk tboronczyk    101 Aug 13 21:28 authors.metadata.json
-rw-r--r--. 1 tboronczyk tboronczyk  27410 Aug 13 21:28 customers.bson
-rw-r--r--. 1 tboronczyk tboronczyk    101 Aug 13 21:28 customers.metadata.bson
-rw-r--r--. 1 tboronczyk tboronczyk 320673 Aug 13 21:28 orders.bson
-rw-r--r--. 1 tboronczyk tboronczyk     98 Aug 13 21:28 orders.metadata.bson
-rw-r--r--. 1 tboronczyk tboronczyk    899 Aug 13 21:28 system.indexes.bson
-rw-r--r--. 1 tboronczyk tboronczyk  17814 Aug 13 21:28 titles.bson
-rw-r--r--. 1 tboronczyk tboronczyk    100 Aug 13 21:28 titles.metadata.json
[tboronczyk@benito ~]$
```

The exported collection data is organized by database in the dump directory

The path to the collection files is then given to mongorestore to import the data dumped by mongodump. The database to which the collections will be inserted is named using the --db argument:

```
mongorestore --authenticationDatabase admin --username backupusr
--password "" --drop --db packt dump/packt
```

mongorestore only inserts the data; if documents with the same _id field already exist in a collection then those records are skipped, not updated. This may or may not be desired depending on the circumstances. So to be sure that the restored data matches what was exported, the --drop argument is used, which instructs mongorestore to drop the existing collection first before importing the backup.

Apart from mongodump and mongorestore, there is also mongoexport and mongoimport. mongoexport exports a collection's data to either a JSON or CSV file and mongoimport imports data from these formats. Keep in mind however that JSON's type system (and certainly "types" in CSV) is less granular than BSON's and some fidelity can be lost. For reliable backups, mongodump and mongorestore are preferred.

The default export format of mongoexport is JSON. To export a collection's data to CSV instead, use the --csv argument:

```
mongoexport --db packt --collection titles --csv --out titles.csv
```

Specific fields can be targeted for export as well by providing a comma-separated list of names using the --fields argument:

```
mongoexport --db packt --collection titles --fields isbn,title,
authors,year,language,pages --csv --out titles.csv
```

Some arguments worth noting when importing data with mongoimport are --type, which specifies the import file's type (either JSON for CSV), --headerline – to skip the first row of data in the case of column headers in a CSV file, --fields – to import only specific fields from the file, and --upsert, which performs an upsert action on existing documents instead of skipping them:

```
mongoimport --db packt --collection titles --fields isbn,title,
authors --type csv --upsert < titles.csv
```

See also

Refer to the following resources for more information on backing up and restoring MongoDB databases:

- The mongodump manual page (man 1 mongodump)
- The mongorestore manual page (man 1 mongorestore)
- The mongoexport manual page (man 1 mongoexport)
- The mongoimport manual page (man 1 mongoimport)
- MongoDB Manual: MongoDB Backup Methods (http://docs.mongodb.org/manual/core/backups)
- BSON: Binary JSON (http://bsonspec.org/)

Configuring a MongoDB replica set

This recipe teaches you how to configure replication using MongoDB replica sets.

When replication is performed using replica sets, one installation of MongoDB identifies as the primary server while others in the cluster are secondaries. The primary server accepts writes, which are replicated to the secondaries, while the secondaries service read requests. If the primary server goes down, the secondary servers automatically call a quorum and promote one of the secondaries to fill the primary's role. The old primary rejoins the cluster when it comes back on line. This configuration provides redundancy, distributed read/write access, and automatic failover for high-availability.

Getting ready

This recipe demonstrates configuring replica sets using three systems. The first system will be the cluster's primary server and we assume that its IP address is 192.168.56.100. The other two systems will be secondary servers using the addresses 192.168.56.102 and 192.168.56.103. MongoDB should be installed on all three systems. You'll also need administrative access to complete the configuration and access to a user account with membership in the userAdmin role.

MongoDB replication relies on hostnames. Before you begin this recipe, make sure that the systems are accessible to one another by the hostname. If the systems are inaccessible and you are unable to add the necessary records to your network's DNS, you can override local resolution for the hosts in question by adding entries to /etc/hosts, similarly to the following:

```
192.168.56.100 benito benito.localdomain
192.168.56.101 javier javier.localdomain
192.168.56.102 geomar geomar.localdomain
```

How to do it...

Follow these steps to configure replication using MongoDB replica sets:

1. On the primary system, navigate to /var/lib/mongodb and use openssl to create a shared secret. This secret serves as the password each server will use to authenticate itself as a member of the replication cluster:

```
cd /var/lib/mongodb
openssl rand 756 -base64 -out rs0.key
```

2. Secure the file's permissions; it should be owned by `mongodb` and only readable by its owner:

```
chown mongodb.mongodb rs0.key
chmod 600 rs0.key
```

3. Open `/etc/mongod.conf` with your text editor:

```
vi /etc/mongod.conf
```

4. Locate the `replSet` option, uncomment it, and assign it the value `rs0`:

```
# Arg is <setname>[/<optionalseedhostlist>]
replSet = rs0
```

5. Uncomment the `keyFile` option and provide the path to the file containing the shared password:

```
# Private key for cluster authentication
keyFile = /var/lib/mongodb/rs0.key
```

6. Save your changes and close the file.
7. Restart the MongoDB server:

```
systemctl restart mongod.service
```

8. Copy the shared secret to each of the secondary systems:

```
scp rs0.key 192.168.56.101:/var/lib/mongodb/rs0.key
scp rs0.key 192.168.56.102:/var/lib/mongodb/rs0.key
```

9. Repeat steps 2-7 on each of the other secondary systems.

10. Connect to the primary MongoDB server and create an account with membership in the `clusterManager` role to be used for configuring and managing the replica cluster:

```
db.createUser({
  user: "repladmin",
  pwd: "dupl1C@t3",
  roles: [{ role: "clusterManager", db: "admin" }]
})
```

11. Authenticating yourself using the `repladmin` user:

```
db.auth("repladmin", "dupl1C@t3")
```

12. Use the `rs.initiate()` method to initialize the cluster:

```
rs.initiate()
```

13. Register the secondary members using `rs.add()`:

```
rs.add("192.168.56.101")
rs.add("192.168.56.102")
```

How it works...

Clusters must contain an odd number of servers because there has to be a majority vote to approve a secondary's proposal to take on the role of primary if the primary server becomes unavailable. Three servers were used, which is the minimum number for a cluster that provides proper redundancy and availability.

Cluster members identify themselves to one another using a shared replica set name and password, which we provide in each server's `mongod.conf` configuration file. The name is specified using the `replSet` option:

```
replSet = rs0
```

The password value can be anything up to 1,024 characters. For security reasons, a long random string is preferred for resistance against brute force and dictionary attacks. We can generate such values using `openssl rand`:

```
openssl rand 756 -base64 -out rs0.key
```

`rand` generates the number of random bytes we request, in this case 756 bytes. `-base64` encodes them using the Base64 encoding scheme to represent the bytes safely as plain text. Encoding incurs some overhead, and Base64 encodes three bytes as four characters and pads the result when less than three bytes are available. So, Base64-encoding the 765 random bytes results in 1,024 characters of text suitable for our needs.

The resulting key file containing the password is copied to each system. Its ownership is set to the system's `mongodb` user and access permissions to the file are revoked for everyone except that user:

```
chown mongodb.mongodb rs0.key
chmod 600 rs0.key
```

The file is specified in the configuration file using the `keyFile` option:

```
keyFile = /var/lib/mongodb/rs0.key
```

Management of the cluster requires permissions assigned to the `clusterManager` role, so we then created an account with membership in that role, and then we authenticated ourselves using the new account:

```
db.createUser({
  user: "repladmin",
  pwd: "dupl1C@t3",
  roles: [{ role: "clusterManager", db: "admin" }]
})
db.auth("repladmin", "dupl1C@t3")
```

We started the cluster using `rs.initiate()` on the primary server and then registered the secondary servers using `rs.add()`:

```
rs.initiate()
rs.add("192.168.56.101")
rs.add("192.168.56.102")
```

After `rs.initiate()` is invoked, you'll notice the mongo client's prompt changes to `rs0:primary` to notify us that we're connected to the primary server in the `rs0` replication group. If you were to log in to a secondary server, the prompt would read `rs0:secondary`.

Alternatively, the cluster can be configured by passing an object that specifies the secondary servers as an argument to `rs.initiate()`. The object's `_id` property is the name of the set and the `members` property is an array of secondary hosts:

```
rs.initiate({
  _id : "rs0",
  members : [
    {_id : 0, host : "192.168.56.100"},
    {_id : 1, host : "192.168.56.101"},
    {_id : 2, host : "192.168.56.102"}
  ]
})
```

See also

Refer to the following resources for more information on working with MongoDB replica sets:

- MongoDB Manual: Replication (`http://docs.mongodb.org/manual/core/replication-introduction`)
- MongoDB Replication and Replica Sets (`http://www.youtube.com/watch?v=CsvbG9tykC4`)

Setting up an OpenLDAP directory

This recipe teaches you how to install OpenLDAP, an open-source implementation of an X.500 directory server. The X.500 series of protocols was developed in the late 1980s to support the storage and lookup of names, e-mail addresses, computer systems, and other entities in a hierarchical fashion. Each entry is a node in a directory information tree (DIT) and is identified by its distinguished name (DN). Information about the entry is represented as key/value pairs known as attributes.

Getting ready

This recipe requires a CentOS system with a working network connection and administrative privileges either by using the `root` account or `sudo`.

How to do it...

Follow these steps to set up an OpenLDAP directory:

1. Install the `openldap-server` and `openldap-clients` packages:

```
yum install openldap-servers openldap-clients
```

2. Copy the database configuration file included with OpenLDAP to the server's data directory. Ensure the file is owned by the `ldap` user:

```
cp /usr/share/openldap-servers/DB_CONFIG.example
/var/lib/ldap/DB_CONFIG
```

```
chown ldap.ldap /var/lib/ldap/DB_CONFIG
```

3. Use `slappasswd` to generate a password hash for OpenLDAP's `Manager` account. Enter the desired password when prompted:

```
slappasswd
```

4. Start the LDAP server and optionally enable it to start automatically whenever the system reboots:

```
systemctl start slapd.service
systemctl enable slapd.service
```

5. Open port `389` in the system's firewall to allow outside connections to the server:

```
firewall-cmd --zone=public --permanent --add-service=ldap
firewall-cmd --reload
```

6. Create the file `config.ldif` using the following content. The DIT's suffix is based on the domain `ldap.example.com` and the value for `olcRootPW` is the password hash obtained in step 3:

```
dn: olcDatabase={2}hdb,cn=config
changetype: modify
replace: olcSuffix
olcSuffix: dc=ldap,dc=example,dc=com
-
replace: olcRootDN
olcRootDN: cn=Manager,dc=ldap,dc=example,dc=com
-
add: olcRootPW
olcRootPW: {SSHA}cb0i4Kwzvd5tBlxEtwB50myPIUKI3bkp
dn: olcDatabase={1}monitor,cn=config
changetype: modify
replace: olcAccess
olcAccess: {0}to * by dn.base="gidNumber=0+uidNumber=0,
 cn=peercred,cn=external,cn=auth" read by dn.base="cn=
 Manager,dc=ldap,dc=example,dc=com" read by * none
```

7. Invoke `ldapmodify` to execute the operations in `config.ldif`:

```
ldapmodify -Y EXTERNAL -H ldapi:/// -f config.ldif
```

8. Use `ldapadd` to import the `cosine`, `inetorgperson`, and `nis` schemas found in `/etc/openldap/schema`:

```
cd /etc/openldap/schema
ldapadd -Y EXTERNAL -H ldapi:/// -f cosine.ldif
ldapadd -Y EXTERNAL -H ldapi:/// -f inetorgperson.ldif
ldapadd -Y EXTERNAL -H ldapi:/// -f nis.ldif
```

9. Create the file `root.ldif` with the following content:

```
dn: dc=ldap,dc=example,dc=com
objectClass: dcObject
objectClass: organization
o: My Company's LDAP Database
```

10. Use `ldapadd` to import `root.ldif`, authenticating yourself with the `Manager` account:

```
ldapadd -D "cn=Manager,dc=ldap,dc=example,dc=com" -W -H
ldapi:/// -f root.ldif
```

How it works...

We first installed the `openldap-server` package, which contains the LDAP server (`slapd`) and some supporting utilities, and the `openldap-clients` package, which installed the basic utilities used for working with the directory server:

```
yum install openldap-servers openldap-clients
```

OpenLDAP uses the Berkeley DB (BDB/HDB) database for backend data storage, indexing, and caching. The database is configured separately from the directory server and an example configuration file is installed along with the server. We copied the example into the server's data directory but left it with its default values; the defaults are fine to start with although you'll want to review the settings periodically after you deploy OpenLDAP to ensure the best performance (`man 5 slapd-bdb` provides descriptions of the file's configuration options):

```
cp /usr/share/openldap-servers/DB_CONFIG.example
/var/lib/ldap/DB_CONFIG
```

The directory's administrative user `Manager` doesn't have an assigned password at first. OpenLDAP expects the password to be hashed so we created a suitable value using `slappasswd`:

slappasswd

The default hashing algorithm used by `slappasswd` is salted SHA (SSHA) as indicated by the `{SSHA}` prefix in its output. It's possible to hash the password using a different algorithm if required by specifying it using the `-h` argument. The possible values are `{CRYPT}`, `{MD5}`, `{SMD5}` (salted MD5), `{SHA}`, or `{SSHA}`. The salted algorithms are preferred over their nonsalted counterparts because the randomly generated salt `slappasswd` incorporates into the hash makes the hash resistant to rainbow attacks.

OpenLDAP has deprecated its file-based configuration approach in favor of online configuration, storing parameters in a config DIT so that they can be updated without needing to restart the directory server for the changes to take effect. So after starting the server, we wrote the necessary operations to `config.ldif` that will make our updates and then executed them as a batch with `ldapmodify`:

ldapmodify -Y EXTERNAL -H ldapi:// -f config.ldif

The `-H` argument provides one or more URIs for the servers we want to connect to. We can specify the transport protocol, hostname or IP address, and port, but the URI is not a full RFC-4516 style LDAP URI (other components such as the base DN are given using other arguments). The supported protocols are `ldap`, `ldaps` (LDAP over SSL), and `ldapi` (LDAP over IPC/unix-socket). No hostname is required to access the local host, so just `ldapi://` is used.

The `-Y` argument specifying `EXTERNAL` as the authentication mechanism allows the use of mechanisms external to the server's SASL methods. When paired with `ldapi`, `EXTERNAL` uses our login session's username to authenticate us.

The default behavior for `ldapmodify` is to read input from STDIN, but the `-f` argument can specify an input file instead. Since the statements are rather verbose, using an input file is a great idea because you can review them for any mistakes beforehand. If you do want to provide them via STDIN however, I recommend that you use the `-c` argument to run `ldapmodify` in "continuous mode". The program terminates when it encounters an error by default, but in continuous mode it will keep running. This will give you the opportunity to resubmit the operation if there's a problem, without reconnecting:

```
ldapmodify -Y EXTERNAL -H ldapi:/// -c
```

Our first operation changed the DIT's suffix from the default `dc=my-domain,dc=com` to something more appropriate. The recipe uses `ldap.example.com` for example purposes, but of course you may substitute your own domain accordingly:

```
dn: olcDatabase={2}hdb,cn=config
changetype: modify
replace: olcSuffix
olcSuffix: dc=ldap,dc=example,dc=com
```

The suffix is stored in the `olcSuffix` attribute of the `olcDatabase={2}hdb,cn= config` entry and represents the top level of the DIT. Traditionally, the suffix is based on a domain name and is expressed as a series of domain components (DC), so the domain `ldap.example.com` becomes `dc=ldap,dc=example,dc=com`.

The suffix appears in a few other places, so we needed to update those as well – the `olcRootDN` attribute, which lists the name of the DIT's administrative user, and in the permission statement in `olcAccess` that grants access to `Manager` and the system's `root` account. Additionally, we added the `olcRootPW` attribute that stores the Manager's password hash. We don't have to specify the DN multiple times for attributes on same entry. Rather, we can separate the operations with a single hyphen:

```
replace: olcRootDN
olcRootDN: cn=Manager,dc=ldap,dc=example,dc=com
-
add: olcRootPW
olcRootPW: {SSHA}3NhShraRoA+MaOGSrjWTzK3fX0AIq+7P
dn: olcDatabase={1}monitor,cn=config
changetype: modify
replace: olcAccess
olcAccess: {0}to * by dn.base="gidNumber=0+uidNumber=0,
 cn=peercred,cn=external,cn=auth" read by dn.base="cn=
 Manager,dc=ldap,dc=example,dc=com" read by * none
```

Next, we imported the `cosine`, `nis`, and `inetorgperson` schemas. Creating new schemas from scratch can be a daunting task as a fair amount of planning is required to identify what types are needed and what PEN/OIDs should be allocated. Importing these schemas provided with OpenLDAP gives us access to various useful predefined types:

```
ldapadd -Y EXTERNAL -H ldapi:/// -f cosine.ldif
ldapadd -Y EXTERNAL -H ldapi:/// -f inetorgperson.ldif
ldapadd -Y EXTERNAL -H ldapi:/// -f nis.ldif
```

`cosine` defines a standard X.500 directory services schema that was originally developed for the COSINE PARADISE Project and is outlined in RFC-4524. It gives us types such as `document` and `domain` objects and attributes such as `host`, `mail`, and `documentAuthor`. `inetorgperson` defines the `inetOrgPerson` class, a person object that attempts to "meet the requirements found in today's Internet and intranet directory service deployments" as described by RFC-2798 and RFC-4524. `nis` defines a Network Information Services schema with user and host attributes useful for setting up centralized authentication, such as `uidNumber`, `gidNumber`, `ipNetworkNumber`, and `ipNetmaskNumber`.

If you look at the contents of these files, you'll find that object identifiers (OIDs) play an important role in schema definitions, providing globally unique identification of various object classes and attributes. OIDs are a string of numbers separated by dots, read left to right, with each position representing a level in the distributed hierarchy. Top levels of the hierarchy are maintained by various standards bodies and registry authorities, and Internet Assigned Numbers Authority (IANA) allows individuals to register for their own branch under the OID `1.3.6.1.4.1`. For example, `1.3.6.1.4.1.4203` is assigned to the OpenLDAP project.

Finally, we need to define the domain component object (`dcObject`) first. This object is the root of our local branch of the directory under which future entries can be added. If your experience centers mostly on working with relational databases such as MySQL or with modern NoSQL databases such as MongoDB, you can think of `dcObject` as the database:

```
dn: dc=ldap,dc=example,dc=com
objectClass: dcObject
objectClass: organization
o: My Company's LDAP Database
```

While using `ldapadd` to import the definition, we provided the `-D` argument to specify the `Manager` account and `-W` to be prompted for the account's password:

```
ldapadd -D "cn=Manager,dc=ldap,dc=example,dc=com" -W -H ldapi:///
-f root.ldif
```

See also

Refer to the following resources for more information on working with OpenLDAP:

- The `ldapmodify` manual page (`man 1 ldapmodify`)
- OpenLDAP (`http://www.openldap.org/`)
- Understanding the LDAP Protocol, Data Hierarchy, and Entry Components (`http://www.digitalocean.com/community/tutorials/understanding-the-ldap-protocol-data-hierarchy-and-entry-components`)
- How to Use LDIF Files to Make Changes to an OpenLDAP System (`http://www.digitalocean.com/community/tutorials/how-to-use-ldif-files-to-make-changes-to-an-openldap-system`)
- How to Get Your Own LDAP OID (`http://ldapwiki.willeke.com/wiki/How%2To%2Get%2Your%20Own%2LDAP%20OID`)

Backing up and restoring an OpenLDAP database

This recipe teaches you how to back up an OpenLDAP database by exporting the directory to an LDIF file, which can then be imported later to restore the database.

Getting ready

This recipe requires a CentOS system with a working network connection and administrative privileges either using the `root` account or `sudo`.

How to do it...

To back up an LDAP directory, export the directory using the `slapcat` utility:

```
slapcat -b "dc=ldap,dc=example,dc=com" -l backup.ldif
```

To rebuild the directory from an export, follow these steps:

1. Stop the LDAP server:

   ```
   service stop slapd.service
   ```

2. Import the file using `slapadd`:

   ```
   slapadd -f backup.ldif
   ```

3. Ensure the data files are owned by the `ldap` user:

   ```
   chown -R ldap.ldap /var/lib/ldap/*
   ```

4. Restart the LDAP server:

   ```
   service restart slapd.service
   ```

How it works...

`slapcat` exports the LDAP database's contents to LDIF-formatted output. The content is sent to STDOUT by default, so you should either capture it using the shell's redirect operators (> or >>) or using the command's -l (lowercase L) argument, which specifies the name of an output file:

```
slapcat -b "dc=ldap,dc=example,dc=com" -l backup.ldif
```

The suffix of the targeted directory is given using the -b argument. If there are any subordinate directories, they'll be exported as well by default. To eliminate subordinates from the export and to export only the top-level directory contents, use the -g argument:

```
slapcat -b "dc=ldap,dc=example,dc=com" -g -l backup.ldif
```

`slapcat` returns entries in the order it encounters them while scanning the database. This means it's possible for an object's definition to appear in the export after that of an entity who's attributes reference it. This isn't a problem for `slapadd` because of how it imports data as opposed to `ldapadd`, so the former utility should be used to restore the directory. Otherwise you'll have to edit the file to ensure the ordering won't pose a problem; something I'm sure you'll agree isn't appealing given the format's verbosity:

```
slapadd -f backup.ldif
```

When performing exports and imports, the LDAP server should not be running. This makes any write actions impossible during the process to guarantee the integrity and consistency of the data.

`slapadd` writes files directly to the server's data directory so that the files will be owned by `root` (the user account used to run `slapadd`), so their ownership needs to be set to `ldap` after the import but before the server is started so that the process can access them:

```
chown -R ldap.ldap /var/lib/ldap/*
```

See also

Refer to the following resources for more information on working with OpenLDAP backups:

- OpenLDAP FAQ-O-Matic: How do I backup my directory (`http://www.openlda p.org/faq/data/cache/287.html`)
- OpenLDAP Administrator's Guide: Maintenance (`http://www.openldap.org/do c/admin24/maintenance.html`)

8

Managing Domains and DNS

This chapter contains the following recipes:

- Setting up BIND as a resolving DNS server
- Configuring BIND as an authoritative DNS server
- Writing a reverse lookup zone file
- Setting up a slave DNS server
- Configuring `rndc` to control BIND

Introduction

In this chapter, you'll find recipes that cover working with BIND in various capacities to manage your domain infrastructure better. You'll learn how to configure BIND as a resolving DNS server capable of caching lookup results which can help reduce latency, and also how to configure BIND as an authoritative DNS server to provide authoritative responses publicly for your domain or for resources on your private intranet. Also discussed are handling reverse lookup requests and ensuring your resources remain accessible by configuring redundant, secondary authoritative DNS servers that perform master/slave-style transfers of zone records. Finally, you'll learn how to set up and use `rndc`, a very useful administration client for BIND servers.

Setting up BIND as a resolving DNS server

This recipe teaches you how to set up a resolving DNS server using BIND. Domain Name Service (DNS) is the unsung workhorse of the Internet, which translates memorable names such as `facebook.com` and `google.com` to IP addresses such as `172.217.18.238` and `31.13.76.68`.

Communication across the Internet uses IP addresses to identify systems, but numbers are hard for people to remember. For example, it's easier for us to remember `google.com` than `172.217.18.238` (or the IPv6 address `2607:f8b0:4006:80e::200e`). So, when you type `google.com` in your browser's address bar, your system queries a DNS server to resolve the name to its IP address and then requests the page from the web server at that address. When you write an e-mail, a DNS server retrieves the IP address of the recipient's mail server before the message is sent.

A resolving DNS server maintained by your service provider is probably the first server to receive such lookup requests and it will respond immediately if it already happens to know the address. If not, it contacts the DNS servers in the requested domain's parent zone and receives either a referral to the authoritative DNS server of the requested domain or to servers in the next zone in the DNS hierarchy. If the request reaches the top of the hierarchy without being referred to an authoritative server, then the domain doesn't exist. Otherwise, the authoritative server sends the address back to your resolving server. The resolver then caches the response so that future lookups will complete faster.

Depending on your network and how many servers are involved in resolving an address, DNS lookups can become a significant source of latency. Address records should be found within the first one or two hops, and the resolving server should be physically close to the user for best performance. Because of this, setting up a local DNS server to cache lookup results can greatly improve how users experience the speed of your network.

Getting ready

This recipe requires a CentOS system with a working network connection. It assumes that the system is configured with the IP address `192.168.56.10`. Administrative privileges are also required, either by logging in with the `root` account or through the use of `sudo`.

How to do it...

Follow these steps to install BIND as a resolving DNS server:

1. Install the `bind` and `bind-util` packages:

   ```
   yum install bind bind-utils
   ```

2. Open BIND's configuration file at `/etc/named.conf` with your text editor:

   ```
   vi /etc/named.conf
   ```

3. Find the `listen-on` option inside the braces of `options`. Update its list to reflect the system's IP addresses BIND will use:

   ```
   listen-on port 53 { 127.0.0.1; 192.168.56.10; };
   ```

4. Change the value of `listen-on-v6` similarly if you want to service IPv6 requests. Otherwise, update the value to `none`:

   ```
   listen-on-v6 port 53 { none; }
   ```

5. Update the `allow-query` option with the list of IP addresses that BIND is allowed to accept requests from:

   ```
   allow-query { localhost; 192.168.56.0/24; };
   ```

6. Save your changes to the configuration file and close it.

7. Start BIND with `systemctl`, optionally enable it to start automatically when the system reboots:

   ```
   systemctl start named.service
   systemctl enable named.service
   ```

8. Enable FirewallD's `dns` service to open port 53 to TCP and UDP traffic:

   ```
   firewall-cmd --zone=public --permanent --add-service=dns
   firewall-cmd --reload
   ```

9. Request a lookup using `dig` to test the configuration:

   ```
   dig @192.168.56.10 google.com A
   ```

How it works...

BIND is configured as a resolving DNS server by default but we still want to update a few options to define how it accepts lookup requests. The first change is to the `listen-on*` options found in the `options` section which specify the port and network interface BIND listens on for requests. `listen-on` applies to IPv4 networks and `listen-on-v6` applies to IPv6. In both cases, the standard port for DNS traffic is port `53`:

```
listen-on port 53 { 127.0.0.1; 192.168.56.10; };
listen-on-v6 port 53 { none; }
```

Next, we updated the `allow-query` option, providing a whitelist of systems that BIND may accept requests from. Addresses can be provided individually or written in CIDR notation:

```
allow-query { localhost; 92.168.56.0/24; }
```

Using the predefined values such as `any`, `localhost`, `localnets`, and `none` is also acceptable. Intuitively, `any` represents all addresses, allowing BIND to listen on all of the system's configured addresses or accept requests from any source, whereas `none` disallows everything. `localhost` represents all of the system's addresses and `localnets` represents all addresses on all of the networks the system is a member of.

Be careful that the `local` in `localhost` and `localnets` doesn't give you a false sense of security. If your system is connected to multiple networks, for example, a public network (such as the Internet) and a private internal network, both of them are considered local. Allowing access from untrusted networks is a serious risk without the necessary security measures in place because an open DNS server can be abused by malicious users intent on carrying out several types of denial of service attacks.

After BIND's configuration is updated and it's up and running, we can test everything by sending a lookup request with `dig` and inspect the response:

```
dig @192.168.56.10 google.com A
```

Requests can be sent to a specific DNS server with `dig` by providing the targeted server's address prefixed by `@`. If a DNS server isn't given in the invocation, `dig` will send the request to the servers listed in your system's `/etc/resolve.conf` file.

After the address of the DNS server, we gave the resource name we're interested in followed by the desired record type. In the preceding example, the Address (A) record for `google.com` is sought. Other types can be queried too, such as the Name Server (NS) and Mail Exchange (MX) records.

```
[tboronczyk@ns1 ~]$ dig @192.168.56.10 google.com A

; <<>> DiG 9.9.4-RedHat-9.9.4-29.el7 <<>> @192.168.56.10 google.com A
; (1 server found)
;; global options: +cmd
;; Got answer:
;; ->>HEADER<<- opcode: QUERY, status: NOERROR, id: 45141
;; flags: qr rd ra; QUERY: 1, ANSWER: 1, AUTHORITY: 4, ADDITIONAL: 5

;; OPT PSEUDOSECTION:
; EDNS: version: 0, flags:; udp: 4096
;; QUESTION SECTION:
;google.com.                     IN      A

;; ANSWER SECTION:
google.com.             300     IN      A       216.58.219.238

;; AUTHORITY SECTION:
google.com.             172800  IN      NS      ns4.google.com.
google.com.             172800  IN      NS      ns1.google.com.
google.com.             172800  IN      NS      ns2.google.com.
google.com.             172800  IN      NS      ns3.google.com.

;; ADDITIONAL SECTION:
ns2.google.com.         172800  IN      A       216.239.34.10
ns1.google.com.         172800  IN      A       216.239.32.10
ns3.google.com.         172800  IN      A       216.239.36.10
ns4.google.com.         172800  IN      A       216.239.38.10

;; Query time: 459 msec
;; SERVER: 192.168.56.10#53(192.168.56.10)
;; WHEN: Sat Aug 13 21:42:00 EDT 2016
;; MSG SIZE  rcvd: 191

[tboronczyk@ns1 ~]$
```

dig queries the DNS servers and displays their response

The response from `dig` is organized into several sections. The **ANSWER SECTION** shows the A record we requested. The **AUTHORITY SECTION** lists the authoritative DNS servers configured for the requested domain, and the **ADDITIONAL SECTION** shows the IP addresses of the authoritative servers. Various metadata is included throughout, such as which flags were set in the request, which DNS server was queried, and how long the lookup took to complete.

When you're satisfied with the testing results, you can configure the systems on your network to use the new DNS server. This is typically done by adding a `nameserver` entry in each system's `/etc/resolv.conf` file that provides the DNS server's address:

```
nameserver 192.168.56.10
```

`resolv.conf` may be dynamically generated depending on how the system's interfaces are configured. If this is the case, any changes you make in the file will be overwritten. You'll need to inspect the interfaces' configuration files (for example, `/etc/sysconf/network-scripts/ifcfg-enp0s3`), and if `PEERDNS` is set to `yes` then `resolv.conf` is maintained by the network manager. Add the `DNS` entry in the interface's configuration and the DNS server's address will make its way into `resolve.conf` the next time the interface is brought up:

```
DNS=192.168.56.10
```

Bounce the interface after updating the configuration for the change to take effect and verify the contents of `resolve.conf`:

```
ifdown enp0s3 && ifup enp0s3
cat /etc/resolv.conf
```

Resolving DNS servers are sometimes called recursive servers because they send lookup requests to each level in the zone hierarchy until they find an answer. Forwarding DNS servers function similarly to resolving/recursive servers, in that both types accept lookup requests and cache the results for expediency; however, forwarding servers send their requests to another DNS server and wait for the response, delegating the resolution process instead of tracking down the answer itself. This can offload a lot of the network chatter produced by a resolving DNS server trying to service a request.

To configure BIND to run as a forwarding DNS server, open `/etc/named.conf` again and add the `forwarders` and `forward` options to the `options` block:

```
forwarders { 8.8.8.8; 8.8.4.4; };
forward only;
```

The `forwarders` option provides a list of DNS servers responsible for resolving lookup requests. The example identifies Google's public DNS servers but your service provider should also maintain public DNS servers that you can use if you prefer.

`forward only` forces BIND to forward requests to the responsible servers listed in `forwarders`. Only when the responsible server fails to return an address or a referral, will BIND contact the root servers for the domain's authoritative DNS servers and service the request itself. Recursion isn't completely turned off on a forwarding server but it is greatly reduced.

See also

The following resources will provide you with more information on how DNS works and how to configure BIND:

- The `dig` manual page (`man 1 dig`)
- An Introduction to DNS Terminology (`http://www.digitalocean.com/communi ty/tutorials/an-introduction-to-dns-terminology-components-and-conce pts`)
- DNS for Rocket Scientists (`http://www.zytrax.com/books/dns/`)
- How DNS Works (`http://howdns.works/`)
- BIND 9 Administrator Reference Manual (`http://www.isc.org/downloads/bin d/doc/`)
- RHEL 7 Networking Guide: BIND (`https://access.redhat.com/documentatio n/en-US/Red_Hat_Enterprise_Linux/7/html/Networking_Guide/sec-BIND.ht ml`)
- DNS & BIND by Cricket Liu and Paul Albitz (`http://shop.oreilly.com/produ ct/9785961575.do`)

Configuring BIND as an authoritative DNS server

A benefit to hierarchical structures is that the responsibility for subordinate nodes can be delegated. Although the Internet Corporation for Assigned Names and Numbers (ICANN) has authority over the DNS directory, it delegates the responsibility to accredited registrars for top-level domains, such as `com`, `net`, and `org`, and delegates to the appropriate governmental agencies for country top-level domains, such as `ca`, `de`, and `es`. Registrars delegate responsibility to you when you register a domain and you may further delegate the responsibility for your subdomains however you please. Each boundary formed by delegating responsibility creates what is known as a DNS zone.

This recipe teaches you how to configure BIND to operate as an authoritative DNS server for your zone. If you recall the previous recipe's discussion on how a DNS request propagates, you'll remember that authoritative servers have the final say for a resolution. This is because its information comes from outside the DNS system, from an administrator who manually configures the zone's information. You'll also learn how to write a zone file with information such as mapping hostnames to IP addresses, which, I promise, isn't as scary as it might look at first glance.

Getting ready

This recipe requires a CentOS system with BIND configured as a resolving DNS server, as described in the previous recipe (BIND's configuration will be updated to operate as an authoritative server). Administrative privileges are also required, either by logging in with the root account or through the use of sudo.

Following the advice of RFC-2606 (Reserved Top Level DNS Names), I'll use the example.com domain for illustration. If you have your own domain name then feel free to substitute. Also for the sake of illustration, the recipe will reflect a network of various servers that handle the different services one commonly finds in a domain, such as e-mail servers and web servers. The systems are as follows:

- ns1: Hosts the domain's primary authoritative DNS server with the IP address 192.168.56.10 (this is the system we'll be working on)
- ns2: Hosts a secondary authoritative DNS server with the address 192.168.56.20
- mail: Hosts the primary e-mail server with the address 192.168.56.12
- mail2: Hosts a secondary e-mail server with the address 192.168.56.22
- www: Hosts a web and FTP server with the address 192.168.56.100

How to do it...

Follow these steps to configure BIND as an authoritative DNS server:

1. Open /etc/named.conf with your text editor:

   ```
   vi /etc/named.conf
   ```

2. Verify that the listen-on* and allow-query options are configured as described in the previous recipe:

   ```
   listen-on port 52 { 127.0.0.1; 192.168.56.10; };
   listen-on-v6 port 52 { none; };
   allow-query { 192.168.56.0/24; };
   ```

3. Change the value of the recursion option to no to disable BIND's recursive lookup behavior completely:

   ```
   recursion no;
   ```

4. At the end of the file, add the following zone configuration:

   ```
   zone "example.com." in {
       type master;
       file "/var/named/zones/example.com.fwd";
       allow-transfer { none; };
   };
   ```

5. Save your changes and close the file.

6. Create the /var/named/zones directory:

   ```
   mkdir /var/named/zones
   ```

7. Create the zone file `/var/named/zones/example.com.fwd` with the following content (our discussion in *How it works...* will help you understand the meaning of each record):

```
$TTL 1d
$ORIGIN example.com.
; start of authority resource record
@       IN SOA    ns1 hostmaster.example.com. (
                  2016041501 ; serial
                  12h        ; refresh
                  5m         ; retry
                  2w         ; expire
                  3h)        ; negative TTL
; nameserver records
        IN NS     ns1
        IN NS     ns2
ns1     IN A      192.168.56.10
ns2     IN A      192.168.56.20
; mail records
@       IN MX     10 mail
        IN MX     20 mail2
mail    IN A      192.168.56.12
mail2   IN A      192.168.56.22
; webserver records
@       IN A      192.168.56.100
www     IN CNAME  @
ftp     IN CNAME  @
```

8. Ensure that the directory and zone file have the correct ownership and access permissions:

```
chown root.named /var/named/zones
chmod 750 /var/named/zones
chmod 640 /var/named/zones/*
```

9. Restart BIND for the configuration changes to take effect:

```
systemctl restart named.service
```

10. Request a lookup using dig to test the configuration:

```
dig @192.168.56.10 example.com SOA
```

How it works...

The only records an authoritative DNS server should serve are those with authoritative information about its zones, so we began by disabling `recursion` in BIND's configuration file. When disabled, BIND won't forward requests or try to resolve a lookup request for non-authoritative records:

```
recursion off;
```

Then we added a short section at the end of the configuration file that specifies how the BIND server should function for the `example.com.` zone:

```
zone "example.com." in {
    type master;
    file "/var/named/zones/example.com.fwd";
    allow-transfer { none; };
};
```

The section starts with the keyword `zone` to denote a zone configuration and is followed by the zone's name given as a fully qualified domain name (FQDN). FQDNs always end with a dot because they include all of the delegated paths, including the root. Since the root of the DNS system doesn't have a name, its separator appears as a trailing dot. Thus, `example.com.` is fully qualified but `example.com` is not. (Some people misuse the term FQDN when they're really talking about partially qualified domain names. This is one of my irrational pet peeves so consider yourself warned.)

Thinking about how you navigate the filesystem can help you understanding the difference between the fully qualified and partially qualified names. Navigation, when the absolute (fully qualified) path `/var/named` is given, begins at the root of the filesystem, descends into the `var` directory, and then into `named`. The root directory has no name other than its separator. However, the relative (partially qualified) path `var/named` doesn't start with the separator. Its navigation begins where the current directory happens to be at the moment. Domain names are similar, but they list traverse the hierarchy backwards toward the root, and the dot is used as a separator instead of a slash.

The `type master` option specifies this server as the zone's primary authoritative DNS server. A common deployment strategy sets up several authoritative servers in a master/slave configuration. An administrator updates the zone information on the primary, which is identified as the master; the information is then transferred to one or more slaves acting as secondary authoritative DNS servers. You'll learn how to set this up in the *Setting up a slave DNS server* recipe, but for now we'll only focus on the primary server.

The `allow-transfers` option lists the slave systems this server is allowed to respond to when a request is received for zone information transfers, but since we don't (yet) have a secondary authoritative DNS server configured, we've used `none` to disable transfers. This helps to protect us from a specific type of denial of service attack. Resource records are small enough to fit in a UDP packet or two during normal lookup activity, but zone transfers transmit all of the records in bulk over TCP. Malicious users repeatedly sending transfer requests in quick succession can saturate your network.

The zone's information is stored in a text file known as a **zone file** whose location is given with the `file` option. The convention followed in this chapter places the files in a `zone` directory under `/var/named` and uses `fwd` and `rev` as file extensions to indicate whether the file is a forward lookup or a reverse lookup zone file. Thus, our file is saved as `/var/named/zones/example.com.fwd`.

This recipe's file is a forward zone file because it maps names to their IP addresses. A reverse lookup zone maps the inverse relationship, which is addresses to names. They are discussed in the *Writing a reverse lookup zone file* recipe.

 I've seen a handful of different conventions followed when it comes to naming zone files. Some administrators use `zon` or `zone` as the file's extension. Some will separate the zone files in the directories named `fwd-zone` and `rev-zone`. Honestly, it really doesn't matter what you do as long as you stay consistent `systemctl restart named.servicent` and your files are well organized.

`$TTL` is the first directive given in the zone file and gives the default length of time a resolving DNS server may cache records it receives from the authoritative server. Specific records may provide their own TTL, which overrides this default value:

```
$TTL 14400
```

The $ORIGIN directive provides the FQDN identifying the zone. Any @ appearing in the file will be replaced by the value of $ORIGIN:

```
$ORIGIN example.com.
```

The remaining entries are collectively called resource records and are made up of a series of fields in the order `name ttl class type values`. The `name` field gives the name of the resource that owns the record. If blank, its value defaults to the name used in the previous record. `ttl` is also optional, defaulting to the value of $TTL. And for our purposes, `class` will always be `IN` because we're writing the Internet resource records. The other classes are `CH` for Chaos and `HS` for Hesiod but they aren't in widespread use.

The first record in the file must be the start of authority (`SOA`) record which identifies that this server is the authoritative DNS server for the zone. The values for a `SOA` record are the name of the primary authoritative server for the zone (we supplied ns1), an e-mail address for the person responsible for the zone (`hostmaster.example.com.`), a serial number (`2016041501`), refresh duration (`12h`), retry duration (`5m`), expiration duration (`2w`), and the length of time negative responses (sent when the requested record doesn't exist) from the server can be cached (`3h`). Records are usually written as single-line entries, but parentheses permit us to split the record over several lines:

```
;  start of authority resource record
@       IN SOA    ns1 hostmaster.example.com. (
                  2016041501 ; serial
                  12h        ; refresh
                  5m         ; retry
                  2w         ; expire
                  3h)        ; negative TTL
```

The @ variable that would normally appear in the e-mail addresses is changed to a dot in `hostmaster.example.com.` because @ has special meaning in zone files. Also notice which names are fully qualified. Names that aren't fully qualified will have the FQDN appended automatically, so ns1 is understood as `ns1.example.com.`. If the e-mail address's domain part wasn't fully qualified then `hostmaster.example.com` would be treated as `hostmaster.example.com.example.com.`, which certainly isn't what we want.

Values beyond that in the SOA record are primarily of interest to the slave DNS servers. The refresh value informs the slave how often it should try to refresh its copy of the zone file. The retry duration tells the slave how long it should wait between connection attempts if the master is unreachable, and the expiry value specifies how long the slave can satisfy lookup requests as an authoritative server with its copy of the zone file if contact with the master is completely lost. The negative TTL is the length of time a resolver should cache negative responses from a DNS server, for example, NXDOMAIN and NODATA responses.

The serial number is an arbitrary that 10-digit value slaves can use to differentiate this version of the zone file from previous versions. Anytime you update the file, you must also update the serial number. A popular convention is to use the current date followed by a sequence counter. For example, April 15, 2016 is written as 20160415 and then two additional digits are added to identify multiple updates during the same day (2016041501, 2016041502, 2016041503, and so on).

Next, we gave the NS records that identify the zone's authoritative DNS servers. The SOA and NS records are mandatory in every zone file:

```
; nameserver records
        IN NS    ns1
        IN NS    ns2
ns1     IN A     192.168.56.10
ns2     IN A     192.168.56.20
```

The NS records identify the names of the authoritative servers. In the preceding example, we defined n1 and n2 as the zone's authoritative DNS servers which are understood as ns1.example.com. and ns2.example.com. since they are not fully qualified. The A records map a name to its address (AAAA is used for IPv6 addresses). The records we wrote in the example say ns1.example.com. can be reached at 192.168.56.10 and ns2.example.com. can be reached at 192.168.56.20.

The NS records belong to the zone but I left the first field of the NS records blank since the field defaults to the name used in the last record. In this case, the name happens to be @ from the SOA record (which is $ORIGIN). Any of the following alternatives mean the same and are equally acceptable:

```
@ IN NS n1
$ORIGIN IN NS n1
example.com. IN NS n1
```

However, be careful because the MX records also belong to the zone. As we begin the next set of records, the last name is ns2 from that server's A record. This means the first MX record must provide either @, $ORIGIN, or example.com..

The MX records define the names of the servers responsible for handling e-mail for the zone. The mailers are assigned a relative preference and a client will try to communicate with the mail server with the lowest preference first. If the server is unreachable, the client attempts to connect to the next lowest until it exhausts the list:

```
; mail records
@       IN MX   10 mail
        IN MX   20 mail2
mail    IN A    192.168.56.12
mail2   IN A    192.168.56.22
```

Our configuration defines the principal mail server mail.example.com. with the IP address 192.168.56.12 and a relative preference of 10. The second server, perhaps a backup in the event of an outage, is mail2.example.com. at 192.168.56.22 with a preference of 20.

Last, we defined records that identify our zone's web server and other aliases for the system:

```
; webserver records
@       IN A     192.168.56.100
www     IN CNAME @
ftp     IN CNAME @
```

The ubiquity of `www` appearing at the beginning of URLs has waned since the good old days of the dot-com era. Still, many zones resolve the addresses both with and without `www` to the same IP. Our configuration does the same, returning `192.168.56.100` for lookups of both `example.com` or `www.example.com`. This is accomplished by creating the `A` record that maps the domain to the web server's address and then a Canonical Name (`CNAME`) record that aliases `www` to the domain's `A` record. Our configuration also aliases `ftp` to the `A` record so that users can upload their site's files to the web server using the address `ftp.example.com`.

See also

Refer to the following resources for more information on running a DNS server and managing your domain:

- BIND 9 Administrator Reference Manual (`http://www.isc.org/downloads/bind/doc`)
- Five Basic Mistakes Not to Make in DNS (`http://archive.oreilly.com/pub/a/sysadmin/27/4/26/5-basic-mistakes-not-to-make-in-dns.html`)
- BIND for the Small LAN (`http://www.madboa.com/geek/soho-bind`)
- RFC-1034: Domain Concepts and Facilities (`https://tools.ietf.org/html/rfc134`)
- RFC-1035: Domain Names-Implementation and Specification (`https://tools.ietf.org/html/rfc135`)
- RFC-1912: Common DNS Operational and Configuration Errors (`https://tools.ietf.org/html/rfc1912`)

Writing a reverse lookup zone file

Until now we've treated DNS requests as forward facing lookups, translating resource names like `www.example.com` to an IP address. However, services can also ask a DNS server to resolve information in the opposite direction by providing an IP address and want to know what name it's associated with. Reverse lookups such as these are especially useful for logging or authentication and security purposes. For example, a system can query a DNS server to verify that a client really is connecting from the system they claim. To accommodate such requests, this recipe shows you how to write a reverse lookup zone file.

Getting ready

This recipe requires a CentOS system with BIND installed and configured as described in the previous recipes. Administrative privileges are also required, either by logging in with the `root` account or through the use of `sudo`.

How to do it...

Follow these steps to add a reverse lookup zone:

1. Open BIND's configuration file:

   ```
   vi /etc/named.conf
   ```

2. Add the following zone entry:

   ```
   zone "56.168.192.in-addr.arpa." in {
       type master;
       file "/var/named/zones/example.com.rev";
       allow-transfer { none; };
   };
   ```

3. Save your changes and close the configuration file.

4. Create the `/etc/named/zones/example.com.rev` file with the following content:

   ```
   $TTL 1d
   $ORIGIN 56.168.192.in-addr.arpa.
   ; start of authority
   @   IN SOA  ns1.example.com. hostmaster.example.com. (
               2016041501 ; serial
               12h          ; refresh
               5m           ; retry
               2w           ; expire
               3h)          ; error TTL
   ; nameservers
       IN NS   ns1.example.com.
       IN NS   ns2.example.com.
   10  IN PTR  ns1.example.com.
   20  IN PTR  ns2.example.com.
   ; mail servers
   12  IN PTR  mail.example.com.
   22  IN PTR  mail2.example.com.
   ; web servers
   100 IN PTR  example.com.
   ```

```
100 IN PTR   www.example.com.
100 IN PTR   ftp.example.com.
```

5. Ensure that the zone file has the correct ownership and access permissions:

```
chown root.named /var/named/zones/example.com.rev
chmod 640 /var/named/zones/example.com.rev
```

6. Restart BIND for the configuration changes to take effect:

```
systemctl restart named.service
```

7. Perform a reverse DNS lookup using `dig` to test the zone:

```
dig @192.168.56.10 -x 192.168.56.100
```

How it works...

Reverse lookup zones are just like any other zones defined by a zone file. So, hopefully nothing in this recipe came as a big surprise to you. Nevertheless, there are still a few points worth reviewing.

First, the zone's name is constructed by combining the network's address with the special domain `in-addr.arpa`, which is used to define reverse-mapped IP addresses (`ip6.arpa` is used for IPv6). The order of the address's octets is reversed to maintain consistency with domain names that read from the most specific to the most broad. Thus, `56.168.192.in-addr.arpa.` is the FQDN for reverse lookups on addresses in the `192.168.56/24` address space:

```
zone "56.168.192.in-addr.arpa." in {
    type master;
    file "/etc/named/zones/example.com.rev";
    allow-transfer { none; };
};
```

This recipe names the zone file as `example.com.rev` so that it will sort alongside the forward zone file `example.com.fwd` in directory listings. Other conventions might name the file as `56.168.192.in-addr.arpa.zone`. Again, regardless of whatever convention you choose, the key thing is to be consistent.

Keep in mind the expansion and substitution rules we've discussed when writing a reverse zone file, most importantly that partially qualified names are interpreted in the context of $ORIGIN. We can get away writing just the primary authoritative DNS server's hostname in a forward lookup zone's SOA record, but we need to make sure that the names are fully qualified in a reverse file to prevent them from being treated as ns1.56.168.192.in-addr.arpa.:

```
; start of authority
@   IN SOA  ns1.example.com. hostmaster.example.com. (
            2016041501 ; serial
            12h        ; refresh
            5m         ; retry
            2w         ; expire
            3h)        ; error TTL
```

A pointer record (PTR) relates an IP address back to a resource name. Apart from the SOA and NS records (as they are mandatory records in any zone file), the only other type of record that can appear in a reverse file is PTR. A consequence of this is that multiple records are needed to correctly inverse any aliases created with the CNAME records in the forward file. Since we used www and ftp as aliases for example.com., which resolve to 192.168.56.100, three records for the address appears in the reverse zone file as follows:

```
100 IN PTR  example.com.
100 IN PTR  www.example.com.
100 IN PTR  ftp.example.com.
```

We can test the zone configuration with dig using the −x argument:

```
dig @192.168.56.10 −x 192.168.56.100
```

−x lets dig know that we're performing a reverse lookup. We provide the IP address as we would normally write it and dig will reverse its octets and append the in-addr.arpa domain for us when it sends the request.

See also

Refer to the following resources for more information on working with reverse zones and lookups:

- BIND 9 Administrator Reference Manual (http://www.isc.org/downloads/bind/doc/)

- DNS Reverse Mapping (http://www.zytrax.com/books/dns/ch3/)
- Classless in-addr.arpa. delegation (http://www.indelible.org/ink/classl ess)

Setting up a slave DNS server

Redundancy is important to ensure key services remain available in the event of an issue. As DNS is one of the most critical components of a network, whether it's a private intranet or the public Internet, having only one authoritative DNS server is unwise. In fact, IANA's *Technical Requirements for Authoritative Name Servers* document states that there must be a minimum of two different authoritative name servers for the zone. This recipe shows you how to configure a second BIND installation to act as a secondary authoritative server that receives its zone information from the primary in a master/slave configuration. A lookup request can then be satisfied by either server and be considered an authoritative response.

Getting ready

This recipe requires two CentOS systems with BIND installed and configured as described in earlier recipes. Use the network described by the *Configuring BIND as an authoritative DNS server* recipe. This recipe assumes that the system to serve as the master is configured as 192.168.56.10 and the slave is 192.168.56.20. Administrative privileges are also required, either by logging in with the root account or through the use of sudo.

How to do it...

Follow these steps to configure BIND as a secondary authoritative DNS server that receives its zone information from the primary:

1. On the system running the slave instance of BIND, open named.conf and configure the example.com. zone as follows:

```
zone "example.com." in {
    type slave;
    file "/var/named/slaves/example.com.fwd";
    masters { 192.168.56.10; };
    allow-transfer { none; };
    notify no;
};
```

2. Configure its reverse zone as follows:

```
zone "56.168.192.in-addr.arpa." in {
    type slave;
    file "/var/named/slaves/example.com.rev";
    masters { 192.168.56.10; };
    allow-transfer { none; };
    notify no;
};
```

3. Save your changes and close the file.
4. Restart the slave for the configuration changes to take effect:

```
systemctl restart named.service
```

5. On the system running the master instance of BIND, open `named.conf`.
6. Update the `example.com.` zone's `allow-transfer` entry with the addresses of the slave. The zone's configuration should look like this:

```
zone "example.com." in {
    type master;
    file "/var/named/zones/example.com.fwd";
    allow-transfer { 192.168.56.20; };
};
```

7. Make the same change to the reverse zone configuration:

```
zone "56.168.192.in-addr.arpa." in {
    type master;
    file "/var/named/zones/example.com.rev";
    allow-transfer { 192.168.56.20; };
};
```

8. Save the changes and close the file.
9. Restart the master for the configuration changes to take effect:

```
systemctl restart named.service
```

10. On the slave, test the configuration using `dig` to request a zone transfer:

```
dig @192.168.56.10 example.com. AXFR
```

How it works...

Slave servers request a zone transfer when notified by the primary authoritative DNS server that the zone's records have changed and when the copy of the zone file maintained by the slave expires according to the SOA record. In this recipe, we began with two systems running BIND and edited their configurations to allow the transfer. We began on the system targeted as the slave, configuring both the forward and reverse lookup zones we've worked with earlier:

```
zone "example.com." in {
    type slave;
    file "/var/named/slaves/example.com.fwd";
    masters { 192.168.56.10; };
    allow-transfer { none; };
    notify no;
};
zone "56.168.192.in-addr.arpa." in {
    type slave;
    file "/var/named/slaves/example.com.rev";
    masters { 192.168.56.10; };
    allow-transfer { none; };
    notify no;
};
```

The type slave option instructs this server to act as a secondary server for the zone. Since designating the master and slave is done on a per-zone basis, it's possible for the same instance of BIND to be the master for one zone and a slave for another. The masters option provides the address of the primary server.

The file option provides the location where BIND will write the transferred zone information. Not only is it good for the organization to keep the transferred zones separate from any primary zone files on the system, but it's also good for security. BIND needs write permissions to the directory to save the transferred files, but the primary zone files should be read-only to anyone except the administrator (that is, root) as a safeguard from any tampering. Our configuration saves them to /var/named/slaves, which was created when we installed the bind package and already has the appropriate permissions.

The allow-transfers option lists the systems this server is allowed to respond to for zone transfer requests. To protect ourselves from possible abuse, we set the value to none, which disallows transfers from the secondary server. All transfers will be serviced by the primary authoritative DNS server, and even then it will only send them to the slave.

BIND sends a notification to the secondary authoritative servers listed in a zone's NS records each time the zone is reloaded. There's no reason for the slave to send a notification to other secondaries (if you configure more than one slave) because they are already notified by the primary, so we turned off this behavior with `notify no`.

However, if you want you can send notifications to other servers along with those listed in the zone file with the `also-notify` option. This is useful if you have additional secondary servers which you don't want to make public with NS records or if you want to notify some other automated process. Simply provide the addresses of the servers you want to notify with `also-notify`:

```
also-notify { 192.168.56.200; 192.168.68.200; };
```

To notify only those servers listed in `also-notify` and not the secondary authoritative servers, set `notify` to `explicit`:

```
also-notify { 192.168.56.200; 192.168.68.200; };
notify explicit;
```

Next, we updated the master's configuration, giving the slave's address with `allow-transfers` to permit the master to respond to zone transfer requests from the slave:

```
zone "example.com." in {
    type master;
    file "/var/named/zones/example.com.fwd";
    allow-transfer { 192.168.56.20; };
};
```

After restarting BIND for our changes take effect, we can test the configuration by using `dig` to request a zone transfer from the master while on the slave system:

```
dig @192.168.56.10 example.com. AXFR
```

 Remember to increment the serial number in the SOA record whenever you update a zone configuration. The slave checks the serial before updating its zone information and won't update it if the value hasn't changed.

See also

Refer to the following resources for more information on configuring and working with zone transfers:

- BIND 9 Administrator Reference Manual (`http://www.isc.org/downloads/bind/doc/`)
- DNS for Rocket Scientists (`http://www.zytrax.com/books/dns/`)
- Technical requirements for authoritative name servers (`http://www.iana.org/help/nameserver-requirements`)
- How the AXFR protocol works (`http://cr.yp.to/djbdns/axfr-notes.html`)
- A Pattern for DNS Architecture (`http://www.allgoodbits.org/articles/view/5`)
- Securing an Internet Name Server (`http://resources.sei.cmu.edu/library/asset-view.cfm?assetid=52493`)

Configuring rndc to control BIND

`rndc` is the client utility for managing BIND servers. However, before you can use it, both `rndc` and BIND need to be configured. This recipe shows you how to configure them and then shows you a few commands for managing the server's cache.

Getting ready

This recipe requires a CentOS system with BIND installed and configured as described in the previous recipes. Administrative privileges are also required, either by logging in with the `root` account or through the use of `sudo`.

How to do it...

Follow these steps to configure `rndc`:

1. Use the `rndc-confgen` utility to generate the necessary key file:

   `rndc-confgen -a -c /etc/rndc.key`

2. Create the `/etc/rndc.conf` file with the following content:

   ```
   include "/etc/rndc.key";
   options {
       default-key "rndc-key";
       default-server 127.0.0.1;
       default-port 953;
   };
   ```

3. Ensure the correct ownership and access permissions for `rndc.key` and `rndc.conf`:

   `chown root.named /etc/rndc*`
   `chmod 640 /etc/rndc*`

4. Open `/etc/named.conf` and add the following configuration settings after the closing brace of the `options` block:

   ```
   include "/etc/rndc.key";
   controls {
       inet 127.0.0.1 port 953 allow { 127.0.0.1; } keys {
       "rndc-key"; };
   };
   ```

5. Restart BIND for the configuration changes to take effect:

   `systemctl restart named.service`

6. Test the configuration by using `rndc` to request BIND's status:

   `rndc status`

How it works...

Communication between `rndc` and BIND requires a shared key for authorization. So, first we used `rndc-confgen` to create one. In a normal operation without arguments, the program generates the key and necessary configuration fragments and dumps everything to the screen. You can cut and paste sections of the output into the appropriate files, but if you only have access with a terminal and keyboard then this could prove difficult. Instead, we ran the program with `-a` for it to generate the key's definition and dump it to its own configuration file and we'll type the other configuration pieces manually. The `-c` argument simply specifies our desired name for the key definition's file:

```
rndc-confgen -a -c /etc/rndc.key
```

 Some people report that `rndc-confgen` appears to crash on their system. If you experience this, the most likely reason is that it's waiting for sufficient data to generate the secret, but the entropy pool for `/dev/random` is starved which causes `rndc-confgen` to wait. Terminate the process and try again using `-r` to specify `/dev/urandom` as an alternate source:

```
rndc-confgen -a -c /etc/rndc.key -r /dev/urandom
```

A quick peek inside `/etc/rndc.key` reveals the key's definition as follows:

```
key "rndc-key" {
    algorithm hmac-md5;
    secret "YBmUKeobRMlAOUjCqMcb6g==";
};
```

`rndc` uses a configuration file of its own. So, next we created `/etc/rndc.conf`:

```
include "/etc/rndc.key";
options {
    default-key "rndc-key";
    default-server 127.0.0.1;
    default-port 953;
};
```

We include the key definition from `rndc.key` and specify it as the default key for `rndc` to use. We also specified the local loopback address as the default server and 953 as the default port. With these configuration options, `rndc` attempts to connect to the locally running BIND server without the need for us to provide extra arguments at the command line.

Last, we BIND to allow and authenticate rndc's connection requests. So, we again include the key definition and add a `controls` block in `named.conf`:

```
include "/etc/rndc.key";
controls {
    inet 127.0.0.1 port 953 allow {127.0.0.1;} keys {"rndc-key";};
};
```

The `inet` statement specifies which addresses are allowed to connect and the keys they need to authenticate. The first address lists which address BIND will listen on for connection requests. The configuration is intentionally restrictive for the sake of security and only allows us to use `rndc` locally—BIND listens on the local address and services commands sent from the local address.

If you want to use `rndc` for remote administration, I recommend you against opening access and instead use SSH to log into the remote system and it's copy of `rndc`. BIND's control channel remains closed to anyone up to no good, you don't need to distribute copies of the key file, and communication between the two systems is encrypted:

```
ssh 192.168.56.10 rndc status
```

You can save typing by creating an `alias`:

```
alias rndc-ns1="ssh 192.168.56.10 rndc" rndc-ns1 status
```

When invoked without a subcommand, `rndc` displays a usage message enumerating the actions we can perform. The `status` command outputs BIND's current status including how many zones are configured, if any zone transfers are in progress, and in the case of a resolving DNS server, how many queries it's currently trying to resolve through recursion:

> **rndc status**

```
[root@ns1 ~]# rndc status
WARNING: key file (/etc/rndc.key) exists, but using default configuration file (
/etc/rndc.conf)
version: 9.9.4-RedHat-9.9.4-29.el7_2.3 <id:8f9657aa>
CPUs found: 4
worker threads: 2
UDP listeners per interface: 1
number of zones: 8
debug level: 0
xfers running: 0
xfers deferred: 0
soa queries in progress: 0
query logging is OFF
recursive clients: 0/0/1000
tcp clients: 0/100
server is up and running
[root@ns1 ~]#
```

rndc is used to manage BIND DNS servers

You may find the `flush` command useful if you're running a resolving DNS server. It removes all of the cached lookup information from BIND's cache. If you want to clear only the records related to a particular domain, you can use `flushname`:

> **rndc flushname google.com**

The `reload` and `refresh` commands are useful with authoritative servers. The `reload` command causes BIND to reparse zone files after they've been updated without restarting the server. Unless a specific zone is given, all zones will be reloaded:

> **rndc reload example.com.**

In the case of slave DNS servers, we can force BIND to update its copy of a zone file if it's stale using the `refresh` command:

> **rndc refresh example.com.**

See also

Refer to the following resources for more information on using `rndc`:

- The `rndc` manual page (`man 8 rndc`)
- RHEL 7 Networking Guide: BIND (`https://access.redhat.com/documentation/en-US/Red_Hat_Enterprise_Linux/7/html/Networking_Guide/sec-BIND.html`)

9
Managing E-mails

This chapter contains the following recipes:

- Configuring Postfix to provide SMTP services
- Adding SASL to Postfix with Dovecot
- Configuring Postfix to use TLS
- Configuring Dovecot for secure POP3 and IMAP access
- Targeting spam with SpamAssassin
- Routing messages with Procmail

Introduction

In this chapter, you'll find recipes to help you set up and secure e-mail services for your domain. You'll learn how to set up Postfix to run as an SMTP server and then learn how to configure it to support SASL authentication and TLS encryption. Then we'll configure Dovecot which will provide users access to their e-mail over the POP3 and IMAP protocols. Finally, you'll learn how to set up SpamAssassin and Procmail to reduce the amount of spam that makes it way to your inbox.

Configuring Postfix to provide SMTP services

This recipe teaches you how to configure Postfix as a basic e-mail server for your domain. E-mail is one of the oldest Internet services and has become one its most pervasive services. Moreover, e-mail can be one of the most difficult services to manage.

Using the Simple Mail Transport Protocol (SMTP), an e-mail message passes through many processes from its starting point on its way to your inbox. When someone writes you a message, they use an e-mail client to compose the message. The client sends the message to their mail server which looks up the MX records for your domain and relays the message to your mail server for delivery. Once the message is received by your mail server, it's delivered to your mail directory on the server. At least that's the basic idea. A message can be relayed by any number of intermediate servers between the sender's server and your mail server; servers can be configured to send mail, receive mail, or both. Different protocols are used to retrieve the messages from the server (POP3 and IMAP) than those used to send them, and trying to stay one step ahead of spammers can add a fair amount of complexity.

 Because of the complexity of the e-mail ecosystem and being a mail server administrator is often more than a full-time job, I can only present to you the basics. Later recipes will teach you how to add authentication and encryption to your setup, there will still be much to explore and learn. I strongly recommend that you take advantage of the additional resources mentioned in the *See also* section after each recipe.

Getting ready

This recipe requires a CentOS system with a working network connection. Administrative privileges are also required, either by logging in with the root account or through the use of sudo. You'll want to have a couple of user accounts available on the system for testing purposes as well.

Because MX records are used to resolve the mail server's address during the delivery process, it's assumed that you have either completed the previous chapter's recipes or have, otherwise, configured your own DNS records. The IP address 192.168.56.20 is used here in keeping with the example network outlined in the *Configuring BIND as an authoritative DNS server* recipe in Chapter 8, *Managing Domains and DNS*.

How to do it...

Follow these steps to set up Postfix:

1. Use a text editor to open Postfix's configuration file /etc/postfix/main.cf:

```
vi /etc/postfix/main.cf
```

2. Find the example `myhostname` parameters. Delete the leading # character to uncomment one of the examples and update its value with your qualified hostname:

```
myhostname = mail.example.com
```

3. Locate the example `mydomain` parameter and uncomment and edit it, setting your domain name as its value:

```
mydomain = example.com
```

4. Find the `inet_interfaces` parameters. Place an # in front of the `localhost` entry to comment it out and then uncomment the `all` entry:

```
inet_interfaces = all
#inet_interfaces = $myhostname
#inet_interfaces = $myhostname, localhost
#inet_interfaces = localhost
```

5. Find the `mydestination` parameters and comment out the first entry. Uncomment the one that includes `$mydomain` in its list:

```
#mydestination = $myhostname, localhost.$mydomain,  localhost
mydestination = $myhostname, localhost.$mydomain,  localhost,
$mydomain
#mydestination = $myhostname, localhost.$mydomain,  localhost,
#          $mydomain mail.$mydomain, www.$mydomain,  ftp.$mydomain
```

6. Find the example `mynetworks` parameters. Uncomment one of the entries and edit it so that the value reflects your network:

```
mynetworks = 192.168.56.0/24, 127.0.0.0/8
```

7. Find the example `home_mailbox` parameters and uncomment the entry with the `Maildir/` value:

```
home_mailbox = Maildir/
```

8. Save your changes and close the file.

9. Start the Postfix server and optionally enable it to start automatically whenever the system reboots:

```
systemctl start postfix.service
systemctl enable postfix.service
```

10. Open port 25 in the system's firewall to allow outside connections to Postfix:

```
firewall-cmd --zone=public --permanent --add-service=smtp
firewall-cmd --reload
```

How it works...

CentOS systems have Postfix installed by default, using it as a local mail transfer agent. To reconfigure it to act as our domain's mail server, we updated several parameters in its configuration file, /etc/postfix/main.cf.

First, we updated the myhostname parameter to provide our system's qualified domain name (the hostname and domain name):

```
myhostname = mail.example.com
```

> Comments in the configuration file refer to a FQDN, but we know better because FQDNs require a trailing dot. If you do provide a true FQDN as the value, Postfix will fail to start stating that the parameter's value is bad.

The mydomain parameter specifies the domain that this system is a member of and that Postfix is handling e-mail for. Although Postfix will try to determine the domain name based on the system's qualified hostname, it's not a bad idea to explicitly define it with mydomain to be certain it's correct:

```
mydomain = example.com
```

The inet_interface parameter identifies the network interfaces that Postfix will listen on for connections. The original configuration accepts connections only from the localhost; so we updated it to listen on all interfaces, although you may want to specify something more specific if your system is connected to multiple networks:

```
inet_interfaces = all
```

The mydestination parameter lists the zones for which Postfix will accept mail for final delivery. We changed the original configuration to include our domain:

```
mydestination = $myhostname, localhost.$mydomain, localhost,   $mydomain
```

If necessary, you should add other values to the list to identify all of the system's hostnames, similar to what's shown in the last example, `mydestination`, in the set. This is important to prevent Postfix from trying to relay messages to itself, thinking they're destined for a different domain when they're really not:

```
mydestination = $myhostname, localhost.$mydomain, localhost,
$mydomain, mail.$mydomain, www.$mydomain, ftp.$mydomain
```

The `mynetworks` parameter identifies the trusted networks Postfix can relay messages for. This is the first line of defense against spammers abusing your mail server because Postfix will refuse to accept messages for delivery if they're not for our domain and if they're received from a system outside one of the trusted networks:

```
mynetworks = 192.168.56.0/24, 127.0.0.0/8
```

Finally, we set the messages' delivery destination using the `home_mailbox` parameter:

```
home_mailbox = Maildir/
```

Messages are traditionally appended to the user's file in `/var/spool/mail` in what is known as the **mbox** format. The Maildir format stores messages individually in a subdirectory in the user's Maildir directory. Postfix delivers mail to the spool by default. We can convert messages between the two formats, but choosing Maildir now makes things a bit easier when we configure user access over IMAP in a later recipe.

Once Postfix is restarted, we can send a test message to verify that the server's configuration is correct. There are several ways to do this of course. The easiest is to use a command-line e-mail client such as `mailx` to send the message. `mailx` isn't installed by default but is available via `yum`:

```
yum install mailx
```

Invoke `mailx` to send a message. The `-s` argument provides the message's subject and `-r` provides the sender's address (your own e-mail address). Then the recipient's address follows after the arguments:

```
mailx -r abell@example.com -s "Test email" tboronczyk@example.com
```

`mailx` reads the message from `stdin`. A simple "hello world" or "this is a test" should be sufficient for testing purposes; when you're done typing, type a period on its own line or press *Ctrl + D*:

If all goes well, `mailx` sends the mail to Postfix for delivery which in turn delivers it to the user's mail directory in `/home/<username>/Maildir/new`. Check the directory and output the file's contents to make sure the message was delivered:

```
ls /home/tboronczyk/Maildir/new
cat /home/tboronczyk/Maildir/new/146284221.Vfd00I188f5ceM9593.mail
```

```
[tboronczyk@mail ~]$ cd ~/Maildir/new/
[tboronczyk@mail new]$ ls
146284221.Vfd00I188f5ceM9593.mail
[tboronczyk@mail new]$ cat 146284221.Vfd00I188f5ceM9593.mail
Return-Path: <abell@example.com>
X-Original-To: tboronczyk@example.com
Delivered-To: tboronczyk@example.com
Received: by mail.example.com (Postfix, from userid 105)
        id 0C2389A8; Thu, 12 May 2016 18:24:19 -0400 (EDT)
Date: Thu, 12 May 2016 18:24:18 -0400
From: abell@example.com
To: tboronczyk@example.com
Subject: Test email
Message-ID: <57350292.xugTnWfbNXisQ/h/%abell@example.com>
User-Agent: Heirloom mailx 12.5 7/5/10
MIME-Version: 1.0
Content-Type: text/plain; charset=us-ascii
Content-Transfer-Encoding: 7bit

Hello world! This is a test.

[tboronczyk@mail new]$
```

Received messages are delivered to the user's Maildir directory

Alternatively, we can connect directly to Postfix using a Telnet client. Typing raw commands to send an e-mail is slightly more involved than sending one using `mailx`, but is preferred because it offers you more flexibility and greater visibility into how Postfix responds. This can prove invaluable when trying to troubleshoot a problem.

No Telnet client is installed by default, so first you'll need to use `yum` to install `telnet`:

```
yum install telnet
```

Then use `telnet` to connect to the server on port 25, the port reserved for SMTP:

```
telnet mail.example.com 25
```

The `MAIL FROM` command is used to provide the sender's e-mail address and `RCPT TO` to provide the recipient's address. After each is entered, Postfix should respond with a `250 Ok` status:

```
MAIL FROM: tboronczyk@example.com
250 2.1.0 Ok
RCPT TO: abell@example.com
250 2.1.0 Ok
```

`DATA` begins the message's content. Postfix accepts everything we type as the message until we type a single period on its own line:

```
DATA
352 End data with <CR><LF>.<CR><LF>
Subject: Test email
Hello world! This is a test.
.
250 2.0.0 Ok: queued as 705486E22E
```

Then, to close the connection, type `QUIT`:

```
QUIT
221 2.0.0 Bye
Connection closed by foreign host.
```

See also

Refer to the following resources for more information on working with Postfix:

- RHEL 7 System Administrator's Guide: Mail Transport Agents (`https://access.redhat.com/documentation/en-US/Red_Hat_Enterprise_Linux/7/html/System_Administrators_Guide/s1-email-mta.html`)
- RFC-5321: Simple Mail Transport Protocol (`https://tools.ietf.org/html/rfc5321`)
- Mbox vs Maildir: Mail Storage Formats (`http://www.linuxmail.info/mbox-maildir-mail-storage-formats/`)
- Setup a Local Mail Server in CentOS 7 (`http://www.unixmen.com/setup-a-local-mail-server-in-centos-7`)

Adding SASL to Postfix with Dovecot

If a mail server relays a message to another domain (that is, the recipient's address is not in our domain) and the message originates from outside our network, the server is known as an open relay. Spammers are constantly on the lookout for open relays because such permissive behavior is easy to take advantage of, and Postfix tries to protect us by default by only relaying messages that come from our network. Unfortunately, it's not practical to restrict legitimate users from sending e-mail through the server only when they're on our network. This recipe teaches you how to add Simple Authentication and Security Layer (SASL) authentication to Postfix's configuration using Dovecot. Postfix will then happily relay messages for our users authenticated users, regardless of their network location, while still refusing to do so for anyone else.

Getting ready

This recipe requires a CentOS system with Postfix configured as described in the previous recipe. Administrative privileges are also required, either by logging in with the root account or through the use of `sudo`.

How to do it...

Follow these steps to secure Postfix to SASL:

1. Install the `dovecot` package:

   ```
   yum install dovecot
   ```

2. Open the `/etc/dovecot/conf.d/10-master.conf` file with your text editor:

   ```
   vi /etc/dovecot/conf.d/10-master.conf
   ```

3. Locate the `unix_listener` section for `/var/spool/postfix/private/auth`. Uncomment the section by removing the leading # characters:

```
# Postfix smtp-auth
unix_listener /var/spool/postfix/private/auth {
  mode = 0666
}
```

4. Update `mode` to `0660` and add the parameters `user` and `group` to the section with the value `postfix`:

```
# Postfix smtp-auth
unix_listener /var/spool/postfix/private/auth {
  mode = 0660
  user = postfix
  group = postfix
}
```

5. Save your changes and close the file.

6. Open the `/etc/dovecot/conf.d/10-auth.conf` file with your text editor:

```
vi /etc/dovecot/conf.d/10-auth.conf
```

7. Locate the `auth_mechanisms` option and add `login` to its value:

```
auth_mechanisms = plain login
```

8. Save the changes and close the file.

9. Start the Dovecot server and optionally enable it to start automatically whenever the system reboots:

```
systemctl start dovecot.service
systemctl enable dovecot.service
```

10. Open the `/etc/postfix/main.cf` file with your text editor:

```
vi /etc/postfix/main.cf
```

11. At the end of the configuration file, add the following options and values:

```
smtpd_sasl_auth_enable = yes
smtpd_sasl_type = dovecot
smtpd_sasl_path = private/auth
smtpd_sasl_security_options = noanonymous
```

12. Save the changes and close the file.
13. Restart Postfix:

```
systemctl restart postfix.service
```

How it works...

Dovecot is a primarily a mail retrieval server offering users access to their e-mail using the POP and IMAP protocols, and it also allows Postfix to hook into its SASL authentication mechanism. We'll need a retrieval server for users to fetch their e-mail from the system, and Dovecot and Postfix integrate nicely, so choosing Dovecot over other options makes sense.

Dovecot's configuration is organized into various files, each file addressing a particular feature or bit of functionality. For this recipe, we needed to update the master configuration file /etc/dovecot/conf.d/10-master.conf and the authentication configuration file /etc/dovecot/conf.d/10-auth.conf.

In 10-master.conf, we located the unix_listener parameter that defines the SMTP authentication service that will be shared with Postfix. Uncommenting it will create the socket file /var/spool/postfix/private/auth over which Dovecot and Postfix will communicate. We then updated the mode parameter and added the user and group parameters to secure the socket's ownership and access permissions:

```
unix_listener /var/spool/postfix/private/auth {
  mode = 0660
  user = postfix
  group = postfix
}
```

In 10-auth.conf, we located the auth_mechanism parameter and added login to its value. This parameter sets the list of mechanisms Dovecot uses, and login is the mechanism used specifically for SMTP authentication:

```
auth_mechanisms = plain login
```

plain allows users to provide their username and password in plain text. login is also considered a plain text mechanism, but don't worry; you'll learn how to secure that in the next recipe.

The final bit of configuration involves adding the necessary SASL-related parameters to Postfix's `main.cf` file:

```
smtpd_sasl_auth_enable = yes
smtpd_sasl_type = dovecot
smtpd_sasl_path = private/auth
smtpd_sasl_security_options = noanonymous
```

`smtpd_sasl_auth_enable` enables SASL authentication and `smtpd_sasl_type` informs Postfix that it will be using Dovecot's authentication service. The `smtpd_sasl_path` parameter specifies the path to the socket file that is used to communicate with Dovecot relative to Postfix's working directory. `smtpd_sasl_security_options` prohibits anonymous connections and requires everyone to be authenticated.

Postfix expects the username and password to be Base64 encoded so that we need to encode them before we can test our configuration with Telnet. `base64` can be used, but be careful not to introduce a trailing newline when you provide the original values. After invoking `base64`, you can enter your username or password on `stdin` and immediately press *Ctrl + D* twice, but do not press *Enter*. You may want to redirect base64's output to a separate file you can dump later to more readily distinguish the encoded value from the original, since they'll appear to run together in the terminal without the newline:

```
base64 > ./username
tboronczyk
base64 > ./password
P@$$W0rd
cat ./username ./password
```

> Despite the hassle of "newline vigilance", this approach is better than piping the value as follows:
>
>
>
> ```
> echo -n tboronczyk | base64
> ```
>
> The command's invocation will be retained in your shell's history. While this is fine for usernames, sensitive data such as passwords should never be provided on the command line as part of a command for this very reason.

After connecting to the server with `telnet` on port 25, send the `AUTH LOGIN` command to initiate the authentication. Postfix should respond with `VXNlcm5hbWU6` which is the Base64 encoded value for `Username:`:

```
AUTH LOGIN
334 VXNlcm5hbWU6
```

Provide your encoded username and press *Enter*. Postfix then responds with `UGFzc3dvcmQ6`, which, as you probably have already guessed, is the encoded version of `Password:`. After you provide the encoded password, you'll be informed if the authentication was successful:

```
[abell@mail ~]$ telnet mail.example.com 25
Trying 192.168.56.20...
Connected to mail.example.com.
Escape character is '^]'.
220 mail.example.com ESMTP Postfix
AUTH LOGIN
334 VXNlcm5hbWU6
YWJlbGw=
334 UGFzc3dvcmQ6
UEAkJFcwcmQ=
235 2.7.0 Authentication successful
MAIL FROM: abell@example.com
250 2.1.0 Ok
RCPT TO: tboronczyk@example.com
250 2.1.5 Ok
DATA
354 End data with <CR><LF>.<CR><LF>
Subject: This is a test.

Hello world! This is another test email.
.
250 2.0.0 Ok: queued as 21D2F64B
QUIT
221 2.0.0 Bye
Connection closed by foreign host.
[abell@mail ~]$
```

The authentication exchange expects credentials to be Base64 encoded

See also

Refer to the following resources for more information on Postfix, Dovecot, and SASL:

- The Dovecot Homepage (http://www.dovecot.org/)
- RFC 4422: Simple Authentication and Security Layer (https://tools.ietf.org/html/rfc4422)
- Postfix SASL How-To (http://www.postfix.org/SASL_README.html)
- 25, 465, 587... What Port Should I Use? (http://blog.mailgun.com/25-465-587-what-port-should-i-use/)

Configuring Postfix to use TLS

Implementing authentication for mail relaying is an important step in securing your mail server. But as you learned in the previous recipe, the user's name and password are sent in clear text. Base64-encoding encodes binary data using only ASCII characters, which allows for non-ASCII characters in a user's password for example, but encoding isn't encryption. If traffic between the user's mail client and the server happens over an untrusted network, a malicious user can easily capture the credentials and masquerade as the user. This recipe further secures Postfix by configuring Transport Layer Security (TLS) encryption to protect the communication from eavesdropping.

Getting ready

This recipe requires a CentOS system with Postfix configured as described in previous recipes. Administrative privileges are also required, either by logging in with the `root` account or through the use of `sudo`.

How to do it...

Follow these steps to configure Postfix to use TLS:

1. Generate a new key file and security certificate with `openssl`:

```
openssl req -newkey rsa:2048 -nodes \
  -keyout /etc/pki/tls/private/mail.example.key \
  -x509 -days 730 -subj "/CN=mail.example.com" -text \
  -out /etc/pki/tls/certs/mail.example.pem
```

2. Use your text editor to open the /etc/postfix/main.cf file:

```
vi /etc/postfix/main.cf
```

3. At the end of the file, add the following options and values:

```
smtpd_tls_security_level = may
smtpd_tls_cert_file = /etc/pki/tls/certs/mail.example.pem
smtpd_tls_key_file = /etc/pki/tls/private/mail.example.key
```

4. Save your changes and close the file.
5. Restart Postfix:

```
systemctl restart postfix.service
```

How it works...

An encryption key and a security certificate that confirms the ownership of the key are needed for SSL/TLS communications. A self-signed certificate is sufficient for personal use or for use with services on a private network, so this recipe shows us how to generate this ourselves using openssl:

```
openssl req -newkey rsa:2048 -nodes \
  -keyout /etc/pki/tls/private/mail.example.key \
  -x509 -days 730 -subj "/CN=mail.example.com" -text \
  -out /etc/pki/tls/certs/mail.example.pem
```

The req option makes a new certificate request and -newkey asks openssl to generate a new private key and to use that key when it signs the certificate (this is what we mean when we say self-signed certificate). rsa:2048 says the key will be a 2,048-bit RSA key. 2,048-bit keys are generally considered sufficiently resistant against attacks until around the year 2030 based on estimates of the rate at which computing power increases. 3,072-bit keys are considered suitable beyond that. -nodes prevents the key file from being encrypted with a passphrase. It's important not to encrypt the key file with a passphrase because Postfix needs to access the key. If it were encrypted, we'd need to provide the passphrase to decrypt the key every time we start Postfix.

-x509 specifies that the certificate will be an X.509 certificate (the type used by SSL and TLS connections) and -days sets the certificate's expiration date to a number of days in the future, in this case 730 days (3 years). -subj is used to specify the value for the certificate's CN (common name) field, which should be the hostname or the IP address of the system the certificate identifies. Alternatively, you can omit the argument and openssl will prompt you interactively for values for a number of other fields as well. Finally, the -text argument specifies that the certificate should be encoded as text as this is the format Postfix expects:

```
[root@mail ~]# openssl req -newkey rsa:2048 -nodes -keyout /etc/pki/tls/private/
mail.example.key -x509 -days 730 -text -out /etc/pki/tls/certs/mail.example.pem
Generating a 2048 bit RSA private key
...............................+++
.........................................+++
writing new private key to '/etc/pki/tls/private/mail.example.key'
-----
You are about to be asked to enter information that will be incorporated
into your certificate request.
What you are about to enter is what is called a Distinguished Name or a DN.
There are quite a few fields but you can leave some blank
For some fields there will be a default value,
If you enter '.', the field will be left blank.
-----
Country Name (2 letter code) [XX]: US
State or Province Name (full name) []: New York
Locality Name (eg, city) [Default City]: Syracuse
Organization Name (eg, company) [Default Company Ltd]: ACME Corp
Organizational Unit Name (eg, section) []: Information Technology
Common Name (eg, your name or your server's hostname) []: mail.example.com
Email Address []: admin@example.com
[root@mail ~]#
```

More identifying information can be embedded within a certificate

A self-signed certificate basically says, *here's my encryption key. You know it's mine because I said so.* If your system's services are intended for public consumption, you'll most likely need to invest in a certificate signed by a trusted Certificate Authority (CA). Trusted certificates say, *you can trust the key is mine because a mutual friend will vouch for me.* To obtain a trusted certificate, you need a certificate signing request (CSR):

```
openssl req -new -newkey rsa:2048 -nodes \
  -keyout mail.example.key -out mail.example.csr
```

Then, you send your money and the CSR to the CA. After a short wait, you'll receive your certificate.

 By depending on the CA and the specifics of the request, trusted certificates can become quite expensive. And trust isn't what it used to be either. A scandal erupted when it was uncovered that employees at a prominent CA were signing forged certificates, reportedly for internal testing purposes. One can only wonder at the lack of oversight given to the Web of trust. Hopefully, the worst is behind us. Browser vendors are starting to push for stricter guidelines and more auditing. There are also projects such as *Let's Encrypt* which enable secure trusted certificates to be automatically generated for free.

Next, we added the necessary configuration parameters to Postfix's `main.cf` file:

```
smtpd_tls_security_level = may
smtpd_tls_cert_file = /etc/pki/tls/certs/mail.example.pem
smtpd_tls_key_file = /etc/pki/tls/private/mail.example.key
```

`smtp_tls_security_level` configures Postfix's enforcing behavior in relation to the encrypted connection. `may` enables opportunistic TLS—the server advertises that encryption and clients can take advantage of it but its use is not required. You may also set the parameter to `encrypt` to make the use of encryption mandatory.

`smtpd_tls_cert_file` and `smtpd_tls_key_file` specify the paths to the self-signed certificate and the encryption key we generated earlier, respectively. If you're using trusted certificates then you'll also need to provide the `smtpd_tls_CAfile` parameter with a value that identifies the signing CA's public certificate.

If you find that negotiating the secure connection is slow, there are a few tuning parameters you can try. For example, we can explicitly specify the source of entropy that Postfix is using with `tls_random_source`:

```
tls_random_source = dev:/dev/urandom
```

Also, we can cache details of the encrypted session between the server and mail client. The `smtpd_tls_session_cache_database` parameter defines the file in which Postfix will store the cached details and `smtpd_tls_session_cache_timeout` specifies how long the session can be cached. This reduces the overhead of establishing a new session each time the client connects:

```
smtpd_tls_session_cache_database =
  btree:/var/lib/postfix/smtpd_tls_cache
smtpd_tls_session_cache_timeout = 3600s
```

To test the configuration, you can connect using telnet and issue the `STARTTLS` command. Postfix should respond that it's ready to start negotiating the secure connection:

```
STARTTLS
220 Ready to start TLS
```

See also

Refer to the following resources for working with Postfix and TLS:

- Postfix TLS Support (`http://www.postfix.org/TLS_README.html`)
- Wikipedia: Public Key Infrastructure (`https://en.wikipedia.org/wiki/Public_key_infrastructure`)
- OpenSSL Essentials: Working with SSL Certificates, Private Keys, and CSRs (`https://www.digitalocean.com/community/tutorials/openssl-essentials-working-with-ssl-certificates-private-keys-and-csrs`)

Configuring Dovecot for secure POP3 and IMAP access

When you check your e-mail, the e-mail program connects to your mail server to see if there are any new messages in your mail directory. If its configured to used the Post Office Protocol (POP3), it downloads the messages locally and deletes them from the server. If it's configured to use Internet Message Access Protocol (IMAP), the mail remains on the server and you manage it remotely.

Dovecot handles both protocols out of the box. Since we've already installed Dovecot for its SASL functionality, we could just open the standard ports for POP3 and IMAP traffic in the system's firewall and be done. However, the connections would be unencrypted and information would be transmitted across the network in plain text. This recipe teaches you how to secure these connections with SSL.

Getting ready

This recipe requires a CentOS system with Postfix and Dovecot configured as described in previous recipes. Administrative privileges are also required, either by logging in with the root account or through the use of sudo.

How to do it...

Follow these steps to configure access to Dovecot:

1. Open /etc/dovecot/dovecot.conf with your text editor:

   vi /etc/dovecot/dovecot.conf

2. Locate the protocols parameter. Remove the leading # character and set its value to imaps pop3s:

   protocols = imaps pop3s

3. Save the changes and close the file.

4. Open /etc/dovecot/conf.d/10-ssl.conf with your text editor:

   vi /etc/dovecot/conf.d/10-ssl.conf

5. Locate the ssl parameter and set its value to yes:

   ssl = yes

6. Locate the ssl_cert and ssl_key parameters. Update their values with the paths to your certificate and key files (note that both paths are preceded with <):

   ssl_cert = </etc/pki/tls/certs/mail.example.pem
   ssl_key = </etc/pki/tls/private/mail.example.key

7. Save the changes and close the file.

8. Restart Dovecot for the changes to take effect:

```
systemctl restart dovecot.service
```

9. Open port `993` for IMAP over SSL and port `995` for POP3 over SSL in the firewall:

```
firewall-cmd --permanent --add-service=imaps \
  --add-service=pop3s
firewall-cmd --reload
```

How it works...

Dovecot makes it easy to secure the traffic for POP3 and IMAP connections; in fact, configuring it only took a few seconds. We first edited the `protocols` parameter `/etc/dovecot/dovecot.conf` to let Dovecot know that we want these protocols to be secured:

```
protocols = imaps pop3s
```

Then we updated `/etc/dovecot/conf.d/10-ssl.conf` to enable SSL to use the `ssl` parameter and to identify a certificate and encryption key using `ssl_cert` and `ssl_key`. Since Postfix and Dovecot are running on the same system and we already generated a key and certificate for Postfix, we can reference the same files in Dovecot's configuration. Dovecot uses the leading < in front of the paths to specify that it should use the file's content for the parameter's value and not the literal string itself:

```
ssl = yes
ssl_cert = </etc/pki/tls/certs/mail.example.pem
ssl_key = </etc/pki/tls/private/mail.example.key
```

Dovecot will still allow non-SSL access to POP and IMAP (on ports `110` and `143`, respectively) from connections originating from the localhost, but once we restart it for the configuration changes to take effect, all other users will need to use SSL to access their messages.

We can use `mailx` to test the configuration. First, we'll check POP3:

```
mailx -f pop3s://tboronczyk@mail.example.com
```

The -f argument specifies the directory that mailx will read from to retrieve our messages. Given as a URI, the value instructs mailx to read the default directory for our user on the mail.example.com system using POP3 over SSL (pop3s).

The command is the same to check IMAP apart from changing the URI's protocol:

```
mailx -f imaps://tboronczyk@mail.example.com
```

Because we're using a self-signed certificate, mailx will complain that the certificate has not been marked as trusted by the user and prompt us whether we want to continue. Respond with y to this and you'll then be prompted for the user's password. mailx then displays the user's inbox. Exit the program by entering quit at the prompt:

```
[tboronczyk@mail ~]$ mail -f pop3s://tboronczyk@mail.example.com
Error in certificate: Peer's certificate issuer has been marked as not trusted
by the user.
Continue (y/n)? y
Password:
Heirloom Mail version 12.5 7/5/10.  Type ? for help.
"pop3s://tboronczyk@mail.example.com": 1 message 1 new
>N  1 abell                  Thu May 12 22:43   /549   "test"
& quit
[tboronczyk@mail ~]$
```

mailx can be used to test our configuration of POP3 and IMAP over SSL

If mailx complains that it's missing the nss-config-dir variable, you can define it on the command line using -S. The value should be a path to the certificate databases that mailx can use to verify certificate trust:

```
mailx -S nss-config-dir=/etc/pki/nssdb \
    -f pop3s://tboronczyk@mail.example.com
```

When we first configured Postfix, we adjusted its home_mailbox parameter to store messages in separate directories. I acknowledged this was optional at that time but it would make things easier and cleaner when we set up retrieval access. If you didn't set home_mailbox at that time, incoming messages are appended to the user's mail spool file under /var/spool/mail and some additional configuration is necessary for Dovecot to access them. These changes can be made in /etc/dovecot/conf.d/10-mail.conf.

Alternatively, you can convert the spool file to separate messages in a `Maildir` directory at this time. First, install the `mb2md` package:

```
yum install ftp://ftp.pbone.net/mirror/atrpms.net/el7-
x86_64/atrpms/stable/mb2md-3.20-2.at.noarch.rpm
```

Open the `/etc/postfix/main.cf` file and locate the `home_mailbox` parameter. Remove the leading # character from the entry with the value `Maildir/`:

```
home_mailbox = Maildir/
```

Save your changes and then restart Postfix for the update to take effect. Then, for each account, invoke `mb2md` to convert the spool file. The utility needs to be run as the target user, so use `su` to temporarily switch to that user's context:

```
su -l -c "mb2md -m" tboronczyk
```

See also

Refer to the following resources for more information on the different topics discussed in this recipe, including Dovecot, POP3, and IMAP.

- The `mailx` manual page (`man 1 mailx`)
- The Dovecot Homepage (`http://www.dovecot.org/`)
- RFC 3501: Internet Message Access Protocol (`https://tools.ietf.org/html/rfc351`)
- RFC 1939: Post Office Protocol (`https://tools.ietf.org/html/rfc1939`)
- Converting Mbox Mailboxes to Maildir format (`http://batleth.sapienti-sat.org/projects/mb2md/`)

Targeting spam with SpamAssassin

Some estimates propose that over 90% of all e-mail is unsolicited advertisements (spam)! Regardless of whether these estimates are correct or not, there's no denying that spam is a huge problem. Unwanted messages cause extra load on mail servers, consume storage space, and can even be a security risk. Also, while there have been many attempts to legally manage spam, such attempts have largely failed.

This recipe teaches you how to set up SpamAssassin to identify spam messages. SpamAssassin filters incoming messages by checking for various spam hallmarks, such as missing headers and invalid return addresses, and uses heuristics to analyze the message content. Each check contributes to the message's overall spam score, and if this score exceeds the defined threshold then the message is labeled spam.

Getting ready

This recipe requires a CentOS system with Postfix configured as described in the previous recipe. Administrative privileges are also required, either by logging in with the root account or through the use of sudo.

How to do it...

Follow these steps to identify spam using SpamAssassin:

1. Install the spamassassin package:

   ```
   yum install spamassassin
   ```

2. Start SpamAssassin and optionally enable it to start automatically whenever the system reboots:

   ```
   systemctl start spamassassin.service
   systemctl enable spamassassin.service
   ```

3. Create SpamAssassin's Bayesian classifier database:

   ```
   sa-learn --sync
   ```

4. Create an unprivileged system user account that Postfix can use to communicate with SpamAssassin:

   ```
   useradd -r -s /sbin/nologin spamd
   ```

5. Open Postfix's master.cf file for editing:

   ```
   vi /etc/postfix/master.cf
   ```

6. Locate the line that defines the `smtp` service and append the `-o` argument specifying `spamassassin` as a content filter:

```
smtp inet n - n - - smtpd -o content_filter=spamassassin
```

7. At the end of the configuration file, add the definition for the `spamassassin` filter:

```
spamassassin unix - n n - - pipe user=spamd argv=/usr/bin/spamc -e
/usr/sbin/sendmail -oi -f ${sender}   ${recipient}
```

8. Save your changes and close the file.
9. Restart Postfix for the updates to the configuration to take effect:

```
systemctl restart postfix.service
```

How it works...

The initial installation of SpamAssassin is pretty straightforward. We installed the `spamassassin` package and started and enabled the `spamassassin` service which runs the `spamd` daemon. The client program `spamc` is used to communicate with the daemon, and the rest of the recipe's steps focused on configuring Postfix to use `spamc` to score the e-mail message.

We created a new user account named `spamd` for Postfix to use when it invokes `spamc`. The account is intended to be a noninteractive system account, so we provided the `-r` argument. This causes no `home` directory to be created and the account's user ID to be assigned a value less than 100. The `-s` argument gives `/sbin/nologin` as the account's shell to prevent someone from logging in using the account:

```
useradd -r -s /sbin/nologin spamd
```

For Postfix to pass messages to SpamAssassin, we need to define a new `spamassassin` service in its `master.cf` configuration file and ask Postfix to use the service as a content filter. The organization of `master.cf` is much different from the configuration files we've seen before—each line defines a process in the mail delivery pipeline and certain properties about it.

The first active entry in the file is for the `smtp` service and looks like this:

```
smtp inet n - n - - smtpd
```

The first column is the name of the service and the second column specifies how the service will communicate. For example, `inet` signifies that the process uses a TCP/IP socket while `unix` signifies that it uses a local unix-domain socket. The next three columns indicate whether the process is private (only accessible to Postfix), runs without administrative privileges, and is chrooted. Their values can be `y` for yes, `n` for no, or `–` for Postfix's default value. The remaining columns provide a wakeup timer for processes that run at time intervals, the limit for the number of instances that can be running at the same time, and the command that's invoked to provide the service.

To set our `spamassassin` service as a filter, we updated the `smtp` service's command with the `-o` option to set the `content_filter` parameter with the name of our service:

```
smtp inet n – n – – smtpd –o content_filter=spamassassin
```

Then we defined the `spamassassin` service at the bottom of the file:

```
spamassassin unix – n n – – pipe user=spamd argv=/usr/bin/spamc –e
/usr/sbin/sendmail –oi –f ${sender} ${recipient}
```

The `pipe` command is part of Postfix's delivery system with the purpose of piping messages to external processes. The `user` argument specifies the name of the user account the invoked process will run under and `argv` is the command and its arguments that will be run. Our definition references the `spamd` user we created earlier and pipes the message to the `spamc` client.

After the message is reviewed by `spamd`, `spamc` returns the message to stdout by default. To avoid losing the message, we pipe the output to another process to deliver the message. `-e` instructs `spamc` to pipe the output for handling, in this case to a program named `sendmail`.

Sendmail is another mail server that's quite older than Postfix. It dominated the e-mail landscape for decades, and as such many programs attempt to interface with it to send mail. This instance of `sendmail` is actually Postfix's Sendmail compatibility interface which allows other processes to think they're calling Sendmail when in fact they're really working with Postfix. The `-oi` argument for `sendmail` instructs the mail server to treat lines with a single dot as regular input and not interpret it as the end of the message. The `-f` argument sets the from address of the message to the value of `${sender}`, a special variable populated by Postfix with the sender's e-mail address, and the message is sent to `${recipient}`, the recipient's e-mail address.

To test the configuration, we can send an e-mail message with the following subject—it's a known value that SpamAssassin always marks as spam:

XJS*C4JDBQADN1.NSBN3*2IDNEN*GTUBE−STANDARD−ANTI−UBE−TEST− EMAIL*C.34X

```
[abell@mail ~]$ telnet mail.example.com 25
Trying 192.168.56.20...
Connected to mail.example.com.
Escape character is '^]'.
220 mail.example.com ESMTP Postfix
MAIL FROM: abell@example.com
250 2.1.0 Ok
RCPT TO: tboronczyk@example.com
250 2.1.5 Ok
DATA
354 End data with <CR><LF>.<CR><LF>
Subject: XJS*C4JDBQADN1.NSBN3*2IDNEN*GTUBE-STANDARD-ANTI-UBE-TEST-EMAIL*C.34X

This message should be marked as spam by Spamassassin.
.
250 2.0.0 Ok: queued as A3A297BCF2
quit
221 2.0.0 Bye
Connection closed by foreign host.
[abell@mail ~]$
```

An e-mail is sent with a known signature in the subject line to test SpamAssassin

When you check the message in your inbox, you'll notice that SpamAssassin will have prepended [SPAM] to the subject line, allowing you to easily identify unwanted messages. It also adds additional headers to the message that summarizes its findings that lead it to the conclusion that the message is spam:

```
[tboronczyk@mail new]$ cat 1463277851.Vfd00I18a1d4cM247193.mail
Return-Path: <abell@example.com>
X-Original-To: tboronczyk@example.com
Delivered-To: tboronczyk@example.com
Received: by mail.example.com (Postfix, from userid 997)
        id 35CC6819DA; Sat, 14 May 2016 22:04:11 -0400 (EDT)
X-Spam-Checker-Version: SpamAssassin 3.4.0 (2014-02-07) on mail
X-Spam-Flag: YES
X-Spam-Level: ************************************************
X-Spam-Status: Yes, score=1002.7 required=5.0 tests=ALL_TRUSTED,GTUBE,
        MISSING_DATE,MISSING_FROM,MISSING_HEADERS,MISSING_MID autolearn=no
        autolearn_force=no version=3.4.0
X-Spam-Report:
        * -1.0 ALL_TRUSTED Passed through trusted hosts only via SMTP
        *  1.2 MISSING_HEADERS Missing To: header
        * 1000 GTUBE BODY: Generic Test for Unsolicited Bulk Email
        *  0.1 MISSING_MID Missing Message-Id: header
        *  1.0 MISSING_FROM Missing From: header
        *  1.4 MISSING_DATE Missing Date: header
Received: from unknown (unknown [192.168.56.10])
        by mail.example.com (Postfix) with SMTP id C3642819DA
        for <tboronczyk@example.com>; Sat, 14 May 2016 20:45:56 -0400 (EDT)
Subject: [SPAM] XJS*C4JDBQADN1.NSBN3*2IDNEN*GTUBE-STANDARD-ANTI-UBE-TEST-EMAIL*C
.34X
X-Spam-Prev-Subject: XJS*C4JDBQADN1.NSBN3*2IDNEN*GTUBE-STANDARD-ANTI-UBE-TEST-EM
AIL*C.34X
Message-Id: <20160515020411.35CC6819DA@mail.example.com>
Date: Sat, 14 May 2016 22:04:11 -0400 (EDT)
From: abell@example.com

This message should be marked as spam by Spamassassin.
[tboronczyk@mail new]$
```

SpamAssassin updates a message's subject line and adds additional headers to explain why it thinks the message is spam

Keep in mind that the world of spam is constantly in flux; programmers are working hard to build better spam filters, but spammers are working just as hard to find ways to circumvent them. For this reason, it's important to keep SpamAssassin's database up to date. A cron job is added when SpamAssassin is installed that will update its database daily, but you can also run an update manually any time you like by running:

```
sa-update
```

If SpamAssassin is falsely identifying a large amount of legitimate messages as spam or vice versa, you can train it's Bayesian classifier to better identify unwanted messages using `sa-learn`. We can provide a collection of messages we know are spam and identify them as such with the `--spam` argument, and good messages with `--ham` for the program to study:

```
sa-learn --ham /home/tboronczyk/Maildir/cur
sa-learn --spam /home/tboronczyk/Mail/.Spam
```

`sa-learn` keeps track of the messages it's seen. If you have previously indicated that a message is spam and then later use it as ham, the program will remove it from its spam database, and vice versa if you indicate an e-mail is good but later decide it should be used as spam.

See also

Refer to the following resources for more information on working with SpamAssassin:

- The `sa-learn` manual page (`man 1 sa-learn`)
- SpamAssassin Home Page (`http://spamassassin.apache.org/`)
- Rum SpamAssassin with Postfix (`http://howto.gumph.org/content/run-spam assassin-with-postfix/`)
- Stop Spam on your Postfix Server with SpamAssassin (`https://www.linux.com/learn/stop-spam-your-postfix-server-spamassassin`)
- Bayes Theorem Explained Like You're Five (`https://www.youtube.com/watch?v=2Df1sDAyRvQ`)

Routing messages with Procmail

Depending on your preferences, tagging messages as spam may not be enough. Maybe you'll want to set up a rule in your e-mail client that moves any unwanted messages from your inbox to a dedicated spam directory. Or maybe you want such routing to happen automatically on the server. We can configure this using Procmail, a mail filtering and delivery agent.

In this recipe, we'll look at how to configure Procmail to route messages. We'll scan incoming mail, looking for a special header that SpamAssassin adds to messages if it thinks they're spam and then deliver them to a separate directory instead of the inbox.

Getting ready

This recipe requires a CentOS system with Postfix configured as described in the previous recipes. Administrative privileges are also required, either by logging in with the root account or through the use of sudo.

How to do it...

Follow these steps to set up Procmail to route messages:

1. Create the /etc/procmailrc file with the following content:

```
MAILDIR=$HOME/Maildir
DEFAULT=$MAILDIR/new
INCLUDERC=/etc/mail/spamassassin/spamassassin-spamc.rc
:0
* ^X-Spam-Status: Yes
.Spam
```

2. Create each user's spam directory:

```
echo Spam >> /home/tboronczyk/Maildir/subscriptions
mkdir /home/tboronczyk/Maildir/.Spam
```

3. If you created the user's spam directory as root, fix the directory and subscription file's ownership and permissions:

```
chown tboronczyk /home/tboronczyk/Maildir/subscriptions
chmod 0600 /home/tboronczyk/Maildir/subscriptions
chown tboronczyk.tboronczyk /home/tboronczyk/Maildir/.Spam
chmod 0700 /home/tboronczyk/Maildir/.Spam
```

4. Open Postfix's main.cf configuration file with your editor:

```
vi /etc/postfix/main.cf
```

5. Locate the example mailbox_command parameters. Uncomment the second example and correct its path to the procmail executable:

```
mailbox_command = /bin/procmail -a "$EXTENSION"
```

6. Save the changes and close the file.
7. Restart Postfix for the updated configuration to take effect:

```
systemctl restart postfix.service
```

How it works...

Like Postfix, Procmail is installed by default on CentOS systems. However, we need to create its configuration file for it to be useful to us. The main configuration file is `/etc/procmailrc` and we start it by defining the `MAILDIR`, `DEFAULT`, and `INCLUDERC` variables.

```
MAILDIR=$HOME/Maildir
DEFAULT=$MAILDIR/new
INCLUDERC=/etc/mail/spamassassin/spamassassin-spamc.rc
```

`MAILDIR` provides the location of the user's mail directory. `procmailrc` is a global configuration file and we use `$HOME` to denote the user's home directory in which `Maildir` resides. `DEFAULT` provides the default location for incoming mail, which is the mail directory's `new` directory.

`INCLUDERC` gives the name of other files that should be included when Procmail processes the configuration file. In this case, SpamAssassin installs a configuration file to integrate with Procmail which we reference.

The second part of the configuration appears as a cryptic incantation—the definition of a matching rule. In Procmail parlance, they're called recipes:

```
:0
* ^X-Spam-Status: Yes
.Spam
```

More than one rule can be given in the configuration file, in which case they are processed in the order in which they appear, top to bottom.

All rules begin with `:0` and contain conditions followed by an action. Here, the condition starts with `*` to specify a regular expression pattern that Procmail will search the message and its headers for. The action line then lists the directory that matching messages will be delivered to. If it's given as a relative path, the directory considered will be relative to `$MAILDIR`. Thus, the rule asks Procmail to route any messages flagged with the `X-Spam-Status` header by SpamAssassin to the user's `Maildir/.Spam` directory.

The original Maildir specification only allows the `new`, `cur`, and `tmp` directories, but others have augmented it to support additional directories. The user can either create their spam directory through their e-mail client over IMAP, in which case all of the details are worked out by Dovecot. Alternatively, we can create it for them in the filesystem. When we create a directory manually, the `subscriptions` file must list the additional directories, one entry per line, for them to be visible in the user's mail client. The directories themselves are then named with a leading dot:

```
echo Spam >> /home/tboronczyk/Maildir/subscriptions
mkdir /home/tboronczyk/Maildir/.Spam
```

Procmail also allows for per-user actions as well. For example, if only one user wants to have flagged messages moved to their spam folder, the matching rule can be moved from the global configuration under `/etc` to a file named `.procmailrc` in their `home` directory. It's still recommended that you keep the variable definitions in the global configuration so that they'll be available to all users, as Procmail executes the global file first and then the user's local `.procmailrc` if it's available.

Various flags can be given after `:0` that modify how Procmail behaves or how the rule is interpreted. For example, Procmail only search the message's headers by default. To search the message's body, we need to provide the `B` flag. The following rule is an example that searches the message's body for the text "Hello World" and routes the matching messages to `/dev/null`:

```
:0 B
* Hello World
/dev/null
```

Some flags you may find useful are:

- `H`: Search the message's headers
- `B`: Search the message's body
- `D`: Match the regular expression in a case-sensitive manner
- `e`: Only execute the rule if the rule immediately preceding it was unsuccessful
- `c`: Create a copy of the message
- `h`: Only send the message's header to a piped program
- `b`: Only send the message's body to a piped program

If the action begins with | then the value is interpreted as a command and the message is piped to it. Here's an example that sends a copy of any messages received from the human resources department to the printer by piping it through `lpr`:

```
:0 c
* ^From: hr-dept@example.com
| lpr
```

If the action begins with ! then the value is seen as an e-mail and the message is forwarded. This example routes an e-mail from a known recipient to a personal e-mail account instead:

```
:0
* ^From: secret-admirer@example.com
! tboronczyk@another-example.com
```

See also

Refer to the following resources for more information on Procmail:

- The `procmail` manual page (`man 1 procmail`)
- The `procmailrc` file manual page (`man 5 procmailrc`)
- Timo's Promail tips and recipes (`http://www.netikka.net/tsneti/info/proctips.php`)

10
Managing Web Servers

This chapter contains the following recipes:

- Installing Apache HTTP Server and PHP
- Configuring name-based virtual hosting
- Configuring Apache to serve pages over HTTPS
- Enabling overrides and performing URL rewriting
- Installing NGINX as a load balancer

Introduction

This chapter contains recipes for working with the Apache HTTP Server to serve websites. You'll first learn how to install the server as well as PHP, a very common server-side scripting engine used to generate dynamic web content. Then you'll see how to serve multiple sites with the same server instance using name-based virtual hosting, encrypt the connection and serve content over HTTPS, and how to rewrite incoming URLs on the fly. We'll finish with looking at NGINX and its use as a reverse proxy to decrease load on the server while at the same time speeding up access to our sites for the user.

Installing Apache HTTP Server and PHP

You may have heard the acronym LAMP which stands for Linux, Apache, MySQL, and PHP. It refers to the popular pairing of technologies for providing websites and web applications. This recipe teaches you how to install the Apache HTTP Server (Apache for short) and configure it to work with PHP to serve dynamic web content.

First released over twenty years ago, Apache was one of the first web servers and it continues to be one of the most popular. Its task in the LAMP stack is to interact with the user by responding to their requests for web resources. Perhaps one of its selling points is its design that allows its functionality to be expanded with modules. Many modules exist, from mod_ssl, which adds HTTPS support to mod_rewrite, which allows you to modify the request URL on the fly.

PHP is a scripting language for creating dynamic web content. It works behind the scenes and the output of a script is usually served by Apache to satisfy a request. PHP was commonly installed as a module (mod_php) that embedded the language's interpreter into Apache's processing, but nowadays, running PHP as a standalone process is preferred. This is the approach we'll take in this recipe.

Getting ready

This recipe requires a CentOS system with a working network connection. It assumes that the system is configured with the IP address 192.168.56.100. Administrative privileges are also required, either by logging in with the root account or through the use of sudo.

Note that the official CentOS repositories install PHP 5.4. The Remi repositories offer 5.5, 5.6, and 7.0 if you want to install a newer release. To install one of the 5.x versions, open the /etc/yum.repos.d/remi.repo file, locate the enabled option in the [remi-php55] or [remi-php56] section and set its value to 1. For 7.0, update the enabled option found in /etc/yum.repos.d/remi-php70.repo.

 What happened to PHP 6? *It's a long story....* The team of volunteers developing PHP was working on version 6, but the initiative faced many hurdles and was eventually shelved. To prevent confusion between the latest release and any blog postings that were written about PHP 6, it was decided that its version number would be bumped to 7. In short, PHP 6 did exist but never achieved a proper release status and most of the cool features planned for 6 made it into PHP 5.3, 5.4, and 7.0.

How to do it...

Follow these steps to install Apache HTTP Server and PHP:

1. Install the httpd and php-fpm packages:

```
yum install httpd php-fpm
```

2. Open Apache's configuration file with your text editor:

```
vi /etc/httpd/conf/httpd.conf
```

3. Locate the ServerName option. Remove # appearing at the start of the line to uncomment it and then change the option's value to reflect your server's hostname or IP address:

```
ServerName 192.168.56.100:80
```

4. Find the DirectoryIndex option and add index.php to the list:

```
<IfModule dir_module>
    DirectoryIndex index.html index.php
</IfModule>
```

5. At the end of the file, add the following configuration:

```
<IfModule proxy_fcgi_module>
    ProxyPassMatch ^/(.*\.php)$
    fcgi://127.0.0.1:9000/var/www/html/$1
</IfModule>
```

6. Save your changes to the configuration and close the file.

7. Verify that mod_proxy (listed as proxy_module) and mod_proxy_fcgi (proxy_fcgi_module) extension modules are enabled:

```
httpd -M | grep proxy
```

8. Both modules should appear in the output.

9. Start Apache and PHP's FPM service and enable them to start automatically when your system reboots:

```
systemctl start httpd.service php-fpm.service
systemctl enable httpd.service php-fpm.service
```

10. Open port 80 in the system's firewall to allow HTTP requests through:

```
firewall-cmd --zone=public --permanent --add-service=http
firewall-cmd --reload
```

How it works...

There are several ways to integrate PHP with Apache's HTTP server to generate dynamic web content. Historically, using Apache's mod_php module was the way to go, but now the preferred approach is to run PHP as a separate process, which the web server communicates with using the FastCGI protocol. So, we installed the httpd package for the Apache HTTP Server and the php-fpm package for the PHP interpreter and its process manager:

```
yum install httpd php-fpm
```

The PHP FastCGI Process Manager (FPM) is included in the core PHP distributions as of version 5.3. Separating PHP from Apache encourages a more scalable architecture, and using a persistent PHP process reduces CPU overhead because a new interpreter doesn't have to be spawned for each request.

Apache's main configuration file is /etc/httpd/conf/httpd.conf, in which we updated the ServerName option to reflect our server's hostname or IP address. While this step isn't strictly necessary, if we don't set the option then the server will write warning messages to its log files. Besides, it's useful for the server to be able to identify itself:

```
ServerName 192.168.56.100:80
```

Next, we updated for the DirectoryIndex option by adding index.php to its list of values. When the user requests a resource that resolves to a directory, the server will look in that directory for a file that matches one of the names in the DirectoryIndex list. If found, Apache will return that file to satisfy the request. This behavior is what allows visitors to access a website's home page with a URL such as www.example.com rather than www.example.com/index.html:

```
DirectoryIndex index.html index.php
```

The order in which files are listed is significant. For example, if both index.html and index.php exist in the directory then index.html will be returned because it's listed before index.php in the option's list.

Then we navigated to the end of the file to add the following proxy configuration. If the regular expression of ProxyPassMatch matches the incoming request then the server retrieves the given URL and returns that content instead:

```
<IfModule proxy_fcgi_module>
    ProxyPassMatch ^/(.*\.php)$ fcgi://127.0.0.1:9000/var/www/html/$1
</IfModule>
```

Regular expressions are written using a special notation that describes how to match text. Most characters are matched literally, but some have special meaning:

- `.`: This matches any character. The pattern `bu.` matches against the text `bud`, `bug`, `bun`, `bus`, and so on.

- `+`: This matches the preceding element one or more times. The pattern `fe+t` matches `fet`, `feet`, and `feeet` and so on but not `ft`.

- `*`: This optionally matches the preceding element any number of times. The pattern `fe*t` matches `ft`, `fet`, `feet`, `feeet`, and so on.

- `?`: This optionally matches the preceding element once. The pattern `colou?r` matches `color` and `colour`.

- `^`: This anchors the match to the beginning of the line. The pattern `^abc` only matches `abc` if `abc` appears at the beginning of the text (`^` has special significance when used in `[ ]`).

- `$`: This anchors the match to the end of the line. The pattern `xyz$` only matches `xyz` if `xyz` appears at the end of the line.

- `[ ]`: This matches any of the characters given within the brackets. The pattern `co[lr]d` matches `cold` and `cord`. When the first character in `[ ]` is `^` then the list is negated; `co[^lr]d` matches `coed` but not `cold` or `cord`.

- `( )`: This groups elements and captures matches. The pattern `jump(ed)?` matches `jump` and `jumped`.

If you want any of these special characters to be matched literally then you should escape them with a leading backslash, for example `foo\.html` will match `foo.html` instead of `fooahtml`, `foobhtml`, and so on.

Special numeric variables like `$1` and `$2` contain the value of any captured matches. The order in which they are populated are the order in which the parentheses capture a match, thus `(foo)\.(html)` sets `$1` to `foo` and `$2` to `html`.

With this understanding, you should now be able to decipher that the regular expression `^/(.*\.php)$` captures the path and filename of the requested resource that end with the extension `.php`. The `$1` variable represents the captured path, so a request for `/about/staff.php` will be proxied as `fcgi://127.0.0.1:9000/var/www/html/about/staff.php` where PHP's Fast-CGI listener is listening to the local interface on port `9000`.

Apache's functionality is often extended through modules, and as a safeguard it's a good practice to wrap module-specific configuration options in an `IfModule` block. The opening of such blocks contain the name of the module and appear in angle brackets < >. The block's closing appears as </IfModule> just like closing an HTML element.

The directory out of which the server serves files from is set by the option `DocumentRoot`. The default value is `/var/www/html`, so any files we place there or in a subdirectory within it will be accessible. As an example to illustrate this, the distribution includes a sample `index.html` file, which we can use to verify that the server is running correctly; copy the `/usr/share/httpd/noindex/index.html` file to `/var/www/html`:

```
cp /usr/share/httpd/noindex/index.html /var/www/html
```

Then, open your browser and navigate to the domain or IP address of the system. You should see the welcome page:

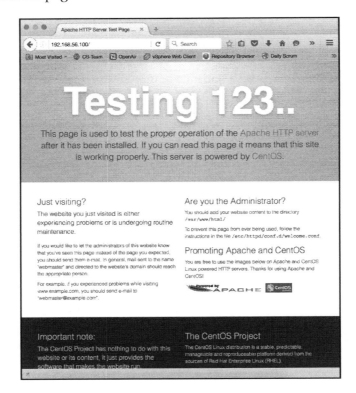

You can copy Apache's default index page to the web directory to test whether the server is up and running

For PHP, you need to place a PHP file where it can be read by the Fast-CGI service. The proxy URL is `fcgi://127.0.0.1:9000/var/www/html/$1`, so that we can place our PHP files in `/var/www/html` as well.

Create the `info.php` file with the following content:

```
<?php
phpinfo();
```

Now save the file and then navigate to the page in your browser. You should see the output of PHP's `phpinfo()` function providing detailed information on how PHP is configured and which of its modules are available:

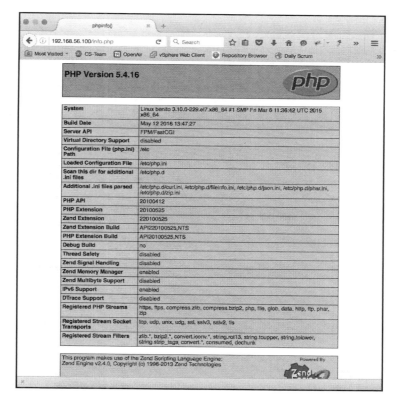

PHP reports information about its environment and the request

For security purposes, it's recommended that you delete the welcome `index.html` file if you copied it over and the `info.php` script after you verify everything works. The information they present can give malicious users more information about the set up of your web server than you'd like them to have.

See also

Refer to the following resources for more information on working with Apache and PHP:

- Apache HTTP Server Project (`http://httpd.apache.org/`)
- The PHP home page (`http://php.net/`)
- Apache `mod_proxy_fcgi` documentation (`http://httpd.apache.org/docs/current/mod/mod_proxy_fcgi.html`)
- Httpd Wiki: PHP-FPM (`http://wiki.apache.org/httpd/PHP-FPM`)
- RFC-2616: HTTP/1.1 (`http://www.rfc-base.org/txt/rfc-2616.txt`)

Configuring name-based virtual hosting

As you may recall from our discussions surrounding DNS in `Chapter 8`, *Managing Domains and DNS* a user's browser needs to translate a website's hostname to its IP address via DNS lookups before it can connect and retrieve the desired web content. You may also recall that this doesn't have to be a one-to-one mapping-more than one site can resolve to the same IP address. Apache is flexible enough so that the same server can serve more than one site by a configuration known as name-based virtual hosting.

This recipe teaches you how to set up name-based virtual hosting. Each site has it's own configuration (often kept in its own configuration file for better organization). Based on the site name that appears in the request, Apache then selects from the available configurations to properly serve the desired site.

Getting ready

This recipe requires a CentOS system with a working network connection and running Apache as described in the previous recipe. Because we'll be connecting to the server via a domain name instead of an IP address, you'll need to make sure the name resolves to the correct address by updating your DNS records or adding entries to /etc/hosts first. Administrative privileges are also required, either by logging in with the root account or through the use of sudo.

How to do it...

Follow these steps to set up name-based virtual hosting:

1. Open Apache's configuration file with your text editor:

   ```
   vi /etc/httpd/conf/httpd.conf
   ```

2. At the bottom of the file, add the following Include option:

   ```
   Include sites/*.conf
   ```

3. Save the updated configuration and close the file.
4. Create the sites directory referenced in the configuration:

   ```
   mkdir /etc/httpd/sites
   ```

5. Create a virtual host configuration file within the new sites directory for your first site:

   ```
   vi /etc/httpd/sites/www.example.conf
   ```

6. Add the following code to the site's configuration file:

   ```
   <VirtualHost *:80>
     ServerName www.example.com
     DocumentRoot "/var/www/example.com/www/html"
     <IfModule proxy_fcgi_module>
       ProxyPassMatch ^/(.*\.php)$
       fcgi://127.0.0.1:9000/var/www/example.com/www/html/$1
     </IfModule>
   </VirtualHost>
   ```

7. Save your changes and close the file.

8. Create the site's document root referenced in the configuration options:

```
mkdir -p /var/www/example.com/www/html
```

9. Repeat steps 4-8 for each additional site you will be hosting, using the host or domain name to create a unique directory path for each site.

10. Restart the HTTP server for the configuration changes to take effect:

```
systemctl restart httpd.service
```

How it works...

Configuring Apache to serve multiple domains is a matter of creating a `VirtualHost` definition for each site. This recipe organizes the definitions in their own file under the directory `/etc/httpd/sites` and then references them in the main `httpd.conf` configuration file using an `Include` directive:

```
Include sites/*.conf
```

How you organize your sites is up to you. This recipe uses a scheme where each site is served from a path based on the domain name followed by the subdomain rooted in `/var/www`. The path `/var/www/example.com/www/html` contains the files for the site at `www.example.com`. Files for the site at `web.example.com` would be placed in `/var/www/example.com/web/html`. The `html` directory is simply the web-accessible root for the site. By including it instead of serving files out of `example.com/www` directly, we can place any supporting files outside the root which aren't mean to be accessed directly (for example, a script with configuration options for a PHP website), but still keep them organized with the rest of the site's files.

 Naming the publicly accessible directory root `html` is a convention, but its one that I find outdated since more than just HTML files are often served. I often name my own root directories `public` or `public_files` and update their references in the configuration file accordingly.

Each definition for a virtual host is contained within a `VirtualHost` block. The opening provides the IP address of the interface on which the server is listening followed by the port number. `*` indicates that the definition applies to all of the system's interfaces and `80` is the default port for HTTP traffic:

```
<VirtualHost *:80>
```

Options that don't appear explicitly in the definition are assumed to have the same settings as found in the main configuration, so at a minimum, the `ServerName` and `DocumentRoot` options need to be defined to make the definition unique. If you're using PHP, you'll want to provide the `ProxyPassMatch` option as well so that the requests are mapped to the correct PHP files:

```
<VirtualHost *:80>
  ServerName www.example.com
  DocumentRoot "/var/www/example.com/www/html"
  <IfModule proxy_fcgi_module>
    ProxyPassMatch ^/(.*\.php)$ fcgi://127.0.0.1:9000/var/www/
    example.com/www/html/$1
  </IfModule>
</VirtualHost>
```

The order in which the virtual host definitions are loaded is somewhat important; the first one loaded acts as the default and will handle any requests that do not match any of the virtual hosts definitions. Prefixing the configuration files numerically, for example `10-www.example.conf`, can help you control the loading order.

Each request is logged to `/var/log/httpd/access_log` and any errors are logged to `error_log`. Of course, this is fine if you're only serving one site. But when serving multiple sites, you may find it beneficial to route log entries to different files for different sites. The `CustomLog` option names a file where the access and general logging messages are written to and the format of the entries. `ErrorLog` specifies the file where the error messages are written. Both of these options can appear in a virtual host's configuration:

```
<VirtualHost *:80>
  ServerName www.example.com
  DocumentRoot "/var/www/example.com/www/html"
  CustomLog "/var/log/httpd/example.com/www/access_log" "%h %u
%t "%r" %>s %b"
  ErrorLog  "/var/log/httpd/example.com/www/error_log"
  <IfModule proxy_fcgi_module>
    ProxyPassMatch ^/(.*\.php)$ fcgi://127.0.0.1:9000/var/www/
    example.com/www/html/$1
  </IfModule>
</VirtualHost>
```

The second argument to `CustomLog` can be the format string itself or an alias that represents the format string. Format strings simply define what details are contained in the logged messages.

There's a slew of format specifiers available which are all documented in the Apache HTTPd Server's documentation. Here's a list of some of the more common ones you may use, while you can find a complete list online at `http://httpd.apache.org/docs/current /mod/mod_log_config.html#formats`):

- `%b`: This is the size of the response (in bytes) served back to the client
- `%D`: This is the time taken to process the request in milliseconds (`%T` represents the time taken in seconds)
- `%h`: This is the IP or hostname of the requesting system
- `%H`: This is the protocol used to make the request
- `%m`: This is the method used to make the request
- `%q`: This is the query string portion of the requested URI
- `%r`: This is the first line of the request
- `%>s`: This is the request's final status code (`%s` represents the initial status for requests that are redirected)
- `%t`: This is the time when the request was received
- `%u`: This is the username for authenticated requests when the request was received
- `%v`: This is the name of the server (`ServerName`) handling the request

The `LogFormat` option names a format string with an alias. For example, the `httpd.conf` file uses `LogFormat` to define strings named as `common` and `combined`, which can be used elsewhere. It's a good idea to define your own alias for your virtual host logging and use the alias in the individual configuration files rather than having cryptic format strings scattered about. In `httpd.conf`, simply add your custom `LogFormat` entry in the same area as the `common` and `combined` entries:

```
LogFormat "%v %h %u %t "%r" %>s %b" vhostcommon
```

Then, you can reference the alias in your sites' configuration files:

```
CustomLog "/var/www/example.com/www/logs/access_log" vhostcommon
```

After making the changes, restart Apache for the configuration to take effect.

Whatever their destination, make sure the ownership/permissions your security context allow Apache runs to write to the log file. If the logs reside under /var/log/httpd then creating the necessary subdirectories should be sufficient. The server will create the log files itself when it starts:

mkidr -p /var/log/httpd/example.com/www

However, if you wish to keep the logs in another directory, perhaps such as /var/www/example.com/www/logs, the server may be blocked from writing to them. SELinux is enabled regardless of the filesystem permissions appearing sane. To fix the situation, first verify the security context with ls -Z:

```
ls -Z /var/www/example.com/www | grep logs
drwxr-xr-x. apache apache unconfined_u:object_r:httpd_sys_content_
t:s0 logs
```

In this case, the logs directory is owned by the apache user, which Apache runs under, and the permissions on the directory should allow the server to create the log files. However, we can also see that the directory has inherited the label that identifies it as web content as indicated by httpd_sys_content_t. To fix the problem, we need to relabel the directory for logging purposes using chcon:

chcon -Rv --type=httpd_log_t /var/www/example.com/www/logs

See also

Refer to the following resources for more information on working with virtual hosting:

- Apache Virtual Host documentation (http://httpd.apache.org/docs/current/vhosts/)
- Apache mod_log_config documentation (http://httpd.apache.org/docs/current/mod/mod_log_config.html)
- VirtualHost examples (http://httpd.apache.org/docs/current/vhosts/examples.html)
- CentOS Wiki: SELinux HowTo (https://wiki.centos.org/HowTos/SELinux)

Configuring Apache to serve pages over HTTPS

HTTP traffic is sent in plain text across the network. In an untrusted environment, a malicious user can monitor and capture the traffic to spy on what sites you're visiting and what content you're reading. While such snooping isn't interesting if the victim is just reading the daily news or watching cat videos on YouTube (), the user's credit card number, shipping address, and other details could be snagged if an e-commerce transaction were to take place unencrypted. To support encrypted traffic, Apache supports HTTPS. This recipe will teach you how to configure HTTPS support and protect your users' traffic from prying eyes no matter how benign the content is.

Getting ready

This recipe requires a CentOS system with a working network connection. It assumes that the system is configured with the IP address 192.168.56.100 and is running Apache as described in the previous recipes. Administrative privileges are also required, either by logging in with the root account or through the use of sudo.

How to do it...

Follow these steps to serve pages over HTTPS:

1. Generate a new key file and security certificate using openssl:

```
openssl req -newkey rsa:2048 -nodes \
  -keyout /etc/pki/tls/private/www.example.key \
  -x509 -days 730 -subj "/CN=www.example.com" -text \
  -out /etc/pki/tls/certs/www.example.pem
```

2. Install the server's SSL module:

```
yum install mod_ssl
```

3. Open the `/etc/httpd/conf.d/ssl.conf` file with your text editor:

   ```
   vi /etc/httpd/conf.d/ssl.conf
   ```

4. Locate the `SSLCertificateFile` option and update its value to point to the self-signed certificate file:

   ```
   SSLCertificateFile /etc/pki/tls/certs/www.example.pem
   ```

5. Locate the `SSLCertificateKeyFile` option and update it to point to the encryption key:

   ```
   SSLCertificateKeyFile /etc/pki/tls/private/www.example.key
   ```

6. Save your changes and close the file.

7. Restart the server for the updated configuration to take effect:

   ```
   systemctl restart httpd
   ```

8. Open port 443 in the firewall to allow HTTPS traffic:

   ```
   firewall-cmd --zone=public --permanent --add-service=https
   firewall-cmd --reload
   ```

How it works...

The Apache HTTP Server comes with a default SSL/TLS configuration contained within a catch-all virtual host definition in `/etc/httpd/conf.d/ssl.conf`. With most of the configuration already done for us, all that's left is to install the SSL module, generate a new key and certificate, and update the configuration to point to our files.

First, we generated a new encryption key and signing certificate. If you've already read the *Configuring Postfix to use TLS* recipe in Chapter 9, *Managing E-mails*, then you already know that the key is needed for secured communication and the certificate confirms the ownership of the key:

```
openssl req -newkey rsa:2048 -nodes \
  -keyout /etc/pki/tls/private/www.example.key \
  -x509 -days 730 -subj "/CN=www.example.com" -text \
  -out /etc/pki/tls/certs/www.example.pem
```

The recipe generates a self-signed certificate which is sufficient for personal use and intranet sites. The `req` option creates a new certificate and `-newkey` generates a new private key. The key is a 2048-bit RSA key and itself is not encrypted (`-nodes`), so we don't need to provide a passphrase to decrypt the key every time we start the web server. The certificate is an X.509 certificate (`-x509`) and is valid for 3 years (`-days 730`). The certificate's `CN` field must match the domain name of the site it will be used for.

In the configuration file, the `SSLCertificateFile` option specifies the file that contains the certificate file and the key is identified using `SSLCertificateKeyFile`:

```
SSLCertificateFile /etc/pki/tls/certs/www.example.pem
SSLCertificateKeyFile /etc/pki/tls/private/www.example.key
```

The server determines which virtual host configuration to use to handle a request by looking at the site's name in the incoming request. However, the original HTTPS implementation encrypted the request in its entirety between the web client and server, including the site's hostname, which raised a chicken and egg problem. The server needed to know which certificate to serve and couldn't know it without reading the request, and the client wanted a certificate that matched the site's domain before it would even send the request. It was impossible to use TLS with name-based virtual hosting and any encrypted site required its own dedicated IP address.

RFC-3546 (Transport Layer Security Extensions) modified the protocol so that the hostname could be sent unencrypted. This allowed the server to select the correct certificate to satisfy the client and opened the door for using TLS with virtual hosting. It took approximately ten years for the major browsers to support the change but we're pretty much there now Internet Explorer as of version 7, Mozilla Firefox as of version 2, and Google Chrome as of version 6 support what is known as Server Name Indication (SNI).

To server your virtual hosts over HTTPS, each site will need its own certificate and key. Then, add the `SSLEngine`, `SSLCertificateFile`, and `SSLCertificateKeyFile` options to the host's configuration. The port number also needs to be changed in the configuration to `443`, the default port for HTTPS traffic:

```
<VirtualHost *:443>
  ServerName www.example.com
  DocumentRoot "/var/www/example.com/www/html"
  CustomLog "/var/log/httpd/example.com/www/access_log" common
  ErrorLog  "/var/log/httpd/example.com/www/error_log"
  SSLEngine on
  SSLCertificateFile /etc/pki/tls/certs/www.example.pem
  SSLCertificateKeyFile /etc/pki/tls/private/www.example.key
  <IfModule proxy_fcgi_module>
    ProxyPassMatch ^/(.*\.php)$ fcgi://127.0.0.1:9000/var/www/
```

```
        example.com/www/html/$1
      </IfModule>
    </VirtualHost>
```

Although self-signed certificates are adequate for personal use and private network/intranet sites, most likely you'll want to use a trusted certificate for sites accessible on a larger scale. However, depending on the Certificate Authority and the specifics of your request, purchasing a trusted certificate can be expensive. If you need only a basic trusted certificate, then you might want to investigate whether Let's Encrypt will meet your needs. Let's Encrypt is a project offering an automated, self-service model for generating trusted certificates for free.

To use *Let's Encrypt*, you'll need to install the `certbot` package available in the EPEL repository (refer to the *Registering the EPEL and Remi repositories* recipe in `Chapter 4`, *Software Installation Management* if you haven't already enabled the repository). Then run the `certbot certonly` command and follow the prompts to request your certificate. Full instructions can be found online in the Let's Encrypt/Certbot User Guide at `http://letsencrypt.readthedocs.io/en/latest/using.html`.

There are a few caveats to Let's Encrypt. First, the certificates are only valid for three months; you'll need to request a new certificate every 90 days. It also won't generate certificates for IP addresses. Also, it rate limits requests which, although necessary to help prevent abuse, causes issues for those using a dynamic DNS service such as DynDNS or NoIP to make their sites accessible. For Let's Encrypt to be a viable option for you, you'll need a proper domain and access to the web system to automate the renewal. If you're running a home server or using a shared hosting provider, then Let's Encrypt is probably not for you.

See also

Refer to the following resources for working with HTTPS:

- SSL/TLS Strong Encryption: How-To (`http://httpd.apache.org/docs/2.4/ssl/ssl_howto.html`)
- How to create an SSL Certificate for Apache on CentOS 7 (`http://www.digitalocean.com/community/tutorials/how-to-create-an-ssl-certificate-on-apache-for-centos-7`)
- How to secure Apache with Let's Encrypt on CentOS 7 (`https://www.digitalocean.com/community/tutorials/how-to-secure-apache-with-let-s-encrypt-on-centos-7`)

Enabling overrides and performing URL rewriting

This recipe teaches you how to use `mod_rewrite`. I mentioned `mod_rewrite` earlier; it is a module for Apache that allows us to modify the URL and resolve it to different resources. There are many reasons one would want to do this. For example, perhaps you moved some files and their URL changed, but you don't want any links that exist elsewhere still pointing to the old destinations to be broken. You can write a rewrite rule that matches the old locations and updates the URL on the fly to successfully satisfy the request. Another example is SEO; you may have long, unfriendly canonical URLs for a resource but want something shorter and more memorable. The friendly URLs can be mapped to the canonical URL behind the scenes.

Getting ready

This recipe requires a CentOS system with a working network connection. It assumes that the system is configured with the IP address `192.168.56.100` and is running Apache as described in the previous recipes. Administrative privileges are also required, either by logging in with the `root` account or through the use of `sudo`.

How to do it...

Follow these steps to perform URL rewriting:

1. Open the `/etc/httpd/conf/httpd.conf` file with your text editor:

   vi /etc/httpd/conf/httpd.conf

2. Locate the `Directory` section that defines various options for your document root. Find its `AllowOverrides` option and update the value from `None` to `All`:

   ```
   <Directory "/var/www/html">
   ...
       AllowOverrides All
   ...
   </Directory>
   ```

3. Save your changes and close the file.

4. Restart Apache for the configuration update to take effect:

```
systemctl restart httpd
```

5. Verify that the mod_rewrite module (identified as rewrite_module) is available:

```
httpd -M | grep rewrite
```

6. Create a file named .htaccess in your document root:

```
vi /var/www/html/.htaccess
```

7. In the .htaccess file, add RewriteEngine to turn on the URL rewriting engine:

```
RewriteEngine on
```

8. Add Rewrite rules that describe the desired redirects. For example, the following rule redirects all requests without a file extension to a PHP file of the given name:

```
RewriteRule ^/?([A-Z]+)$ $1.php [NC,L]
```

9. Save and close the file.

How it works...

The .htaccess files are supplemental configuration files that reside in the sites' directory structure. When configured, Apache searches for an .htaccess file and applies the option settings in it while satisfying a request. Of course, searching and loading configuration values for each request does have a slight performance impact, but its trade-off increases flexibility. For example, the server doesn't need to be restarted for configuration changes in an .htaccess file to take effect. In a shared-hosting environment, savvy clients can tweak the server's behavior for their own sites without asking a server administrator or requiring access to the main configuration files in /etc/httpd (which may contain sensitive configuration values). Even web applications that rely on specific server features might include an .htaccess file with the necessary configuration to make its deployment easier.

Apache doesn't allow the use of the .htaccess files to override the server's configuration by default. To enable it, we need to update the AllowOverrides option in the appropriate context and then restart the server. This recipe made the change in the section that applies to the web root directory:

```
<Directory "/var/www/html">
. . .
    AllowOverrides All
. . .
</Directory>
```

 If you're using virtual hosting, be sure to put the AllowOverrides option in your site's configuration file.

A value of None causes the server to ignore any .htaccess files. Apart from that, not all options are allowed in an .httaccess file. The most common ones found in the files pertain to rewriting requests or directory-specific access. Those that can appear are grouped under different categories and we can specify the category of options that will be allowed to be overridden. The possible group names are as follows:

- AuthConfig: This allows overriding the authorization options (AuthUserFile, AuthDBMUserFile, and so on)
- FileInfo: This allows overriding request-related options (ErrorDocument, Redirect, RewriteRule, and so on)
- Indexes: These allow index-related options to be overridden (DirectoryIndex, IndexOptions, and so on)
- Limit: This allows the access options to be overridden (Allow, Deny, and Order)
- All: This allows overriding all of the option groups

Since `AllowOverrides` applies to the directory level, it's possible to allow or deny different overrides in different directories. For example, overriding can be disabled across a site, but then the authorization options can be overridden for a `private` directory so that the specific authorization databases can be specified:

```
<Directory "/var/www/html">
    AllowOverrides None
</Directory>
<Directory "/var/www/html/priv">
    AllowOverrides AuthConfig
</Directory>
```

 Even if you have full control over Apache and you want to place everything in the main `httpd.conf` files for performance reasons, allowing rewrite options to be overridden with `FileInfo` lets you devise and troubleshoot your rules without restarting the server after each change. You can then migrate the rules to the main configuration file once you're certain they're correct, and turn off overrides.

`rewrite_module` injects itself into the server's request handling workflow and can change what the requested URL looks like on the fly, given what we provide in our ruleset. Although the module is installed by default, we still need to explicitly enable URL rewriting with `RewriteEngine on`. Beyond that, the two most important rewrite options are `RewriteRule` and `RewriteCond`.

The `RewriteRule` option specifies a regular expression against which the URL is compared. If it matches, then the given substitution takes place. Positional variables such as `$1` can be used in the substitution to reference captured pattern matches. In our recipe, the rule matches the path (such as `/about` or `/contactus`) and rewrites it to direct the user to a PHP script of the same name (`about.php` or `contact.php`), thus hiding the fact that we're using PHP from our users:

```
RewriteRule ^/?([A-Z]+)$ $1.php [NC,L]
```

We also can provide flags that affect how the request is returned. The NC flag, for example, performs the pattern matching case insensitively. The L flag stops the engine and returns the URL without any further rule processing. Also common are R, which forces a redirect (an HTTP status code is usually given, for example R=301), and QSA, which appends the query string from the original URL to the new URL.

The RewriteCond option gives a condition that must pass before evaluating a RewriteRule. The condition is a mix of regular expression matching, variables, and test operators. Special variables are available which we can use to reference pieces of the URL, such as the hostname (%{HTTP_HOST}), the requested file (%{REQUEST_FILENAME}), and the query string (%{QUERY_STRING}), or details about the environment/request, such as cookies (%{HTTP_COOKIE}) and user agent strings (%{HTTP_USER_AGENT}). The -d operator tests whether the path is a directory, -f tests whether the path is a file, and ! negates the match. RewriteCond can also accept a handful of flags, such as NC flag to make comparison without regard to case sensitivity and the OR flag to join multiple options in an *or* relationship (multiple options are implicitly treated as *and*).

A very common rewrite that uses both RewriteCond and RewriteRule is one that directs the user to a main index.php file when the request doesn't match an existing file or directory. This is used a lot with web applications that route all requests through a central control point:

```
RewriteCond %{REQUEST_FILENAME} !-f
RewriteCond %{REQUEST_FILENAME} !-d
RewriteRule ^(.*) index.php [L,QSA]
```

The first RewriteCond option checks whether the request is for an existing file and the second checks the same for an existing directory. If the request is neither for a file nor a directory, then the RewriteRule option maps the request to index.php. Any query string that may be present is included and it's marked as the last action, so no further rewriting will be performed.

Many people jokingly refer to rewriting as black magic. Indeed, it's impressive how powerful `mod_rewrite` is and how it transforms requests, and it can be frustrating when you can't seem to figure out the proper incantation to make your rule work as desired. In this case, you may want to turn on logging to gain insight into how the engine views the request. To enable logging, use the `RewriteLog` option to specify a log file where messages can be written to, and use `RewriteLogLevel` to specify the verbosity. Typically, a value of 5 for `RewriteLogLevel` is sufficient. They can be added to your `.htaccess` file and removed later after you're confident that your rules are correct:

```
RewriteLog /var/log/httpd/rewrite_log
RewriteLogLevel 5
```

See also

Refer to the following resources for more information on rewriting URLs:

- Apache `mod_rewrite` documentation (http://httpd.apache.org/docs/current/mod/mod_rewrite.html)
- URL rewriting guide (http://httpd.apache.org/docs/2./misc/rewriteguide.html)
- URL rewriting for the fearful (https://24ways.org/213/url-rewriting-for-the-fearful)

Installing NGINX as a load balancer

High traffic websites can be distributed to different servers, either to better spread out the workload or to achieve redundancy. Each server in the cluster of systems would have their own copy of the website or web application's files and be capable of satisfying the user's request. The trick then is to route the user's request to one of these servers in an orderly fashion. There are different approaches to this, but a common one is to set up a load balancer or reverse proxy server.

NGINX is somewhat newer to the scene than Apache; written a little over a decade ago specifically to handle high-load connections, it can function as a web server, proxy, cache, and load-balancer. In this recipe, we'll see how to set up NGINX as a load balancer to proxy requests between the client and a cluster of Apache servers.

Getting ready

This recipe requires a CentOS system with a working network connection. It assumes that you have other systems configured with Apache to serve a website as described in the earlier recipes; we'll refer to these systems using the IP addresses 192.168.56.20 and 192.168.56.30. The package for NGINX is hosted by the EPEL repository; if the repository is not already registered, refer to the *Registering the EPEL and Remi repositories* recipe in Chapter 4, *Software Installation Management*. Administrative privileges are also required, either by logging in with the root account or through the use of sudo.

How to do it...

Follow these steps to set up reverse proxy using NGINX:

1. Install the nginx package from the EPEL repository:

   ```
   yum install nginx
   ```

2. Open the NGINX server's configuration file with your text editor:

   ```
   vi /etc/nginx/nginx.conf
   ```

3. Within the http block, add a new upstream block to identify the servers in your cluster:

   ```
   upstream cluster {
     server 192.168.56.20;
     server 192.168.56.30;
   }
   ```

4. Find the location block and add a proxy_pass option that references the upstream block:

   ```
   location / {
       proxy_pass http://cluster;
   }
   ```

5. Save your changes to the configuration and close the file.
6. Start the server and enable it to start automatically when your system reboots:

   ```
   systemctl start nginx.service
   systemctl enable nginx.service
   ```

7. Open port 80 in the system's firewall to allow HTTP requests through:

```
firewall-cmd --zone=public --permanent --add-service=http
firewall-cmd --reload
```

How it works...

As usual, we began by installing the program's package, this time nginx. The package is available in the EPEL repository. Once installed, we updated its configuration, identifying the servers in our cluster and then proxying requests. First, we added an upstream block:

```
upstream cluster {
  server 192.168.56.20;
  server 192.168.56.30;
}
```

cluster is simply a name we assigned to this group of servers so that we can refer to the group by name. You can have multiple upstream blocks if you are balancing multiple clusters. Each server entry within it gives the IP address or hostname of one of the systems running the site.

Next, we found the main location block and added a proxy_pass parameter. proxy_pass will forward the incoming request to one of the systems in our cluster group and return the response to satisfy the request:

```
location / {
    proxy_pass http://cluster;
}
```

Communication between NGINX and the hosting web servers is done over http since that's the protocol specified in the value for proxy_pass. This is fine because the clustered systems would be running behind the load balancer on a trusted network. If your site is to be served over HTTPS, it's NGINX that will need to handle the TLS negotiation as it's the public server point seen by the client; the client is unaware of anything behind the balancer.

To configure NGINX to handle HTTPS requests, within the server block update the listen options to listen on port 443. Then add entries with the ssl_certificate and ssl_certificate_key options to identify the certificate and key, respectively:

```
server {
    # listen 80 default_server;
    # listen [::]:80 default_server;
    listen 443 ssl default_server;
    listen [::]:443 ssl default_server;
```

```
        ssl_certificate /etc/pki/tls/certs/www.example.pem;
        ssl_certificate_key /etc/pki/tls/private/www.example.key;
    ...
}
```

Once the changes are made and the configuration file is saved, open port 443 in your firewall and restart NGINX:

```
firewall-cmd --zone=public --permanent --add-service=https
firewall-cmd --reload
systemctctl restart nginx.service
```

Round-robin is the default approach for load balancing. This means the first request is proxied to the first server in the cluster, then next to the second server, and so on. When NGINX reaches the end of the list, it starts again from the top of the list, proxying the next request to the first server. There are other strategies we can use, for example, weighted balancing.

To perform weighted balancing, we assign a weight to any of the servers and it will handle that number of requests per iteration. Here, the first server will handle five requests before NGINX proxies anything to the second server:

```
upstream cluster {
    server 192.168.56.20 weight=5;
    server 192.168.56.30;
}
```

When using load balancing, remember that any one web server isn't guaranteed to receive the next request sent by a user. If you're balancing access to a web application that uses sessions, this can be problematic. You may want to consider storing session data on a central system that each web server has access to, perhaps using a database such as Redis or Memcache.

 I recommend that you avoid any balancing strategy that relies on session persistence. The post at http://www.chaosincomputing.com/212/5/stic ky-sessions-are-evil offers a good overview of their problems.

See also

Refer to the following resources for more information on working with NGINX and load balancing:

- The NGINX website (`https://www.nginx.com/`)
- How to install NGINX on CentOS 7 (`https://www.digitalocean.com/community/tutorials/how-to-install-nginx-on-centos-7`)
- Configuring HTTPS servers (`http://nginx.org/en/docs/http/configuring_https_servers.html`)
- Using NGINX as a load balancer (`http://nginx.org/en/docs/http/load_balancing.html`)
- How to store PHP sessions in Memcache (`http://www.scalescale.com/tips/nginx/store-php-sessions-memcached`)

11
Safeguarding Against Threats

This chapter contains the following recipes:

- Sending messages to Syslog
- Rotating log files with logrotate
- Using Tripwire to detect modified files
- Using ClamAV to fight viruses
- Checking for rootkits with chkrootkit
- Using Bacula for network backups

Introduction

From logging your system's activities to sniffing out rootkits, this chapter presents recipes to help protect the investment you've made in your system and its data against various threats. First, you'll learn how to set up a central log server using Syslog, and then, how to rotate log files to make sure that they don't grow out of control. Then, we'll look at how Tripwire is used to detect system intrusion by checking if changes have been made to important system files. This chapter also contains recipes for setting up ClamAV and chkrootkit to keep your system free of viruses, Trojans, rootkits, and other malware. We'll finish with how to set up a centralized backup server using Bacula to safeguard your data from everyday threats such as accidental deletion and hardware failures.

Sending messages to Syslog

Syslog is a process that listens for messages from other applications and writes them to its log files, providing a common service to handle all logging activity. Messages can also be sent to a running instance of Syslog on a remote system acting as a centralized log server for your entire network. Apart from convenience, centralized logging can be useful for security reasons and also because it's harder for an attacker to cover their tracks when it's logged to a second system. In this recipe, you'll learn how to configure local and remote instances of Syslog to run your own log server.

Getting ready

This recipe requires two CentOS systems with working network connections. The recipe will refer to the first system as the local system and assume that it is configured with the IP address 192.168.56.100 and the hostname `benito`. The second system, referred to as the remote system, is assumed to have the address 192.168.56.35 and the hostname `logs`. The systems should be able to access each other by the hostnames; so, you will need to add the appropriate DNS records or override entries in the systems' `/etc/hosts` files. Administrative privileges are also required either by logging in with the `root` account or through the use of `sudo`.

How to do it...

To forward log messages from the local system to the remote system, perform the following steps on the local system:

1. Open Syslog's configuration file using your text editor:

   ```
   vi /etc/rsyslog.conf
   ```

2. At the end of the file, add the following rule:

   ```
   *.*     @logs.example.com
   ```

3. Save the change and close the configuration file.

4. Restart Syslog for the updated configuration to take effect:

```
systemctl restart rsyslog
```

Then, to accept incoming log messages, perform the following steps on the remote system:

1. Open Syslog's configuration file using your text editor:

```
vi /etc/rsyslog.conf
```

2. Locate the $ModLoad directive responsible for loading the imudp module and uncomment it by removing the leading # character. Uncomment the $UDPServerRun directive that immediately follows it as well:

```
$ModLoad imudp
$UDPServerRun 514
```

3. Save the changes and close the configuration file.
4. Restart Syslog for the updated configuration to take effect:

```
systemctl restart rsyslog
```

5. Open the firewall to UDP traffic on port 514:

```
firewall-cmd --zone=public --permanent --add-port=514/udp
firewall-cmd --reload
```

How it works...

Syslog receives messages through several logging facilities, and each message has an assigned priority/severity. Messages can be filtered based on their facility and priority so that the desired messages are relayed while the rest are discarded. A list of facilities and priorities are both outlined in RFC-5424 (the Syslog protocol), and Rsyslog (the version of Syslog available in CentOS) implements most of them.

Facilities offer a broad categorization designed to organize messages by the type of service that generates them. You can think of them as channels, where a message that logs a user's failed login attempt can be sent over the `auth` channel separate from messages logging the restart of a service sent over the `daemon` channel. Rsyslog's facilities are the following:

- `auth`: Security and authorization-related messages
- `cron`: Messages from cron
- `daemon`: Messages from system daemons
- `kern`: Messages from the Linux kernel
- `lpr`: Messages from the system's printer services
- `mail`: Messages from the system's mail services
- `news`: Messages from NTTP services
- `syslog`: Messages generated by Syslog itself
- `user`: User-level messages
- `uucp`: Messages from UUCP services
- `local0–local7`: User-level facilities for messages that aren't handled by the other facilities

Priorities indicate the severity of the message, for example, a situation that generates an error message is more severe than one generating an informational or debugging message. Rsyslog's priorities are as follows:

- `emerg`, `panic`: The system is unusable
- `alert`: Immediate action is required
- `crit`: A critical event happened
- `err`, `error`: An error happened
- `warn`, `warning`: A significant condition is encountered
- `notice`: Notice messages
- `info`: Informational messages
- `debug`: Debugging messages

The rules in Syslog's configuration file specify where a log is written to and they are made up of two parts—the first part is a pattern that identifies a facility and priority. It consists of both the facility and priority names separated by a dot, for example, `auth.warn` or `local2.debug`. More than one facility can be separated by commas, as in `auth,daemon,cron.warn`. Additionally, `*` can be used as a wildcard to match all facilities or priorities. `auth.*` represents messages coming through the `auth` facility of any priority, `*.warn` represents messages with a priority of `warn` or above from any facility, and `*.*` represents all messages regardless of facility or priority.

Messages that match the pattern are processed by the rule's second part, the action. Usually, the action is the location of a file that the message is written to, but it can also discard the message (use ~ as the location), send the message to a named pipe to be handled by an external process (prefix the location with |), or forward the message to another system (give a hostname as the location prefixed with @).

Since Rsyslog is installed, the service's configuration file is `/etc/rsyslogd.conf`. On the local system we added the following rule:

```
*.*     @logs.example.com
```

This rule matches all messages and sends them to the server `logs.example.com`. One @ means messages will be sent using UDP while two means they will be sent using TCP:

```
*.*     @@archive.example.com
```

Then, we uncommented the following configuration on the remote system:

```
$ModLoad imudp
$UDPServerRun 514
```

$ModLoad loads a Syslog module, in this case `imudp`, which handles incoming messages over UDP. The $UDPServerRun directive specifies the port which the module listens to for the messages. Traditionally, Syslog messages are sent to port 514.

> Syslog can be configured to transmit messages using TCP, but unless you have specific need to do so, I recommend that you use UDP. UDP is less reliable, but TCP entails more overhead and can result in more severe network congestion during heavy logging events.

```
#### RULES ####

# Log all kernel messages to the console.
# Logging much else clutters up the screen.
#kern.*                                                /dev/console

# Log anything (except mail) of level info or higher.
# Don't log private authentication messages!
*.info;mail.none;authpriv.none;cron.none              /var/log/messages

# The authpriv file has restricted access.
authpriv.*                                            /var/log/secure

# Log all the mail messages in one place.
mail.*                                                -/var/log/maillog
# Log cron stuff
cron.*                                                /var/log/cron

# Everybody gets emergency messages
*.emerg                                               :omusrmsg:*

# Save news errors of level crit and higher in a special file.
uucp,news.crit                                        /var/log/spooler
```

The configuration file contains rules to direct messages to different files based on their facility and priorities

Many applications are capable of sending messages to Syslog, even if they write to their own log files by default. Some programs do so when given an appropriate argument on the command line, for example, MySQL accepts the `--syslog` argument. Others, such as BIND and Apache, require changes in their configuration files. Even the shell scripts you write can send messages to Syslog using the `logger` command as follows:

```
logger -n logs.example.com -p user.notice "Test notice"
```

`logger` accepts several arguments and then the log message. `-n` specifies the server where the message is sent (messages are sent to the local system's Syslog instance when not provided) and `-p` specifies the facility and priority for the message.

See also

Refer to the following resources for more information on working with Syslog:

- The Rsyslog website (http://www.rsyslog.com/)
- Basic configuration of Rsyslog (https://access.redhat.com/documentation/en-US/Red_Hat_Enterprise_Linux/7/html/System_Administrators_Guide/s1-basic_configuration_of_rsyslog.html)
- RFC5424: The Syslog protocol (http://www.rfc-base.org/txt/rfc-5424.txt)

Rotating log files with logrotate

Log files are important because they provide better insight into what is happening on a system. The debugging and error messages in a log can be used to track down the source of a problem and resolve it quickly. Authentication messages maintain a record of who accessed the system and when, and repeated authentication failures can be a sign that an attacker is trying to gain unauthorized access. However, the usefulness of logs typically diminishes with age, and chatty applications that generate a lot of log entries could, if left unchecked, easily consume all of the system's storage resources. This recipe will show you how to rotate the log files to prevent the files from growing out of control and stale logs from wasting space.

Getting ready

This recipe requires a CentOS system with a working network connection. Administrative privileges are also required either by logging in with the root account or through the use of sudo.

How to do it...

Follow these steps to configure log file rotation using `logrotate`:

1. Create the `/etc/logrotate.d/example` file:

```
vi /etc/logrotate.d/example
```

2. Write the following contents to the file:

```
/var/log/example.log {
    monthly
    rotate 4
    missingok
    notifempty
    create 0600 root root
    postrotate
        kill -HUP $(cat /var/run/example.pid)
    endscript
}
```

3. Save your update and close the file.

How it works...

`logrotate` rotates the log files by renaming them as sequential backups and creating a new file for the application to write to. While rotating `example.log`, it renames `example.log` to `example.log.1`. If `example.log.1` exists, it renames that file to `example.log.2` first (and so on for the other enumerated files).

For the sake of this example, this recipe created a new configuration to rotate the /var/log/example.log file. The main configuration file of logrotate is /etc/logrotate.conf, while additional files can be placed in the /etc/logrotate.d directory. You'll want to check logrotate.d to see if rotation for the application's logs you want to manage is already configured (many packages will drop a configuration file there as a courtesy). You can then update the configuration if the package maintainer's configuration doesn't suit your needs. Directives in the main file set the global behavior, which is overridden on a per-configuration basis by the additional files in logrotate.d.

The configuration supplies the name of the targeted log file followed by a braced set of directives that specifies how logrotate should manage the file. * can be used as a wildcard to match multiple files which is useful when an application writes to more than one log file. For example, the Apache HTTP server logs messages to access_log and error_log in /var/log/http. So it's configuration targets the log files as follows:

```
/var/log/http/*log {
...
}
```

The monthly directive instructs logrotate to rotate the files on a monthly basis. Other options are daily, weekly, and yearly. Alternatively, you can instruct logrotate to manage files based on their size—the size directive specifies a size and logrotate will rotate those files that are larger than that.

```
size 30k
```

If a value is given without a unit, the given value is understood as bytes. logrotate also supports k for kilobytes, M for megabytes, and G for gigabytes.

The `rotate` directive specifies how many log files to keep in the rotation. In our scenario, four files are allowed; so, `example.log.3` overwrites `example.log.4` and there is no `example.log.5`. The `missingok` directive lets `logrotate` know that it's okay to go on if a log file doesn't exist (its default behavior is to raise an error). Also, the `notifempty` directive instructs `logrotate` to skip rotating if the file is empty. The `create` directive instructs `logrotate` to create a new log file after renaming the original and supplies the mode, user, and group for the new file:

```
rotate 4
missingok
notifempty
create 0600 root root
```

```
[tboronczyk@benito ~]$ ls /var/log
anaconda    cron.1    lastlog    messages    secure    spooler.1   wtmp
audit       cron.2    maillog    messages.1  secure.1  spooler.2   yum.log
boot.log    cron.3    maillog.1  messages.2  secure.2  spooler.3
boot.log.1  cron.4    maillog.2  messages.3  secure.3  spooler.4
btmp        dmesg     maillog.3  messages.4  secure.4  tallylog
cron        dmesg.old maillog.4  ppp         spooler   tuned
[tboronczyk@benito ~]$
```

Rotated log files are numbered in sequence

The content of the original `example.log.4` file doesn't have to be lost. One option is to use the `mail` directive to instruct `logrotate` to e-mail its contents to you before overwriting it.

```
mail tboronczyk@example.com
```

Personally though, I recommend using `mail` only if the file is relatively small since sending a large file can cause undue strain on the mail server. Also, a log file that contains sensitive information shouldn't be transmitted by e-mail. For sensitive logs and larger files, I recommend using `prerotate` to invoke `scp` or another utility to copy the file elsewhere before the rotation.

```
prerotate
  scp /var/log/example.log.4
    storage@archive.example.com:example.log-$ (date +%F)
endscript
```

We can specify external actions to be performed before and after the log files are rotated. The `prerotate` directive supplies a set of shell commands that will be executed before the rotation process begins, and the `postrotate` directive supplies commands that will be run after rotation. Both directives use `endscript` to mark the end of the command set as shown in the preceding tip and in the recipe's configuration. The configuration invokes `kill` to send the hang-up signal (HUP) to the example process which would reload that daemon. Some programs might be confused if the log file they're writing to is moved and recreated, and reloading it causes the program to reopen its connection to the log file so that it can continue logging:

```
postrotate
    kill -HUP $(cat /var/run/example.pid)
endscript
```

`logrotate` is run daily via `cron`, so once you've created/adjusted your rotation's configuration you should be finished. The next time `logrotate` runs, it will pick up the update as it re-reads all of the configuration files.

See also

Refer to the following resources for more information on working with `logrotate`:

- The `logrotate` manual page (`man 8 logrotate`)
- Manage Linux log files with Logrotate (`http://www.techrepublic.com/article/manage-linux-log-files-with-logrotate`)
- How to manage system logs (`http://www.tecmint.com/manage-linux-system-logs-using-rsyslogd-and-logrotate/`)

Using Tripwire to detect modified files

This recipe shows you how to set up Tripwire, an auditing tool for detecting changes made to files on your system. Most often, Tripwire is positioned as an intrusion detection system because the unexpected modification of important configuration files is usually a sign of intrusion or malicious activity. Being able to monitor for such changes gives you the ability to detect and put a stop to malicious activity in a timely manner should it occur.

Getting ready

This recipe requires a CentOS system with a working network connection. The tripwire package is found in the EPEL repository, so the repository must be registered as discussed in Chapter 4, *Software Installation Management*. Administrative privileges are also required, either by logging in with the root account or through the use of sudo.

How to do it...

Follow these steps to monitor for system intrusions using Tripwire:

1. Install the tripwire package from the EPEL repository:

   ```
   yum install tripwire
   ```

2. Run tripwire-setup-keyfiles to generate Tripwire's keyfiles and configuration and policy files:

   ```
   tripwire-setup-keyfiles
   ```

You will be prompted to provide a passphrase for the site keyfile and local keyfiles and then to give the site passphrase again to sign the configuration and policy files that are generated.

3. Initialize Tripwire's database. You will be prompted to provide your local passphrase:

```
tripwire --init 2>output.txt
```

4. Review warnings in the output to identify files that are defined in the policy but do not exist on your system:

```
cat output.txt
```

5. Comment out the entries in /etc/tripwire/twpol.txt that reference the nonexisting files in output.txt. If all of the warnings in output.txt were caused by nonexisting files, then you can automate this step as follows:

```
for f in $(grep "Filename:" output.txt | cut -f2 -d:); do
    sed -i "s|\($f\) |#\\1|g" /etc/tripwire/twpol.txt
done
```

6. Regenerate the signed policy file. Provide the password for the site keyfile when prompted:

```
twadmin --create-polfile -S /etc/tripwire/site.key
/etc/tripwire/twpol.txt
```

7. Delete the original database and initialize a new one. This time, the process should finish without generating any warnings:

```
rm /var/lib/tripwire/benito.twd
tripwire --init
```

How it works...

Tripwire audits your system to detect which files have changed. The idea behind this is, if an attacker gains access to your system, they'll inevitably create or modify keyfiles to secure their presence. However, it would be trivial for an attacker to modify Tripwire's policy files to create the illusion that nothing has changed; so, the configuration and policy files are signed with a keyfile. The configuration file, policy file, and the keyfile are all generated when we run:

```
tripwire-setup-keyfiles
```

Because the default policy tries to be as comprehensive as possible for most users, there will be entries that aren't applicable to our CentOS system. If we were to run with the unmodified defaults then Tripwire would report the missing files, and sifting through the list of false positives would make it more difficult to identify if someone deleted a file of legitimate concern. Rather than reviewing the policy file manually, especially if you're not an expert and familiar with some of the files, the best approach is to run an initial scan on a system that is known to be clean and then let Tripwire report the nonexistent files. This will help save time as we try to tailor the policy to our system.

Initializing Tripwire's database is done using `tripwire --init`. The program will scan the system, comparing the filesystem with what it knows about in the policy file and collect statistics on the files that do exist. These statistics are stored in the database as a baseline metric for comparison the next time Tripwire runs to see if there have been changes. The recipe redirected the error output containing the list of missing files to a separate text file for two reasons: the list will be lengthy and it's sometimes easier to page through a file than scroll the terminal session, and we can script the process of customizing the policy based on that output:

```
tripwire --init 2>output.txt
```

`sed` is the traditional search-and-replace workhorse and `grep` is great for finding and extracting lines of interest, so we can use these two tools to update the policy `/etc/tripwire/twpol.txt`. First, we need to know what the messages in `output.txt` look like:

```
cat output.txt
```

```
### Warning: File system error.
### Filename: /usr/share/grub/i386-redhat/fat_stage1_5
### No such file or directory
### Continuing...
```

Nonexistent files generate a warning when initializing the Tripwire database

If all of the warnings in the output file are related to nonexistent files then it's safe to automate updating the policy. This is why we then carefully reviewed the contents before continuing.

We use `grep` to target the lines containing `Filename:` and then use `cut` to split the line on the colon and capture the second part—the name of the nonexistent file. The `for` loop captures each filename and assigns it to the variable `f`, which we can then reference in our pattern to `sed`. The pattern performs a global search and replace, using capturing parentheses and numeric back references to overwrite the filename with a leading `#`:

```
for f in $(grep "Filename:" output.txt | cut -f2 -d:); do
    sed -i "s|\($f\) |#\\1|g" /etc/tripwire/twpol.txt;
done
```

 It's important there is a space in the search space after the filename to make sure we only match the entire file. For example, we want to avoid a scenario where `/etc/rc.d` will also match `/etc/rc.d/init` because of the common prefix.

An unsigned, plain-text copy of the policy is stored at `/etc/tripwire/twpol.txt`. After we make our changes, we want to create a signed policy file which is used by Tripwire for the security reasons mentioned earlier. This is done with `twadmin` and the `--create-policy` argument. The `-S` argument provides the command with the path to our signing key and then we supply the plain-texted copy of the policy as the input:

```
twadmin --create-polfile -S /etc/tripwire/site.key
/etc/tripwire/twpol.txt
```

`twadmin` will sign the policy and write the result to `/etc/tripwire/tw.pol`. After the policy file has been modified we can then reinitialize the database. In fact, any time the policy file is updated you should regenerate the database, which is stored in `/var/lib/tripwire` and is named using the system's hostname:

```
rm /var/lib/tripwire/benito.twd
tripwire --init
```

To scan the system for violations, run Tripwire with the `--check` option:

```
tripwire --check
```

Tripwire reports its findings after a scan is performed

Of course, to be effective, a scan must be performed at least once a day. For this reason, a cron job is installed in `/etc/cron.daily` by the `tripwire` package which runs a Tripwire scan. Depending on how cron is configured, the output of the scan will probably be e-mailed by cron to the system's `root` user (and will most likely end up in `/var/spool/mail/root`). You can edit `/etc/cron.daily/tripwire-check` so that the output is e-mailed to you instead:

```
test -f /etc/tripwire/tw.cfg && /usr/sbin/tripwire --check |
/bin/mailx -s "Tripwire Report" tboronczyk@example.com 2>&1
```

You can also configure Tripwire to send e-mails itself if you prefer. First, you'll want to ensure that Tripwire can send mail to your address. Issue the following to send a test message and then check to make sure it arrives in your inbox:

```
tripwire --test --email tboronczyk@example.com
```

> You can use supply the `--email-report` option when running a manual scan to have Tripwire send its results to your e-mail.
>
>
>
> ```
> tripwire --check --email-report
> ```
>
> By default, Tripwire will attempt to send the e-mail via sendmail (or Postfix's sendmail interface). If you need to send the mail through an SMTP server instead, review the *Email Notification Variables* section in man 4 twconfig.

Specifying the destination e-mail address is a bit more involved in Tripwire's configuration. The tests defined in the Tripwire policy file are grouped into rulesets, which allows files to be grouped together in a logical fashion. For example, there is a ruleset that tests the integrity of the Tripwire binaries themselves, which is separate from the ruleset that tests system administration programs. Each ruleset can have a defined e-mail address to send notifications to, which is great for flexibility where one administrator should be notified of modifications to one set of files and another admin should be notified about others:

```
(
  rulename = "Tripwire Binaries",
  emailto = tboronczyk@example.com,
  severity = $(SIG_HI)
)
```

If you're the only administrator, repeatedly specifying the same address can be tedious. A better approach would define the e-mail address as a global variable and then let the creative use of `sed` come to the rescue.

First, edit `twpol.txt` to include the variable assignment for your e-mail address in the global variable definitions section:

```
@@section GLOBAL
TWROOT=/usr/sbin;
TWBIN=/usr/sbin;
TWPOL="/"/etc/tripwire";
TWD="/var/lib/tripwire";
TWSKEY="/etc/tripwire";
TWLKEY="/etc/tripwire";
TWREPORT="/var/lib/tripwire/report";
HOSTNAME=benito;
EMAILADDR="tboronczyk@example.com";
```

Save the change and close the file. Then, knowing each ruleset contains a `severity` directive, we can use a replacement pattern to insert the `mailto` directive:

```
sed -i "s|\( \+\)\(severity = \)|\\1mailto =  \$(EMAILADDR),\n\\1\\2|g"
/etc/tripwire/twpol.txt
```

The end result should include the `emailto` directive in each ruleset's definition:

```
(
  rulename = "Tripwire Binaries",
  emailto = $(EMAILADDR),
  severity = $(SIG_HI)
)
```

After you inspect the results, resign the policy file and reinitialize the database.

See also

Refer to the following resources for more information on working with Tripwire:

- Introduction to Tripwire (`man 8 twintro`)
- Tripwire configuration manual page (`man 4 twconfig`)
- Tripwire policy manual page (`man 4 twpolicy`)
- Intrusion detection with Tripwire (`http://www.akadia.com/services/tripwire.html`)
- How to set up and use Tripwire (`http://www.linuxjournal.com/article/8758`)

Using ClamAV to fight viruses

The threat from viruses, Trojans, and other forms of malware is real. They have grown exponentially in both quantity and in sophistication, and antivirus software have had to adopt sophisticated detection methods. While there's no guarantee that your system will not fall victim to these unwanted bits of code, remaining mindful when using the Internet and sharing files, implementing common-sense security policies, and using an up-to-date antivirus program can go a long way in protecting you. This recipe will show you how to install ClamAV, the professional-grade open-source antivirus program, keep its threat database up to date, and scan your system.

Getting ready

This recipe requires a CentOS system with a working network connection. The ClamAV packages can be found in the EPEL repository, so the repository must be registered as discussed in Chapter 4, *Software Installation Management*. Administrative privileges are also required either by logging in with the root account or through the use of sudo.

How to do it...

Follow these steps to install ClamAV and scan for viruses and Trojans:

1. Install the clamav and clamav-update packages from the EPEL repository:

   ```
   yum install clamav clamav-update
   ```

2. Open the freshclam configuration file with your text editor:

   ```
   vi /etc/freshclam.conf
   ```

3. Locate the Example line and add an # to the start of its line to comment it out:

   ```
   # Comment or remove the line below
   #Example
   ```

4. Save the update and close the file.

5. Run `freshclam` to update the scanner's threat database:

```
freshclam
```

6. Create a `systemd` service file to manage the `freshclam` daemon for automate updates:

```
vi /lib/systemd/system/freshclam.service
```

7. Use the following for the file's content:

```
[Unit]
Description = freshclam daemon to update clamav
After = network.target
[Service]
Type = forking
ExecStart = /usr/bin/freshclam -d
Restart = on-failure
[Install]
WantedBy=multi-user.target
```

8. Force `systemd` to reload its services:

```
systemctl daemon-reload
```

9. Start the new `freshclam` service and enable it to start when the system reboots:

```
systemctl start freshclam.service
systemctl enable freshclam.service
```

10. Scan the files in your `home` directory for threats using `clamscan`:

```
clamscan -ir /home/tboronczyk
```

How it works...

First, we installed the `clamav` and `clamav-update` packages. The `clamav` package contains the virus scanner while `clamav-update` contains the `freshclam` program, which updates ClamAV's virus definitions to keep it up to date:

```
yum install clamav clamav-update
```

`freshclam` reads its configuration from `/etc/freshclam.conf`. The file contains a line with the word `Example` to prevent users from using the defaults blindly and we must remove it or comment it out before we can use `freshclam`. The defaults settings are fine for our purposes and this is more of an annoyance than anything else, but it does force us to look at the file and see what behavior can be tweaked. Each directive is commented with an explanation and what the default behavior is.

Then, we ran `freshclam` to update the scanner's databases:

`freshclam`

The process outputs its progress to the terminal and you may see several error messages. For example, it may report that it was unable to download a daily file. Don't panic; `freshclam` will try several mirrors. As long as it reports that `main.cvd`, `daily.cvd`, and `bytecode.cvd` are up to date when it's finished you know you have the latest definitions.

We can run `freshclam` any time we want to make sure the definition databases are up to date, but it would be inconvenient to have to always run it manually. When launched with the `-d` argument, `freshclam` will run in the daemon mode and periodically check for updates throughout the day (every two hours by default). To keep things clean, we created a service file to run `freshclam` and registered it with `systemd`:

```
[Unit]
Description = freshclam clamav update daemon
After = network.target
[Service]
Type = forking
ExecStart = /usr/bin/freshclam -d
Restart = on-failure
[Install]
WantedBy=multi-user.target
```

The `[Unit]` section defines the basic attributes of the service, such as its description and that it relies on a network connection. The `[Service]` section defines the service itself, `ExecStart` will run `freshclam` with the `-d` argument, `Type` lets systemd know that the process will fork and run in the background as a daemon, and `Restart` will have systemd monitor the service and restart it automatically if it crashes. The `[Install]` section defines how it will be linked when we run `systemctl enable`.

The system file's content is pretty basic and can be used as a starting point for other custom services you write.

Scanning files for threats is done with `clamscan`:

```
clamscan -ir /home/tboronczyk
```

The `-i` argument instructs the scanner to only output infected files as opposed to the name of every file it scans. `-r` triggers a recursive scan, descending into subdirectories. The path given can be an individual file to scan or a directory, in this case, our home directory:

```
[tboronczyk@benito ~]$ clamscan -i test.txt
test.txt Eicar-Test-Signature FOUND

~~~~~~~~ SCAN SUMMARY ~~~~~~~~
Known viruses: 4644725
Engine version: 0.99.2
Scanned directories: 0
Scanned files: 1
Infected files: 1
Data scanned: 0.00 MB
Data read: 0.00 MB (ratio 0.00:1)
Time: 7.089 sec (0 m 7 s)
[tboronczyk@benito ~]$
```

ClamAV provides a summary of its scan results

You can use EICAR's test files from `http://www.eicar.org/85--Download.html` to verify if ClamAV is working. Read their intended use page for more information at `http://www.eicar.org/86--Intended-use.html`.

ClamAV is generally used in two ways—as a scanner to examine existing files to detect threats or as a filter to detect threats in a stream of data in real time. The easiest way to schedule a reoccurring scan is by setting up a cron job.

To create a personal cron job that runs `clamav` to scan your home directory, use `crontab`:

```
crontab -e
```

`crontab` will launch your default editor for you to enter the job schedule. Then `crontab` will automatically activate the job after you save the schedule and close the file.

An example schedule that runs `clamscan` every day at 3:00 a.m. might look as follows:

```
0 3 * * * clamscan >> $HOME/clamscan.log
```

The first five columns specify the time when the job should run. The first column is the time's minutes, the second is hours, the third is the day of the month, the fourth is the month, and last is the day of the week when the job will run. `*` is used as a shorthand to indicate the entire range, thus the example will run every day of every month. More information can be found in the man page outlining the format of the `crontab` file (`man 5 crontab`).

On a server system, ClamAV is often run as a real-time scanner as a mail filter. Messages are received by the mail server, for example Postfix, and passed off to ClamAV for scanning. Assuming that you're running Postfix, as discussed in `Chapter 9`, *Managing E-mails*, here's what you'll need to do to set up ClamAV and Postfix to work together.

First, we need to install some additional packages. The `clamav-scanner-systemd` package will install the functionality we need to run `clamscan` as a daemon so that it's always available and the `clamav-milter-systemd` package installs a mail filter that acts as a proxy between Postfix and the scanner:

```
yum install clamav-scanner-systemd clamav-milter-systemd
```

Then, edit the configuration file `/etc/clamd.d/scan.conf`. Comment out the `Example` line and uncomment the `LocalSocket` option:

```
LocalSocket /var/run/clamd.scan/clamd.sock
```

The value given with `LocalSocket` is the socket file used by the scanner daemon for communicating with outside processes.

Next, edit the `/etc/mail/clamav-milter.conf` file, which is the configuration file for the `clamav-milter` mail filter. Comment out the `Example` line, uncomment the first `MilterSocket` directive, and add the `ClamdSocket` directive. The value for `ClamdSocket` should be the same as the `LocalSocket` in `scan.conf` but prefixed with `unix:` to denote that it's a Unix socket:

```
MilterSocket /var/run/clamav-milter/clamav.socket
ClamdSocket unix:/var/run/clamd.scan/clamd.sock
```

Start and enable the scanner daemon and the filter services:

```
system start clamd@scan.service clamav-milter.service
system enable clamd@scan.service clamav-milter.service
```

Finally, open `/etc/postfix/main.cnf` and add an `smtpd_milters` entry which lets Postfix know about the filter:

```
smtpd_milters=unix:/var/run/clamav-milter/clamav.socket
```

Don't forget to restart Postfix after updating its configuration:

```
systemctl restart postfix.service
```

See also

Refer to the following resources for more information on working with ClamAV:

- ClamAV documentation (`http://www.clamav.net/documents/installing-clamav`)
- European Institute for Computer Anti-Virus Research (`http://www.eicar.org/`)

Checking for rootkits with chkrootkit

In the unfortunate event that an attacker gains access to your system, one of the first things they'll do is try to hide their intrusion while preserving access for as long as possible, perhaps by installing a rootkit. A rootkit is a program that runs stealthily and gives the attacker administrator access. They embed themselves in the Linux kernel to prevent detection, and there are even rootkits that can hide in a system firmware's dedicated memory allowing an attacker to control the system even when it's powered down. This recipe shows you how to check your system for rootkits using chkrootkit.

Getting ready

This recipe requires a CentOS system with a working network connection. Administrative privileges are also required, either by logging in with the `root` account or through the use of `sudo`.

How to do it...

Follow these steps to use chkrootkit to check for rootkits:

1. Install the gcc and glibc-static packages that are needed to compile chkrootkit binaries:

   yum install gcc glibc-static

2. Download chkrootkit source code:

   curl -O ftp://ftp.pangeia.com.br/pub/seg/pac/chkrootkit.tar.gz

3. Extract the downloaded source code archive and enter into the code's directory:

   tar xzvf chkrootkit.tar.gz
   cd chkrootkit-0.50

4. Run make to compile chkrootkit's binary components:

   make

5. chkrootkit requires netstat to conduct its network tests which is available in the net-tools package:

   yum install net-tools

6. Run chkrootkit to scan for rootkits:

   ./chkrootkit

How it works...

chkrootkit consists of a shell script and a small collection of compiled utilities distributed as source code so we need to compile it. This means you'll need a compiler installed on your system. Minimally, gcc will suffice. Also, we need to install the glibc-static package because the project's Makefile builds a statically compiled binary—all of the binaries' dependencies are compiled in; it doesn't dynamically reference the copy of the system's shared libraries:

   yum install gcc glibc-static

The source code for chkrootkit is available on the project's website. The link used in the recipe is a direct link to the latest source archive and is downloaded using `curl`:

```
curl -O ftp://ftp.pangeia.com.br/pub/seg/pac/chkrootkit.tar.gz
```

Once the download is complete, building chkrootkit's is a matter of extracting the archive, entering into the newly created directory, and running `make`:

```
make
```

When you learned how to compile a program from source code in the *Compiling a program from source* recipe of `Chapter 4`, *Software Installation Management*, you used the common `configure`, `make`, and `make install` approach. However, chkrootkit doesn't ship with a configure script and its `Makefile` doesn't contain an `install` target. All we need to do here to kick off the compilation process is invoke `make` itself.

chkrootkit runs a series of tests to check for known rootkit signatures. Some of these tests use its compiled utilities while others use common system utilities. One of its network tests checks which ports are open using `netstat`, which is not installed by default on CentOS but is available in the `net-tools` package. So, before we can use chkrootkit, we need to install this dependency:

```
yum install net-tools
```

Once everything is installed, we can execute the chkrootkit script. When run without any arguments, chkrootkit executes all of its tests. Otherwise, we can specify one or more tests and only those will run. The `-l` (lowercase L) argument will display a list of possible tests:

```
./chkrootkit -l
```

See also

Refer to the following resources for more information on working with chkrootkit:

- The chkrootkit website (`http://www.chkrootkit.org`)
- Chkrootkit: check your system for hidden rootkits (`https://www.youtube.com/watch?v=IdvdUvNsq4`)

Using Bacula for network backups

The fact of the matter is that we are living in a world that is becoming increasingly dependent on data. Also, from accidental deletion to a catastrophic hard drive failure, there are many threats to the safety of your data. The more important your data is and the more difficult it is to recreate if it were lost, the more important it is to have backups. So, this recipe shows you how you can set up a backup server using Bacula and how to configure other systems on your network to backup their data to it.

Getting ready

This recipe requires at least two CentOS systems with working network connections. The first system is the local system which we'll assume has the hostname benito and the IP address 192.168.56.41. The second system is the backup server. You'll need administrative access on both systems, either by logging in with the root account or through the use of sudo.

How to do it...

Perform the following steps on your local system to install and configure the Bacula file daemon:

1. Install the bacula-client package:

    ```
    yum install bacula-client
    ```

2. Open the file daemon's configuration file with your text editor:

    ```
    vi /etc/bacula/bacula-fd.conf
    ```

3. In the FileDaemon resource, update the value of the Name directive to reflect the system's hostname with the suffix -fd:

    ```
    FileDaemon {
      Name = benito-fd
    . . .
    }
    ```

4. Save the changes and close the file.

5. Start the file daemon and enable it to start when the system reboots:

```
systemctl start bacula-fd.service
systemctl enable bacula-fd.service
```

6. Open the firewall to allow TCP traffic through to port 9102:

```
firewall-cmd --zone=public --permanent --add-port=9102/tcp
firewall-cmd --reload
```

7. Repeat steps 1-6 on each system that will be backed up.

Perform the following steps on the system designated as the backup server to install and configure the Bacula director, storage, and file daemons.

1. Install the `bacula-console`, `bacula-director`, `bacula-storage`, and `bacula-client` packages:

```
yum install bacula-console bacula-director bacula-storage
bacula-client
```

2. Re-link the catalog library to use SQLite database storage:

```
alternatives --config libbaccats.so
```

3. Type 2 when asked to provide the selection number.

4. Create the SQLite database file and import the table schema:

```
/usr/libexec/bacula/create_sqlite3_database
/usr/libexec/bacula/make_sqlite3_tables
```

5. Open the director's configuration file with your text editor:

```
vi /etc/bacula/bacula-dir.conf
```

6. In the `Job` resource where `Name` has the value `BackupClient1`, change the value of the `Name` directive to reflect one of the local systems. Then add a `Client` directive with a value that matches that system's `FileDaemonName`:

```
Job {
  Name = "BackupBenito"
  Client = benito-fd
  JobDefs = "DefaultJob"
}
```

7. Duplicate the `Job` resource and update its directive values as necessary so that there is a `Job` resource defined for each system to be backed up.

8. For each system that will be backed up, duplicate the `Client` resource where the `Name` directive is set to `bacula-fd`. In the copied resource, update the `Name` and `Address` directives to identify that system:

```
Client {
  Name = bacula-fd
  Address = localhost
  ...
}
Client {
  Name = benito-fd
  Address = 192.168.56.41
  ...
}
Client {
  Name = javier-fd
  Address = 192.168.56.42
  ...
}
```

9. Save your changes and close the file.

10. Open the storage daemon's configuration file:

```
vi /etc/bacula/bacula-sd.conf
```

11. In the `Device` resource where `Name` has the value `FileStorage`, change the value of the `Archive Device` directive to `/bacula`:

```
Device {
  Name = FileStorage
  Media Type = File
  Archive Device = /bacula
  ...
```

12. Save the update and close the file.

13. Create the `/bacula` directory and assign it the proper ownership:

```
mkdir /bacula
chown bacula:bacula /bacula
```

14. If you have SELinux enabled, reset the security context on the new directory:

```
restorecon -Rv /bacula
```

15. Start the director and storage daemons and enable them to start when the system reboots:

```
systemctl start bacula-dir.service bacula-sd.service
bacula-fd.service
systemctl enable bacula-dir.service bacula-sd.service
bacula-fd.service
```

16. Open the firewall to allow TCP traffic through to ports $9101-9103$:

```
firewall-cmd --zone=public --permanent --add-port=9101-9103/tcp
firewall-cmd -reload
```

17. Launch Bacula's console interface:

```
bconsole
```

18. Enter `label` to create a destination for the backup. When prompted for the volume name, use `Volume0001` or a similar value. When prompted for the pool, select the `File` pool:

```
label
```

19. Enter `quit` to leave the console interface.

How it works

Configuring Bacula can be a daunting task for the most part because of the suite's distributed architecture and the level of flexibility it offers in organizing and scheduling backup and restore jobs. However, once everything is up and running, I'm sure you'll have peace of mind knowing that your data is safe from accidents and disasters.

Bacula is made up of several components. In this recipe, our efforts were centered on three daemons—the director, the file daemon, and the storage daemon. The file daemon is installed on each of the client systems to be backed up and listens for connections from the director. The director connects to each file daemon as scheduled and tells it which files to backup and where to copy them to (the storage daemon). The storage daemon receives the backed up data and writes it to the backup medium, for example, the disk or tape drive.

First, we installed the file daemon with the `bacula-client` package on our client systems. Then we edited the file daemon's configuration file found at `/etc/bacula/bacula-fd.conf` to specify the name of the process. The convention is to add the suffix `-fd` to the system's hostname:

```
FileDaemon {
  Name = benito-fd
  FDPort = 9102
  WorkingDirectory = /var/spool/bacula
  Pid Directory = /var/run
  Maximum Concurrent Jobs = 20
}
```

After the update is made to the configuration, we started the service and opened the appropriate port in the system firewall. The file daemon is now listening, waiting for the director to connect and tell it what it needs to do.

On the backup server, we installed the `bacula-director`, `bacula-storage`, and `bacula-client` packages. This gives us the director and storage daemon, and another file daemon. The file daemon's purpose here on the backup server is to backup Bacula's catalog:

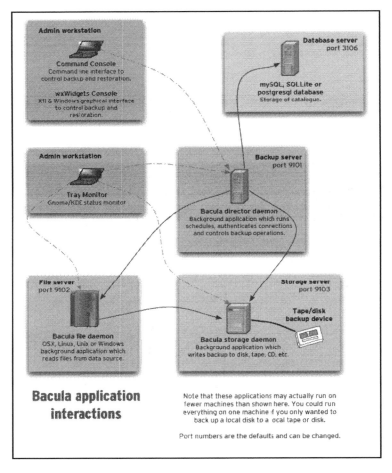

This image reproduced from Bacula's documentation shows how the different applications relate to one another

Bacula maintains a database of metadata about previous backup jobs called the catalog, which can be managed by MySQL, PostgreSQL, or SQLite. SQLite is an embedded database library, meaning the program using it links against the SQLite library and manages its own database files. To support multiple databases, Bacula's code is written so that all the database access routines are contained in separate shared libraries with a different library for each database. Then, when Bacula wants to interact with a database, it does so through `libbaccats.so`, a *fake* library that is nothing more than a symbolic link pointing to one of the specific database libraries. This let's Bacula support different databases without requiring us to recompile its source code.

To create the symbolic link, we used `alternatives` and select the real library that we want to use:

```
alternatives --config libbaccats.so
```

Then, we initialized the database's schema using the scripts that come with Bacula:

```
/usr/libexec/bacula/create_sqlite3_database
/usr/libexec/bacula/make_sqlite3_tables
```

```
[tboronczyk@bacula ~]$ sudo alternatives --config libbaccats.so

There are 3 programs which provide 'libbaccats.so'.

  Selection    Command
-----------------------------------------------------------
     1           /usr/lib64/libbaccats-mysql.so
     2           /usr/lib64/libbaccats-sqlite3.so
*+ 3           /usr/lib64/libbaccats-postgresql.so

Enter to keep the current selection[+], or type selection number: 2
[tboronczyk@bacula ~]$
```

Bacula supports multiple databases without recompiling

This recipe took advantage of Bacula's SQLite support because it's convenient and doesn't require additional effort to set up. If you want to use MySQL, install MySQL as discussed in Chapter 7, *Working with Databases*, create a dedicated MySQL user for Bacula to use, and then initialize the schema with the following scripts:

```
/usr/libexec/bacula/grant_mysql_privileges
/usr/libexec/bacula/create_mysql_database
/usr/libexec/bacula/make_mysql_tables
```

You'll also need to review Bacula's configuration files to provide Bacula with the required MySQL credentials.

Different resources are defined in the director's configuration file at /etc/bacula/bacula-dir.conf, many of which consist not only of their own values but also reference to other resources. For example, the FileSet resource specifies which files are included or excluded in backups and restores, while a Schedule resource specifies when backups should be made. A JobDef resource can contain various configuration directives that are common to multiple backup jobs and also reference particular FileSet and Schedule resources. Client resources identify the names and addresses of systems running file daemons, and a Job resource will pull together a JobDef and Client resource to define the backup or restore task for a particular system. Some resources define things at a more granular level and are used as building blocks to define other resources, creating complex definitions in a flexible manner.

The default resource definitions define basic backup and restore jobs sufficient for this recipe. You'll want to study the configuration and see how the different resources fit together so you can tweak them to better suit your backup needs.

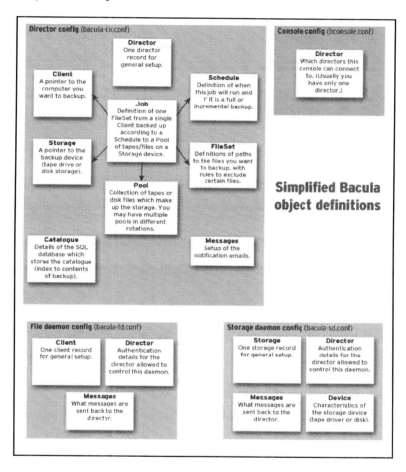

This image, reproduced from Bacula's documentation shows, how the different resources relate to one another

To get started, we customized the existing backup `Job` by changing its name and client. Then we customized the existing `Client` resource by changing its name and address to point to a specific system running a file daemon. The pair of `Job` and `Client` resources were duplicated, a pair for each system we're backing up. Notice that we also left a default `Client` resource that defines `bacula-fd` for the localhost. This is the file daemon that's local to the backup server and will be the target for things such as restore jobs and catalog backups:

```
Job {
  Name = "BackupBenito"
  Client = benito-fd
  JobDefs = "DefaultJob"
}

Job {
  Name = "BackupJavier"
  Client = javier-fd
  JobDefs = "DefaultJob"
}

Client {
  Name = bacula-fd
  Address = localhost
  ...
}

Client {
  Name = benito-fd
  Address = 192.168.56.100
  ...
}

Client {
  Name = javier-fd
  Address = 192.168.56.100
  ...
}
```

If you have a lot of client systems or a lot of job definitions, you can stay better organized by defining these resources in their own files and read them into `bacula-dir.conf`. Create the directory `/etc/bacula/config.d`, and place the individual configuration files there. Then add the following line to `bacula-dir.conf` to read them:

```
@|"find /etc/bacula/config.d -name '*.conf' f -exec echo
@{} \;"
```

To complete the setup, we need to label a backup volume. This task, as with most others, is performed through `bconsole`, a console interface to the Bacula director.

We used the `label` command to define a label for the backup volume, and when prompted for the pool, we assigned the labeled volume to the `File` pool. In a way very similar to how logical volumes work (refer to `Chapter 5`, *Managing Filesystems and Storage*), an individual device or storage unit is allocated as a volume and the volumes are grouped into storage pools. If a pool contains two volumes backed by tape drives for example, and one of the drives is full, the storage daemon will write the backup data to the tape that has space available. Even though in our configuration we're storing the backup to disk, we still need to create a volume as the destination for data to be written to.

At this point, you should consider which backup strategy works best for you. A full backup is a complete copy of your data, a differential backup captures only the files that have changed since the last full backup, and an incremental backup copies the files that have changed since the last backup (regardless of the type of backup). Commonly, administrators employ a combination of these, perhaps making a full backup at the start of the week and then differential or incremental backups each day thereafter. This saves storage space because the differential and incremental backups are smaller and also convenient when the need to restore a file arises, because a limited number of backups need to be searched for the file.

Another consideration is the expected size of each backup and how long it will take for the backup to run to completion. Full backups obviously take longer to run, and in an office with 9-5 working hours, Monday through Friday, it may not be possible to run a full backup during the evenings. Performing a full backup on Fridays gives the backup time over the weekend to run. Smaller, incremental backups can be performed on the other days when time is lesser.

Still another point that is important in your backup strategy is how long the backups will be kept and where they will be kept. This touches on a larger issue, disaster recovery. If your office burns down, a year's worth of backups will be of no use if they were sitting in the office's IT closet. At one employer, we kept the last full backup and last day's incremental on a disk on site. These were then duplicated to tape and shipped off site.

Regardless of the strategy you choose to implement, your backups are only as good as your ability to restore data from them. You should periodically test your backups to make sure you can restore your files.

To run a backup job on demand, enter `run` in `bconsole`. You'll be prompted with a menu to select one of the current configured jobs. You'll then be presented with the job's options, such as what level of backup will be performed (full, incremental, or differential), it's priority, and when it will run. You can type `yes` or `no` to accept or cancel it or `mod` to modify a parameter. Once accepted, the job will be queued and assigned a job ID.

To restore files from a backup, use the `restore` command. You'll be presented with a list of options allowing you to specify which backup the desired files will be retrieved from. Depending on your selection, the prompts will be different. Bacula's prompts are rather clear, so read them carefully and it will guide you through the process.

Apart from the `run` and `restore` commands, another useful command is `status`. It will allow you to see the current status of the Bacula components, if there are any jobs currently running, and which jobs have completed. A full list of commands can be retrieved by typing `help` in `bconsole`.

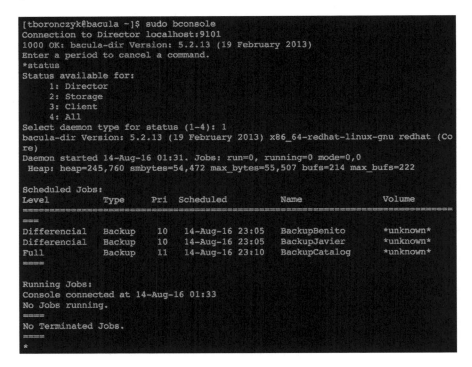

```
[tboronczyk@bacula ~]$ sudo bconsole
Connection to Director localhost:9101
1000 OK: bacula-dir Version: 5.2.13 (19 February 2013)
Enter a period to cancel a command.
*status
Status available for:
     1: Director
     2: Storage
     3: Client
     4: All
Select daemon type for status (1-4): 1
bacula-dir Version: 5.2.13 (19 February 2013) x86_64-redhat-linux-gnu redhat (Co
re)
Daemon started 14-Aug-16 01:31. Jobs: run=0, running=0 mode=0,0
 Heap: heap=245,760 smbytes=54,472 max_bytes=55,507 bufs=214 max_bufs=222

Scheduled Jobs:
Level          Type      Pri  Scheduled          Name             Volume
==================================================================================
=====
Differencial   Backup    10   14-Aug-16 23:05    BackupBenito     *unknown*
Differencial   Backup    10   14-Aug-16 23:05    BackupJavier     *unknown*
Full           Backup    11   14-Aug-16 23:10    BackupCatalog    *unknown*
=====

Running Jobs:
Console connected at 14-Aug-16 01:33
No Jobs running.
=====

No Terminated Jobs.
=====
*
```

bconsole is a console interface to the Bacula director

See also

Refer to the following resources for more information on working with Bacula:

- Bacula documentation (`http://blog.bacula.org/documentation/`)
- How to use Bacula on CentOS 7 (`https://www.digitalocean.com/community/tutorial_series/how-to-use-bacula-on-centos-7`)
- Bacula-Web (a web-based reporting and monitoring tool for Bacula) (`http://www.bacula-web.org/`)

12
Virtualization

This chapter contains the following recipes:

- Creating a new virtual machine
- Cloning a virtual machine
- Adding storage to a virtual machine
- Connecting USB peripherals to a guest system
- Configuring a guest's network interface

Introduction

The recipes in this chapter focus on running a second operating system as a guest using virtualization on your CentOS system. You'll learn how to setup the virtual machine to install a guest operating system, properly create a copy of the machine through cloning, and add additional storage resources. You'll also learn how to share access to USB peripherals attached to the host system and configure the guest's virtual network interface to access the network.

Creating a new virtual machine

This recipe teaches you how to install the KVM virtualization software and create a new virtual machine. Virtualization allows us to take advantage of the hardware resources available to us by running multiple operating systems on the same physical system. The primary operating system is installed "bare-metal" and is known as the host OS. Then, special software is installed that allows the host to provide emulation or direct access to hardware resources. The resources are partitioned as virtual machines and several guest operating systems can then be installed and run on top of the host, each in their own virtual machine.

Getting ready

This recipe requires a CentOS system with a working network connection and a graphical user interface installed (refer to the *Installing the GNOME desktop* and *Installing the KDE Plasma desktop* recipes in Chapter 1, *Getting Started with CentOS*). Administrative privileges are also required, either by logging in with the root account or through the use of sudo.

How to do it...

Follow these steps to install a guest operating system:

1. Install the necessary virtualization packages using package groups:

   ```
   yum groupinstall "Virtualization Platform"
   "Virtualization Client" "Virtualization Tools"
   ```

2. Launch the Virtual Machine Manager application:

   ```
   virt-manager
   ```

3. Create a new virtual machine by selecting **New Virtual Machine** from the **File** menu. This opens the **New VM** wizard.

4. Select the desired installation method and click on **Forward**. For this recipe, we'll choose the **Local install media** option:

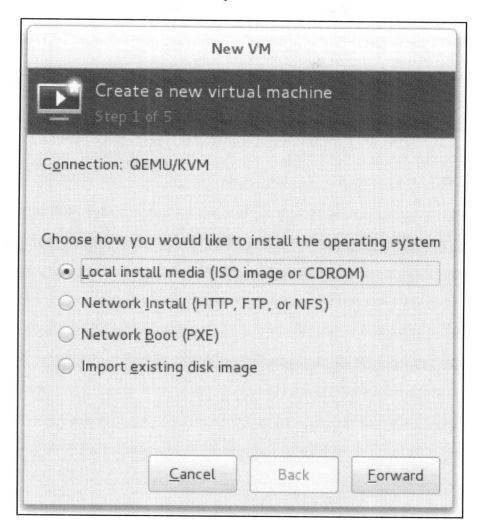

The New VM wizard collects the necessary details to create a new machine

5. Select the media source. If the media is a CD or DVD, select the **Use CDROM or DVD** option. If the media is an ISO file, select the **Use ISO image** option and specify the path to the image file. Then, click on **Forward**:

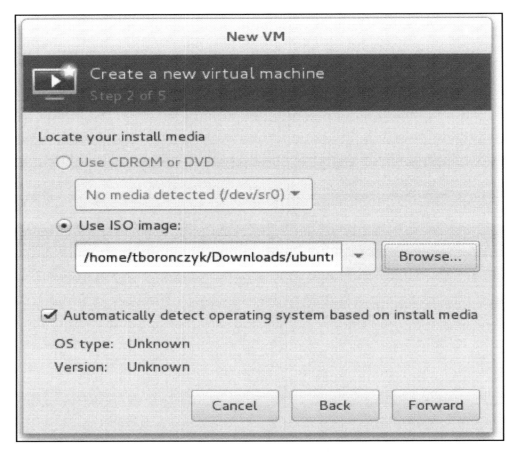

The new machine will use an ISO file as its installation media

6. Set the amount of RAM and the number of CPUs that you want to allocate to the virtual machine and then click on **Forward**:

1 GB of RAM and 1 CPU are allocated to the virtual machine

7. Specify the storage capacity that will be allocated to the machine and then click on **Forward**:

The machine is set up with 8 GB of storage

8. Provide a name to identify the virtual machine and click on **Finish**:

The wizard is ready to create the virtual machine and boot the installation media

9. The virtual machine will automatically start and boot from the specified installation media. You can now proceed with installing your guest operating system in the machine as if it were a physical system:

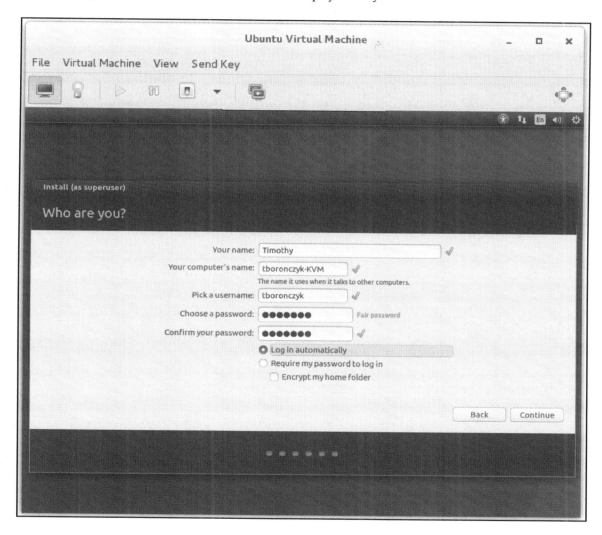

An operating system can be installed on the virtual machine the same way as a physical system

How it works...

The necessary software is installed by installing three package groups; the `Virtualization Platform` group installs the base virtualization libraries, the `Virtualization Client` package installs client programs for creating and managing virtual machines, and the `Virtualization Tools` package installs utilities for maintaining the machines:

```
yum groupinstall "Virtualization Platform"
"Virtualization Client"  "Virtualization Tools"
```

After installing the software, we used the Virtual Machine Manager to create a machine. The machine defines a virtual system, specifying what resources are available to the guest and how the guest may access them. Under the GNOME desktop environment, the manager is launched from the **System Tools** category of the **Applications** menu. In KDE, it's found via the Kickoff Application Launcher under **Applications | System Tools**. The manager can also be launched from the command line with `virt-manager`:

virt-manager

A new virtual machine can be created on the command line as well, using `virt-install` and specifying the resource allocations as arguments. This is especially useful if you want to script the process of spinning up new guests.

The manager's new VM makes it easy to create a new virtual machine definition by prompting us for the necessary resource allocations. For instance, we're asked to provide the amount of RAM, the number of CPUs, and the amount of storage space to make available to the guest. After we provide the values, it creates the machine and starts it, booting from the specified installation media to install the guest operating system. From there, installing the operating system is the same as if you were installing it on a physical system.

To boot a virtual machine, select the desired machine from the available list so that it's highlighted and then click on the play arrow icon in the manager's tool bar. Alternatively, right-click on the list entry and select **Run** from the context menu. This powers on the machine and its status changes to *Running*. When you're finished, you can power the machine off by clicking on the power switch icon in the tool bar or on one of the **Shut Down** options from the context menu. The machine's status changes to *Shut off*. To interact with the guest while it's running, double-click on the entry or highlight it and then click on the Open icon in the manager's tool bar.

> Scrollbars will appear on the side and bottom of the window if the guest's display is too large to show in its entirety. Scaling it to fit within the window can improve your experience. To adjust the display's presentation, select **Display** from **View**.

See also

Refer to the following resources for more information on working with virtual machines:

- The `virt-install` manual page (`man 1 virt-install`)
- The KVM website (`http://www.linux-kvm.org/page/Main_Page`)
- RHEL 7 Virtualization Deployment and Administration Guide (`https://access.redhat.com/documentation/en-US/Red_Hat_Enterprise_Linux/7/html/Virtualization_Deployment_and_Administration_Guide/`)
- Best practices for KVM (`http://www.ibm.com/support/knowledgecenter/linuxonibm/liaat/liaatbpkickoff.htm`)

Cloning a virtual machine

Since a virtual machine is ultimately nothing more than data files, these can easily be copied and shared. This is useful because you can set up a gold server exactly how you want it and then make copies that are used for different purposes. However, using the `cp` command isn't the way to go about it. This recipe shows you the correct way to duplicate a machine with a process called cloning.

Getting ready

This recipe requires a virtual machine set up as described in the previous recipe. While the cloning process doesn't require administrative privileges per se, privileges may be needed to access the machine's files depending on where they are located. By default, the files are stored at `/var/lib/libvirt/images`, which requires administrative access.

How to do it...

Follow these steps to clone a virtual machine:

1. Make sure the machine you want to clone is not running.
2. In Virtual Machine Manager, right-click on the desired machine in the list of available machines and select **Clone** from the context menu. This opens the **Clone Virtual Machine** dialog:

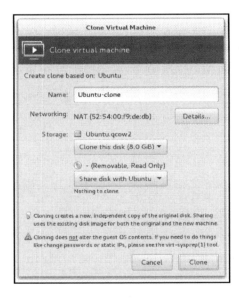

The Clone Virtual Machine dialog makes it easy to clone a machine image

3. Specify a unique name for the new image and click on the **Clone** button. This will create a standalone copy of the virtual machine and selected storage.

How it works...

This recipe used Virtual Machine Manager to create a copy of a machine known as a clone. The machine should be cloned in this manner instead of simply copying the underlying files, because the cloning process also updates various identifiers that should be unique between machines, such as the MAC address of the network interface.

> The `virt-clone` command can be used to clone a guest on the command-line. For more information, refer to the program's man page using `man 1 virt-clone`.

If you want to update various aspects of the cloned machine before booting it, you can use tools such as `virt-sysprep` and `virt-configure`. These programs mount the machine's disk image in a chrooted environment, perform the requested modifications, and then unmount the image. `virt-sysprep` is installed via `libguestfs-tools-c`:

```
yum install libguestfs-tools-c
```

To view a list of the available maintenance actions `virt-sysprep` can perform, invoke the program using `--list-operations`. Each option will be displayed along with a brief description of what it does. To perform an operation, use the `--operation` argument followed by one or more of the operation labels, separated by commas. For example, the following command clears the bash history for any accounts on the system and deletes any files that may be in `/tmp`. The `-a` argument provides the path to the machine's disk image:

```
virt-sysprep -a /var/lib/virt/images/Ubuntu-clone.qcow2
--operations bash-history,tmp-files
```

Depending on what the original machine image was used for, you may find the following cleanup operations useful as well:

- `ca-certificates`: This deletes any CA certificates
- `logfiles`: This deletes log files
- `ssh-hostkeys`: This deletes the SSH host keys
- `ssh-userdir`: This deletes the users' `.ssh` directories
- `user-account`: This deletes all user accounts except for root

There is some overlap in the functionality of `virt-sysprep` and `virt-customize`; however, `virt-customize` performs more general customization operations, while virt-sysprep's actions focus more on cleaning up an image. `virt-customize` can do things like move and set the system's hostname, reset passwords, and install and uninstall packages.

To reset the system's hostname, use the `--hostname` argument and provide the desired name:

```
virt-customize -a /var/lib/virt/images/Ubuntu-clone.qcow2
--hostname ubuntu2
```

The `--install` and `--uninstall` arguments add and remove packages and specify one or more package names separated by commas:

```
virt-customize -a /var/lib/virt/images/Ubuntu-clone.qcow2
--install build-essential
```

Some arguments you may find useful for `virt-customize` are as follows:

- `--chmod`: This changes file permissions
- `--copy`: This creates a copy of a file or directory
- `--delete`: This removes a file or directory
- `--mkdir`: This creates a new directory
- `--move`: This moves a file or directory to a new destination
- `--password`: This updates a user's password
- `--run-command`: This runs a command on the image

See also

Refer to the following resources for more information on cloning and customizing virtual machines:

- The `virt-clone` manual page (`man 1 virt-clone`)
- The `virt-configure` manual page (`man 1 virt-configure`)
- The `virt-sysprep` manual page (`man 1 virt-sysprep`)
- How to clone a KVM virtual machine and reset the VM (http://www.unixarena.com/215/12/how-to-clone-a-kvm-virtual-machines-and-reset-the-vm.html)

Adding storage to a virtual machine

Even if you're not a data hoarder, the time will probably come when you need to add additional storage to a guest system. No worries! This is easy to do! This recipe teaches you how to add and modify the virtual hardware attached to a machine.

Getting ready

This recipe requires a virtual machine set up as described in the previous recipes.

How to do it...

Follow these steps to add storage to a virtual machine:

1. Make sure the virtual machine you want to modify is not running.
2. Open the virtual machine by double-clicking on the desired entry in the list of available machines.
3. Either click on the lightbulb icon in the menu bar or select **Details** from **View** to show the virtual machine's hardware details:

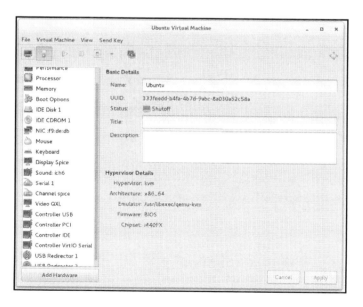

The machine's virtual hardware is displayed and resources can be added, modified, and removed

4. Click on the **Add Hardware** button in the bottom-left corner of the window to open the **Add New Virtual Hardware** window.

5. Select **Storage** from the list of possible resources. Specify the desired storage space to allocate for the new disk and click on **Finish**:

A virtual 8 GB storage drive is added to the machine

6. Leave the hardware view by either clicking on the computer icon in the menu bar or selecting **Console** from **View**.

How it works...

This recipe showed you where to configure the virtual hardware definitions associated with a machine. To increase the storage available to a guest operating system, we navigated to this view and added a new virtual drive. The storage device can be created through the interface, as shown in the recipe, or an existing drive file can be selected and attached to the system.

 If you are creating a new disk, you will want to partition, format, and mount the storage so it can be used. You may find the recipes discussed in Chapter 5, *Managing Filesystems and Storage* helpful.

Other hardware can be managed via the hardware view as well. Most notably, you can add and configure new network interfaces and allocate additional RAM and CPU resources. Increasing the RAM/CPU might be done to run resource-intensive processes on the system—it's better to allocate a smaller amount first and then increase the resources when the need arises.

Another useful configuration is to change the display server. By default, the display is configured to use SPICE, a more robust protocol than VNC. A SPICE server is built into the virtualization platform so that you can connect to the virtual machine using a SPICE client to access its display, even if the guest is only running a console display (refer to https://www.spice-space.org/ to find a SPICE client). If you want to connect using VNC instead, select the **Display Spice** entry in the hardware list and set its **Type** to **VNC server**. Change the **Address** value to **All interfaces** to accept connections from outside the localhost, specify a connection password, and then click on the **Apply** button.

The display's label in the hardware list will change to **Display VNC**:

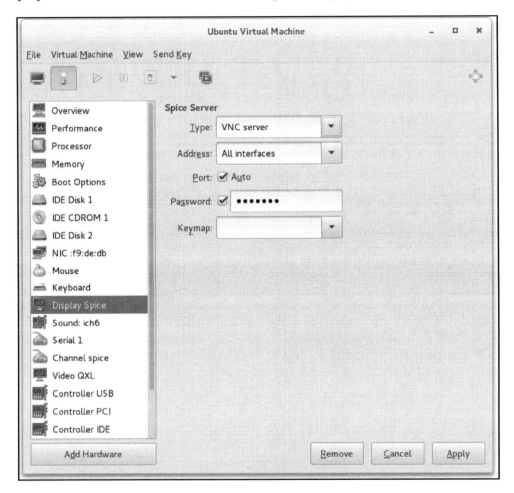

Users can connect to a virtual system's display using a SPICE or VNC client

See also

Refer to the following resources for more information on working with virtual hardware:

- RHEL 7 Virtualization Deployment and Administration Guide: Storage Pools (`https://access.redhat.com/documentation/en-US/Red_Hat_Enterprise_Li nux/7/html/Virtualization_Deployment_and_Administration_Guide/chap-S torage_pools.html`)
- Storage management (`http://libvirt.org/storage.html`)

Connecting USB peripherals to a guest system

This recipe teaches you how to share the USB devices that are connected to the host system with a virtual machine. This means you can use your USB printers, webcams, and storage devices from your guest operating system.

Getting ready

This recipe requires a virtual machine set up as described in the previous recipes.

How to do it...

Follow these steps to connect USB peripherals to a guest system:

1. Make sure the virtual machine you want to modify is not running.
2. Attach the USB device to the physical system.
3. Open the virtual machine by double-clicking on the desired entry in the list of available machines.
4. Show the virtual machine's hardware details by clicking on the lightbulb icon in the menu bar or selecting **Details** from **View**.
5. Click on the **Add Hardware** button to open the **Add New Virtual Hardware** window.
6. Select **USB HOST Device** from the list of resources.

7. Select the desired USB device and then click on the **Finish** button:

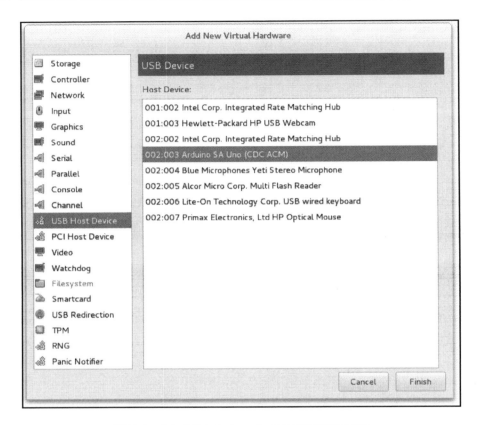

USB devices attached to the host system can be assigned to the virtual machines

8. Leave the hardware view by either clicking on the computer icon in the menu bar or selecting **Console** from **View**.
9. Start the virtual machine and verify that the USB device is available.

How it works...

USB devices attached to the host system can be allocated to a virtual machine through the hardware details. We selected the **USB Host Device** category, which displayed all of the devices currently registered with the host from which we can make our selection. There are a couple of items to be aware of when using USB devices in your guest system. First, only the USB 1.1 protocol is supported. This isn't an issue for most peripherals, such as webcams, printers, and USB microphones, where transfer speed isn't much of a concern. It may be a concern if you intend to attach a USB storage device and transfer large amounts of data. Second, the device must be plugged in and accessible by the host before starting the virtual machine. This is because the virtualization platform running on the host is responsible for provisioning access to the guest.

 This recipe showed you how to assign a USB device connected to the host system to a guest. If you're accessing your virtual machine remotely with a SPICE client, you can plug in USB devices to your local machine and redirect them to the remote guest using USB redirection. More information can be found in the RHEL 7 Virtualization Deployment and Administration Guide.

See also

Refer to the following resources for more information on sharing USB devices:

- RHEL 7 Virtualization Deployment and Administration Guide: USB Devices (https://access.redhat.com/documentation/en-US/Red_Hat_Enterprise_Linux/7/html/Virtualization_Deployment_and_Administration_Guide/sect-Guest_virtual_machine_device_configuration-USB_devices.html)
- USB pass-through with libvirt and KVM (https://david.wragg.org/blog/29/3/usb-pass-through-with-libvirt-and-kvm.html)

Configuring a guest's network interface

This recipe teaches you how to configure the virtual network interface's behavior. By changing the interface's behavior, you can provide the guest direct access or filtered access to the network, and even set up a local network visible only to the host system and other guests.

Getting ready

This recipe requires a CentOS system with a working network connection. It also requires a virtual machine set up as described in the previous recipes.

How to do it...

Follow these steps to configure a guest's network interface:

1. Make sure that the virtual machine you want to modify is not running.
2. Open the virtual machine by double-clicking on the desired entry in the list of available machines.
3. View the virtual machine's hardware details by clicking on the lightbulb icon in the menu bar or selecting **Details** from **View**.
4. Specify the desired **Network source** (NAT or Host device).
5. If selecting a host device, specify the desired mode (Bridged, VEPA, Private, or Passthrough):

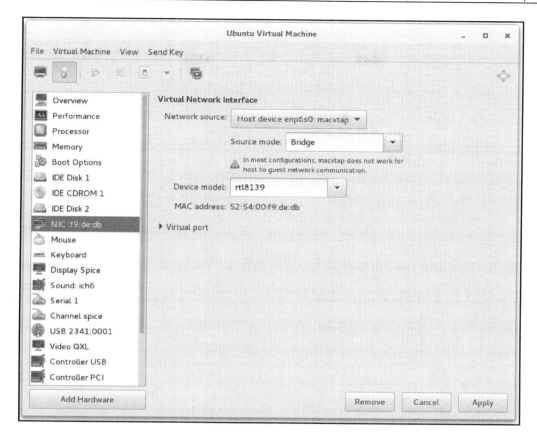

The virtual network interface can be configured to handle the guest's traffic in different ways

6. Click on the **Apply** button to save your configuration.
7. Leave the hardware view by either clicking on the computer icon in the menu bar or selecting **Console** from **View**.
8. Start the virtual machine and proceed to configuring the guest's networking as necessary.

How it works...

Managing a guest's network connectivity is a matter of specifying the behavior of the virtual machine's network adaptor. To do this correctly, we need to first understand what the behaviors are from the options that are available to us.

The first option is **Network Address Translation (NAT)** and that is the default for new virtual machines. The virtualization platform provides a virtual network interface to the guest and handles all of its traffic. The platform marshals the traffic through the host's physical interface, acting very much like a router between the guest and host.

The second option is to tie the virtual interface directly to the host's physical interface. There are four sharing modes, which are as follows:

- **Bridged**: The virtualization platform connects the guest and host interfaces, giving the guest direct access to the Internet. The guest needs to obtain its own IP address and has full access to the network.
- **VEPA**: This is for use with VEPA-capable network devices (special hardware requirements must be met).
- **Private**: The platform creates private network, routing packets so that virtual machines on the same host can communicate with one another and the external network, but connections coming in from the network can't reach the virtual machines.
- **Passthrough**: The host's interface is shared directly (additional technical requirements must be met).

The documentation and terminology are quite technical, given the nature of the subject. Moreover, many people who are not networking experts often have trouble deciding the correct configuration. In my experience, there're two common scenarios in which non-networkers use virtualization-local virtualization to provide an alternate environment and virtualization to provision multiple server systems. If you're using your virtual machine as a typical desktop system where users need Internet access to read e-mail and surf the Web, use NAT networking and configure the guest to use DHCP. If you're running the machines as servers, share the host's adaptor in the Bridged mode and configure the guest with a static IP address.

See also

Refer to the following resources for more information on configuring the virtual network interface:

- libvirt Virtualization API: Networking (`http://wiki.libvirt.org/page/Netwo rking`)
- RHEL 7 Virtualization Deployment and Administration Guide: Network Configuration (`https://access.redhat.com/documentation/en-US/Red_Hat_E nterprise_Linux/7/html/Virtualization_Deployment_and_Administration_ Guide/chap-Network_configuration.html`)

Index

H

host system
  USB peripherals, connecting to 373, 374, 375
HTTPS
  Apache, configuring to serve pages 302, 303, 304
  references 305

I

IMAP access
  Dovecot, configuring for 273, 274, 275, 276
installing
  DHCP server 56, 57, 58, 59, 60
  GNOME desktop 32, 33, 34, 35
  KDE Plasma Workspaces desktop 36, 37, 38
integrity, verifying
  references 108
Internet Corporation for Assigned Names and
        Numbers (ICANN) 233
Internet Message Access Protocol (IMAP) 273
  references 277
iptables
  references 55, 56
  used, for configuring network firewall 52, 53, 54, 55, 56

J

jump to 54

K

KDE Plasma Workspaces desktop
  installing 36, 37, 38
KDE
  URL, for documentation 38
key-based authentication
  references 158
kickstart
  used, for coordinating multiple installations 21, 22, 23

L

Linux Instance
  URL 29
Linux-PAM System Administrator's

URL 80
load balancing
  references 315
log files
  rotating, with logrotate 323, 324, 325, 326, 327
Logical Volume Manager (LVM) 134
logrotate
  references 327
LVM snapshots
  references 145
  working 143, 144, 145
LVM volume
  creating 134, 135, 136, 137
  growing 139, 140, 141, 142
  references 142
  removing 137, 138

M

mbox format 261
messages
  routing, with Procmail 283, 284, 285, 286, 287
modified files
  detecting, Tripwire used 328, 329, 330, 331, 332, 333, 334
MongoDB Backup Methods
  reference link 213
MongoDB database
  backing up 210, 211, 212, 213
  references 209
  restoring 210, 211, 212, 213
  setting up 204, 205, 206, 207, 209
  URL, for documentation 208
MongoDB replica set
  configuring 214, 216, 217
  references 218
multiple installations
  coordinating, kickstart used 21, 22, 23
multiple IP addresses
  binding, to Ethernet device 43, 44, 45
  references 45
MySQL cluster
  references 203
  setting up 196, 197, 198, 199, 200, 201, 202, 203
MySQL database

reference link 100
used, for prioritizing repositories 98, 100
privileges
escalating, with sudo 70, 71, 72, 73
Procmail
messages, routing with 283, 284, 285, 286, 287
reference link 287
program
--disable-FEATURE 111
--enable-FEATURE 111
--prefix 111
compiling, from source 108, 109, 110, 111, 112, 113
PXE Server, on CentOS 7
URL 24

Q

quotas
references 123

R

RAID configurations
RAID-0 128
RAID-1 128
RAID-5 129
RAID-6 129
RAID
references 131
RAM disk
creating 124, 125, 126
references 126
recursive servers 232
redundant array of disks (RAID)
about 126
creating 126, 127, 128, 129, 130, 131
Remi repositories
references 97
registering 94, 95, 96, 97
remote system
Secure Shell (SSH), connecting without
password 155, 156, 157, 158
repositories
prioritizing, priorities plugin used 98, 100
resolving DNS server
setting up, BIND used 228, 229, 230, 231, 232

reverse lookup zone file
references 245, 246
writing 242, 243, 245
rewriting URLs
references 311
RHEL 7 Desktop Migration
URL, for guide 35
RHEL 7
URL, for installation 16, 21, 24
rndc
configuring, to control BIND 250, 251, 252, 253, 254, 255
references 255
rootkits
checking, with chkrootkit 340, 341, 342
RPM packages
verifying 105, 106, 107, 108
Rsyslog
references 323

S

Samba
references 68
Windows share, serving with 64, 65, 66, 67, 68
Secure Shell (SSH) 148
Secure Shell (SSH) access
references 161
restricting, by group 158, 159, 160, 161
restricting, by user 158, 159, 160, 161
Secure Shell (SSH) login
configuring 151, 152, 153, 154
references 154
Secure Shell (SSH)
commands, running through 148, 149, 150, 151
protecting, with Fail2ban 161, 162, 163, 164
references 151
VNC connections, tunneling through 175, 176, 177
Security-Enhanced Linux (SELinux) 87
for security 87, 88, 89, 90, 91, 92
references 92
serve pages
Apache, configuring to over HTTPS 302, 303, 304
Server Name Indication (SNI) 304

85951193R00224

Made in the USA
Lexington, KY
06 April 2018